C000093027

RBI58,515

Presented to the
LIBRARY *of the*
UNIVERSITY OF TORONTO
by

Copp, Clark Pitman Ltd.

PITMAN'S
SHORTHAND INSTRUCTOR
NEW ERA EDITION

PITMAN'S JOURNAL OF COMMERCIAL EDUCATION

THE oldest and largest weekly journal devoted to Pitman's Shorthand and all Commercial Subjects. Every issue contains shorthand reading practice, with key, specially adapted for students at various stages.

2d. Weekly

PITMAN'S SHORTHAND WEEKLY

AN illustrated weekly periodical in beautiful Shorthand, without a key. Provision is made for the beginner, the intermediate student, and the advanced writer.

2d. Weekly

PITMAN'S SHORTHAND INSTRUCTOR

A COMPLETE EXPOSITION OF SIR ISAAC PITMAN'S SYSTEM OF SHORTHAND

NEW ERA EDITION

LONDON
SIR ISAAC PITMAN & SONS, LTD., PARKER STREET, W.C.2
BATH : PHONETIC INSTITUTE
MELBOURNE: THE RIALTO, COLLINS STREET
TORONTO : 70 BOND STREET
NEW YORK : 2 WEST 45TH STREET

PREFACE

THE system of shorthand writing presented in the following pages was invented by Sir Isaac Pitman, who in 1837 published his first treatise on the art. In 1840 the second edition of his work appeared, under the title " Phonography, or Writing by Sound, being also a New and Natural System of Shorthand." In the numerous editions of Phonography published in succeeding years, many improvements were introduced. These were the fruit of long and varied stenographic experiments, and of the valuable criticism and experience of large numbers of expert writers of the system who had applied it to work of every description. No other system of shorthand designed for the English language has been subjected to tests so prolonged, so diverse, and so severe as those which Pitman's Shorthand—as the system is now generally styled —has undergone during the last eighty-six years, with the result that it has been most successfully adapted to the practical requirements of all classes of shorthand writers.

The present edition includes a few alterations that have been made in certain rules of the system. The effect of these alterations is to simplify the work of the student without in any way interfering with the wonderful power of the system in the hands of the expert writer. The object specially borne in mind in preparing the work has been to render it equally suitable for self-tuition and for individual or class instruction under a teacher. No effort has been spared to explain and illustrate the rules in the clearest and simplest manner possible.

Although students, as a rule, experience no difficulty in understanding the method here set forth of " writing by sound," it is desirable that they should have, at the beginning of their study, an intelligent grasp of all that is conveyed by that term. Therefore, before the mastery of the first chapter is attempted, the Introduction which follows this Preface should be read with care.

The advantage of practical ability in the art of shorthand writing is so universally acknowledged in the present day that it is unnecessary to emphasize it. It is obvious, however, that the value of shorthand, whether as a vehicle for private communication or for use in various ways in business or professional life, would be largely diminished if the same system—and that the best—were not employed. This important fact is now generally recognized ; and statistics, the testimony of public men, and general observation, concur in demonstrating that the system which Sir Isaac Pitman invented is taught and used as the shorthand *par excellence* for all who speak the English language. Further and very significant evidence to the merits of his system is the fact that it has been adapted to no fewer than twenty foreign languages.

The Publishers take this opportunity of tendering their sincere thanks to the large number of expert writers and teachers of Phonography who have offered valuable suggestions for the improvement of the present edition.

INTRODUCTION

PHONOGRAPHY, the name originally given to Pitman's Shorthand, has been briefly but accurately defined as " the art of representing spoken sounds by character ; a system of shorthand." The first question that will occur to the student will be, what is the fundamental difference between the shorthand characters and the letters in ordinary writing and printing ? To answer this question it is necessary to consider the alphabet of the language. It is obvious that the usual or Romanic alphabet of twenty-six letters cannot represent by distinct characters the thirty-six typical sounds of the English language. As a consequence, many of the letters of that alphabet are of necessity used to represent different sounds. It is manifest, therefore, that any system of shorthand founded on the common alphabet would prove a very imperfect and cumbrous instrument for recording spoken utterances with certainty and speed—the chief object of shorthand. With such an alphabet either a single sign standing for one of the letters would be required to do duty for several sounds, or more than one character would have to be used to represent a single sound, as is done in ordinary spelling. On the other hand, the three consonants C, Q and X are unnecessary, inasmuch as they represent sounds provided for by other consonants. Two simple illustrations will demonstrate the difference between the ordinary spelling and the phonetic method, which is the distinctive feature of Pitman's Shorthand.

The first illustration deals with consonants, and is concerned with the ordinary spelling of the words

gaol and *gale*, in which the *sounds* of the first consonant are different, although represented in longhand by the same letter. If the common spelling
were followed in shorthand, we should have the
same shorthand symbols for both words. But the
initial sounds in these words are different; in the
first the sound is *jay*, in the second *gay*. For
these dissimilar sounds the Pitman system provides
dissimilar shorthand signs. The second illustration deals with vowels, as, for example, in the
words *tub* and *tube*. If the shorthand symbols
were the equivalents of the letters of the common
alphabet (the final *e* of *tube* being omitted because
it is not sounded), the stenographer would be
obliged to write both words by precisely the same
characters, namely, *t-u-b*. Pitman's Shorthand, however, provides for the representation of the different
sounds *ŭ* and *ū* heard in the respective words, and
these are indicated by different symbols.

The phonetic notation of the system of shorthand
developed in the present work has been found, after
widely extended use, to possess important practical
advantages. By the employment of the phonetic
alphabet, which has been termed the " alphabet of
nature," spoken language can be recorded with
one-sixth of the trouble and time that longhand
requires, by those who use Pitman's Shorthand
simply as a substitute for the ordinary longhand
writing. With the adoption of the systematized
methods of abbreviation developed in the more
advanced stages, this method of shorthand can be
written legibly with the speed of the most rapid
distinct articulation, and it may be read with the
certainty and ease of ordinary longhand writing.

An explanation on one point, however, is desirable.
In the study and use of Pitman's Shorthand it should

be borne in mind that although the system is phonetic it is not designed to represent or record minute shades of pronunciation. The Pitmanic alphabet, in the words of Max-Müller, "comprehends the thirty-six broad typical sounds of the English language and assigns to each a definite sign." It does not seek to mark, for example, the thirty or more variations of sound which have been found to exist in the utterance of the twelve simple vowels. The pronunciation of the vowels, as Max-Müller has shown, varies greatly in different localities and in the various countries of the world in which the English language is spoken, and in which Pitman's Shorthand is practised. The standard of pronunciation, as exhibited in printed shorthand, cannot, therefore, be expected to coincide minutely with the pronunciation of English in all parts. Experience has abundantly proved that the representation of the broad typical sounds of English as provided for in Pitman's Shorthand is ample for all stenographic purposes.

The pronunciation adopted in Pitman's Shorthand Textbooks is based on that given in *The Oxford English Dictionary*, edited by Sir James A. H. Murray, LL.D.

The presence of *r* has a modifying effect upon a preceding vowel. The student's attention is, therefore, directed to the following observations with regard to the consonant *r*, to certain vowels when preceding *r* and to a class of vowels which may be described as more or less obscure.

(*a*) With the exception of *worsted* (the woollen material) and a few proper names, as *Worcester*, wherever the consonant *r* occurs in a word, in Pitman's Shorthand it must be *represented as a consonant.*

(*b*) In such words as *bar, far, mar, tar, jar,* the vowel-sign for *ah* is to be used; but in such words as *barrow, Farrow, marry, carry,* and *Jarrow,* the first vowel-sound is to be represented by the vowel-sign for ă.

(*c*) In such words as *four, fore, roar, lore, wore, shore, door, pour, core, gore, tore, sore,* the vowel-sign for ō is to be used.

(*d*) In such words as *torch, morn, fork,* the vowel-sign for ŏ is to be used.

(*e*) In such words as *air, fair, lair, bare,* the vowel-sign for ā is to be used.

(*f*) In such pairs of words as *fir, fur ; earth, worth ; per, purr ; Percy, pursy ;* the vowel-sound in the first word of the pairs is to be represented by the vowel-sign for ĕ ; the vowel-sound in the second word of the pairs is to be represented by the vowel-sign for ŭ.

(*g*) In words like *custody, custom, baron, felony, colour, factory,* the second vowel-sound is represented by the vowel-sign for ŭ.

(*h*) In words like *village, cottage, breakage,* the second vowel-sound is represented by the vowel-sign for ĕ.

(*i*) In words like *suppose,* the second vowel-sound is represented by the vowel-sign for ō ; but in words like *supposition, disposition,* the second vowel-sound is represented by the vowel-sign for ŭ.

With the accurate employment of the phonographic signs, there need be no uncertainty as to what those employed for a particular word are intended to represent, and, as Max-Müller has testified, " English can be written rationally and read easily " with the Pitmanic alphabet. To use Pitman's Shorthand successfully, the rules of the system must be thoroughly mastered. By the employment of the various abbreviating devices, the most important benefit to be derived from shorthand will be attained, namely, the maximum of speed combined with legibility.

DIRECTIONS TO THE STUDENT

The system of shorthand set forth in the following pages received the name of Phonography (a term derived from two Greek words meaning "sound writing") because it affords the means of recording the sounds of spoken language. From the outset, therefore, the student should remember that he is learning to write by SOUND, *i.e.*, to write words as they are pronounced; that each simple character represents one definite sound and no other; and that the ordinary spelling—with its many irregularities and inconsistencies—as exhibited in printing and in longhand writing, is not to be followed or imitated.

When the student has mastered the value of the phonographic signs, he should use those which represent the equivalent sounds in forming the characters for the words he desires to write. For example, if he wishes to write in Phonography the word *knee* (spelt with four letters, though made up of only two sounds), he uses but two phonographic signs, namely, that for the consonant *n* and that for the vowel *ē*. To spell in this fashion, a mental analysis of the sounds of words must be made, but the ability to do this is very easily acquired, and is soon exercised without conscious effort.

For working the exercises and for ordinary phonographic writing, a pen and ruled paper should be used. Speaking generally, it is not so easy to acquire a neat style of writing by the use of a pencil as it is by the use of a pen. No doubt, the pencil is frequently employed; in some cases, indeed, it may be found impossible to use a pen for note-taking. The student would do well, therefore, to accustom himself to write either with a pen or a pencil in the more advanced stages of his progress, though for writing the exercises given in this book the pen only should be used.

The pen should be held lightly, and in such a manner as to permit of the shorthand characters being easily written. The wrist must not be allowed to rest upon the note-book or desk. In order to secure the greatest freedom of movement, the middle of the fore-arm should rest on the edge of the desk. The writer should sit in front of his work, and should have the paper or note-book parallel with the edge of the desk or table. For shorthand writing, the nib employed should not be too stiff, but should have a sufficiently fine and flexible point to enable the thick and thin characters of the system to be written so as clearly to distinguish the one from the other. Paper with a fairly smooth surface is absolutely essential.

The student should thoroughly master the explanations and rules which precede the respective exercises, and write out several times the illustrative words appearing in the text, afterwards working the exercises. As the secret of success in shorthand is PRACTICE, it is advisable that the various exercises should be written and re-written until they can be done with perfect freedom and accuracy. The perusal of progressive reading lessons in printed shorthand will also be found helpful to the student in forming a correct style of writing; and the practice of writing the characters, at first with careful accuracy, afterwards with gradually accelerated speed, will materially assist him in forming a neat style of shorthand writing.

The system is fully explained in the following pages, and can be acquired from the instruction books alone by anyone who is prepared to devote ordinary perseverance and application to the study. With the assistance of a teacher, however, more rapid and satisfactory advance will be made in the mastery of the art. Should any difficulty be experienced in finding a teacher, the publishers will be pleased to furnish any student with the names and addresses of the nearest teachers of Pitman's Shorthand. It should be pointed out that satisfactory progress in acquiring the art of shorthand will only be made if a certain portion of time is regularly devoted to the study EVERY DAY; or, in the case of school or class instruction, by a thorough and punctual performance of the allotted portions of work forming the course. Study at irregular intervals of time is of little value; but an hour, or a longer period, devoted daily to the task will give the student a knowledge of the system in a comparatively short time, and constant and careful practice will bring speed and dexterity.

CONTENTS

KEY TO PITMAN'S
SHORTHAND INSTRUCTOR
NEW ERA EDITION

Containing a Key to the Exercises.
Price 2s.; cloth, 2s. 6d.

PITMAN'S SHORTHAND
(PHONOGRAPHY)

CHAPTER I
THE CONSONANTS

" Consonants are the result of audible friction or stopping of the breath in some part of the mouth or throat." (*Prof. Sweet.*)

Forms of Consonants. 1. For the representation of all the consonant sounds, (except *w*, *y*, and the aspirate *h*), the simplest geometrical forms are used, namely, the straight line and the shallow curve, as shown in the following diagrams—

Arrangement of Groups. 2. The order of the arrangement of each group of consonants, as exhibited in the Table on a following page, follows the order of the oral movements from the lips inwards in the utterance of their respective sounds. The first pair of consonants, *p*, *b*, are pronounced between the lips, and the next seven pairs at the several barriers further back in the mouth, in the succession indicated in the phonographic alphabet.

Classes of Consonants. 3. The first eight consonants, represented by straight strokes, are called " explodents," because, in pronouncing them, the outgoing breath is forced in a sudden gust through barriers previously closed.

4. The next eight, represented by upright or sloping curves, are called " continuants," because in uttering these the outgoing breath, instead of being

1—(*M*)   1

expelled suddenly, is allowed to escape in a continuous stream through similar barriers partially open.

5. The " nasals," represented by a horizontal curve, are produced by closing the successive barriers in the mouth against the outgoing air-stream, so that it has to escape through the nose.

6. The " liquids " flow into union with other consonants, and thus make double consonants, as in the words cliff, dry, where the l or r blends with the preceding consonant.

7. The " coalescents " precede vowels and coalesce or unite with them.

8. The " aspirate " is a breathing upon a following vowel. Thus by a breathing upon the vowel ă in the word at, the word is changed into hat.

Pairs of Consonants. 9. The first sixteen consonants form pairs; thus, p and b; t and d; ch and j; k and g; f and v; th and th; s and z; sh and zh. The articulations in these pairs are the same; but the sound is light in the first consonant of each pair and heavy in the second. The consonants of each pair are represented by the same stroke, but for the second consonant this is written *thick* instead of *thin;* as \ p, \ b, | t, | d, ⌐ f, ⌐ v, etc. We have, therefore, a *light sign* for the *light sound*, and a *heavy sign* for the *heavy sound*. In this, as in the fact that each pair of consonants is represented by kindred signs, a natural relation is preserved between the *spoken* sound and the *written* sign. Throughout this book whatever relates to the light strokes applies also to the corresponding heavy strokes unless the contrary is stated.

Size of Strokes. 10. The consonants should be written about one-sixth of an inch long, as in these pages. It is of the utmost importance that from the outset the student should learn to form the whole of the strokes uniformly as to length. Whatever size be adopted, all the strokes should be made equal in length. Later there will be introduced a principle for writing strokes half the normal length, and later still another for the making of strokes double the normal length. It is thus imperative that the student should obtain a fixed and strictly uniform length from the start. Care should be taken to form the curved thick letters, when standing alone, thus $\smile$ *v*, $)$ *z*. If made heavy throughout they look clumsy : they should be thick in the middle only, and should taper off at each end, except when a joining such as $\smile$ *v g* or $\searchow$ *b ng* is made. Thick strokes are never written upward. As an aid to remembering the strokes for *th* and *s*, the student should note that $)$ *s* is the curve on the right side of $\wp$ The consonants *l* and *r* form the *left* and *right* sides of an arch $\cap$ The consonant *l* is most commonly written upwards ; but it may be written downward in certain cases in accordance with rules which will be explained later.

Names of Consonants. 11. Until the student is perfectly familiar with the names of the consonants and the characters representing them, he should, in writing out the exercises, name aloud each shorthand stroke as he writes it. The strokes must always be called by their phonetic names : thus, " ch " is to be named *chay;* " g " *gay;* " ng " *ing.* The reason for this is that each phonetic character has a fixed value, and, therefore, requires to be called by a name which indicates the sound that it invariably represents.

Divisions	Character	Name	Letter	As sounded in	
Explodents	\	pee	P	post	rope
	\	bee	B	boast	robe
	|	tee	T	tip	fate
	|	dee	D	dip	fade
	/	chay	CH	chest	etch
	/	jay	J	jest	edge
	—	kay	K	cane	leek
	—	gay	G	gain	league
Continuants	(	ef	F	fat	safe
	(	vee	V	vat	save
	(	ith	TH	thigh	wreath
	(	thee	*TH*	thy	wreathe
	)	ess	S	seal	base
	)	zee	Z	zeal	baize
	)	ish	SH	she	dash
	)	zhee	ZH	treasure	vision
Nasals	⌒	em	M	met	seem
	⌣	en	N	net	seen
	⌣	ing	NG	kingly	long
Liquids	up	el	L	light	tile
	up / down	ar, ray	R	right	tire
Coalescents	up	way	W	wet	away
	up	yay	Y	yet	ayah
Aspirate	up / down	hay	H	high	adhere

Exercise 1

(To be written by the student. The arrow »→ shows the direction in which the stroke is to be written. The curves m, n and ng and the straight strokes k and g are written on the line.)

P, B

T, D

CH, J
(chay)

K, G
(gay)

F, V

TH, *TH*
(ith) (thee)

S, Z
(zee)

SH, ZH
(ish) (zhee)

M

N

NG
(ing)

L

R

R
(ray)

W
(way)

Y
(yay)

H
(hay)

Chay and Ray. 12. These strokes are somewhat similar. They differ, however, in slope and in the direction in which they are written. It is scarcely possible, moreover, to mistake one for the other, inasmuch as *chay* is always written DOWN at an angle of 30° from the perpendicular, and *ray* is always written UP at an angle of 30° from the horizontal; thus ⫽ *chay*, ⫽ *ray*. If the pupil cannot, at the first trial, produce a fair copy of the signs in Exercise 1, he should write them several times, and vary the practice by writing the strokes in irregular order; thus,

— / ⌒ ╲ ╱ ⸮

Exercise 2

Read, copy and transcribe as shown in line 1

1. ╲ ╲ | | ╱ ╱ — — ╱ ╱ ⸮ ╱ ╱
   p   *b*   *t*   *d*   *ch*   *j*   *k*   *g*   *w*   *y*   *h*   *h*   *r*

2. ╲ ╲ ╱ | ⸮ ╲ ╱ | ╱ ╱ — ╱ —

3. ╲ ╲ ╲ (( )))) ⌒ ⌒ ⌒ ⌒

4. ╱ ⌒ (╲ (⌣) ⌒ ( ) ╲)

5. ╲ (╱ ⌒ | ╱ ╱) ⌣)) |

6. ╲ — ⸮ ╲ ╱ ╱ — ╱ ⌣ ╱ |

7. ╱ ╲) (⌒ ⌣ ╲) ( ) ⌣ ⌒ ╲

8. | — | — ╲ ╱ ╲ ╱ ⸮ ╱ ╱ ╱ ╱

Joined Strokes. 13. Strokes when joined must be written without lifting the pen, the beginning of a following stroke joining the end of a preceding stroke, as in the following exercise.

Exercise 3

Read and copy

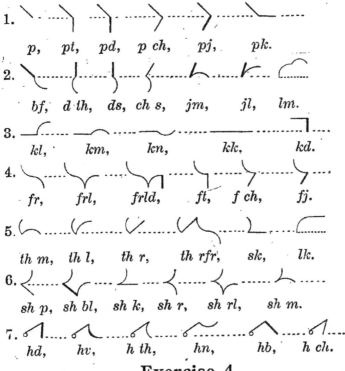

1.   *p,*   *pt,*   *pd,*   *p ch,*   *pj,*   *pk.*

2.   *bf,*   *d th,*   *ds,*   *ch s,*   *jm,*   *jl,*   *lm.*

3.   *kl,*   *km,*   *kn,*   *kk,*   *kd.*

4.   *fr,*   *frl,*   *frld,*   *ft,*   *f ch,*   *fj.*

5.   *th m,*   *th l,*   *th r,*   *th rfr,*   *sk,*   *lk.*

6.   *sh p,*   *sh bl,*   *sh k,*   *sh r,*   *sh rl,*   *sh m.*

7.   *hd,*   *hv,*   *h th,*   *hn,*   *hb,*   *h ch.*

Exercise 4

Read, copy, and transcribe

1.

2.

3.

4.

5.

6.

The student will see the correct angles for the upright and sloping characters if he will copy and practise the following forms in combination—

Summary

1. Pitman's Shorthand is phonetic, words being written according to their sound.
2. The strokes are twenty-six in number, and each stroke has a distinct name and value.
3. To represent the consonants there are mainly two elements, a straight stroke and a shallow curve.
4. The strokes (straight and curved) are thin and thick for the representation of pairs of similar sounds.
5. Thin strokes are written sometimes upward, sometimes downward ; thick strokes are never written upward.
6. Strokes must be of a uniform length, about one-sixth of an inch.
7. Strokes are written by one impression, and the thick curves taper at each end.
8. The stroke representing *chay* is written downward ; the stroke representing *ray* is written upward.
9. Strokes when joined must be written without lifting the pen.

CHAPTER II

THE VOWELS

" If the mouth-passage is left so open as not to cause audible friction, and voiced breath is sent through it, we have a vowel." (*Prof. Sweet.*)

Vowel Sounds. 14. There are six simple long vowel-sounds in the English language, namely—

ah, ā, ē; aw, ō, ōō;

as heard in the words

ba*h*! āle, ēa*ch*; āll, ōa*k*, ōōze.

15. There are six corresponding short vowel-sounds in the language, namely—

ă, ĕ, ĭ, ŏ, ŭ, ŏŏ

as heard in the words

ăt, ĕtch, ĭt, ŏdd, tŭb, bŏŏk.

The long vowels may be remembered by repeating the sentence " *Pa may we all go too ?* " The short vowels may be remembered by repeating the sentence " *That pen is not much good.*"

Vowel Signs. 16. The long vowels are represented by a heavy dot and a heavy dash. The short vowels are represented by a light dot and a light dash.

Vowel Places. 17. There are three places close to each stroke where a vowel sign may be placed, namely, at the beginning, the middle, and the end. The vowels are accordingly called first-place, second-place, and third-place vowels respectively.

The places of the vowels are counted from the point where the stroke begins. In the case of down-strokes, therefore, the vowel places are counted from the top downward. In the case of upstrokes, the

9

·vowel places are counted from the bottom upward. In the case of horizontals, the vowel places are counted from left to right : thus,

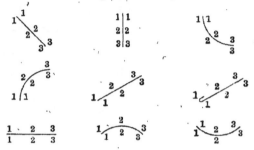

Value of Vowel-Signs. 18. The vowel-signs are put in the places which correspond with their numbers. A heavy dot in the first-place represents the long vowel *ah* ; in the second-place it represents the long vowel *ā* ; in the third-place it represents the long vowel *ē*. A heavy dash in the first place represents the long vowel *aw* ; in the second place it represents the long vowel *ō* ; in the third place it represents the long vowel *ōō*.

19. The light vowel-signs for the short vowels are put in the same places as the heavy vowel-signs for the long vowels ; thus,

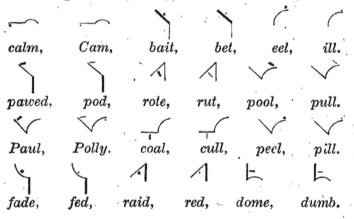

calm,   Cam,   bait,   bet,   eel,   ill.

pawed,   pod,   rote,   rut,   pool,   pull.

Paul,   Polly.   coal,   cull,   peel,   pill.

fade,   fed,   raid,   red,   dome,   dumb.

Vowels preceding and following Strokes. 20. When a vowel-sign is placed on the left-hand side of an upstroke or downstroke, it is read *before* the stroke, as ⌐ *ale*, ⋌ *earth*, ⟍ *ape*, ⟋ *age*, ⎮ *eat*.

When a vowel-sign is placed on the right-hand side of an upstroke or downstroke, it is read *after* the stroke, as ⌐ *lay*, ⟋ *ray*, ⟍ *pay*, ⎮ *jay*, ⟋ *shoe*.

When a vowel-sign is placed above a horizontal stroke it is read *before* the stroke, as ⏤ *ache*, ⏤ *eke*, ⏝ *own*.

When a vowel-sign is placed below a horizontal stroke it is read *after* the stroke, as ⏤ *Kay*, ⏤ *key*, ⌄ *no*.

PRECEDING VOWELS

1. ⟍   ⎮   ⟋   ⟋   ⟍   ⌐

    ebb,   *aid*,   *etch*,   *edge*,   *off*,   *oath*.

2. ⏤   ⏤   ⏜   ⏝   ⏝   ⟋   ⟍

    ache,   *egg*,   *aim*,   *inn*,   *own*,   *awl*,   *ore*.

FOLLOWING VOWELS

3. ⌐   ⟋   ⟋   ⟋   ⟍   ⎮

    low,   *row*,   *woe*,   *ye*,   *bow*,   *day*.

4. ⟍   ⟨   ⏤   ⏤   ⏜   ⏝

    foe,   *they*,   *Kay*,   *gay*,   *mow*,   *knee*.

PRECEDING AND FOLLOWING VOWELS

5. ⟍   ⌐   ⌐   ⟨   ⌐

    ebony,   *Italy*,   *attack*,   *ashore*,   *allay*.

6. ⌐   ⟍   ⏤   ⟍   ⌐

    academy,   *arrow*,   *agony*,   *afar*,   *anatomy*.

Exercise 5

Read, copy, and transcribe

Write the outline of the word first; then put in the vowel-sign.

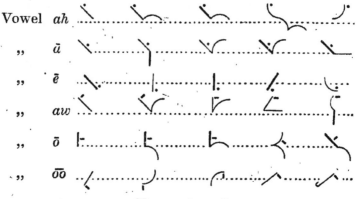

Vowel *ah*

" *ā*

" *ē*

" *aw*

" *ō*

" *ōō*

Exercise 6

Read, copy, and transcribe

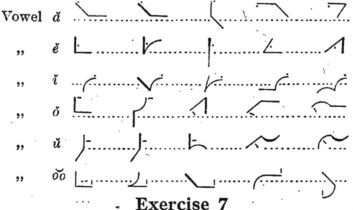

Vowel *ă*

" *ĕ*

" *ĭ*

" *ŏ*

" *ŭ*

" *ŏŏ*

Exercise 7

Write in Shorthand

1. Pay, paid, bay, bait, Tay, tame.
2. Say, essay, Esk, escape, low, load.
3. Show, showed, foe, foam, may, make.
4. Weigh, weighed, eight, Etna, nay, name.

Summary

1. There are six long vowels, represented by a heavy dot and dash, and six corresponding short vowels, represented by a light dot and dash.
2. The vowels are called first-place, second-place, and third-place vowels, respectively.
3. The vowel-places are called first, second, and third-places respectively, and vowel-signs are put in the places which correspond with their numbers.
4. Vowel-places are counted from the point at which the stroke begins.
5. Vowel-signs are read as in reading longhand;
   (a) To downstrokes and upstrokes from left to right; (b) To horizontal strokes from top to bottom, as shown in the following diagrams—

6. In writing a word, the word-form is written first and then the vowel-sign.

CHAPTER III

INTERVENING VOWELS AND POSITION

Intervening Vowels. 21. FIRST- and SECOND-PLACE vowel-signs when occurring between two strokes are written *after the first stroke;* thus, ⌐ *talk,* ⌐ *gate.* THIRD-PLACE vowel-signs are written *before the second stroke* at the end, because the vowel-sign is more conveniently written in that place; thus, ⌐ *deem,* ⌐ *dim,* ⌐ *read,* ⌐ *rid,* ⌐ *pool,* ⌐ *pull.* The vowel-sign is still in the third place, as indicated in the following diagram—

INTERVENING VOWEL PLACES

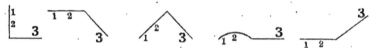

Compound Words. 22. In compound words the vowel-sign is generally placed to the separate words; as, ⌐ *earache.*

Position of Outlines. 23. Just as there are three places in which to put the vowel-signs, so there are three positions in which to write the outlines of words. The *first* position is *above the line;* the *second* position is *on the line;* and the *third* position is *through the line.* The *first sounded vowel* in the word determines the position of the outline.

When the *first sounded vowel* in a word is a *first-place* vowel, the outline is written in the *first position;* as, ⌐ *palm,* ⌐ *talk,* ⌐ *got,* ⌐ *rod,* ⌐ *wrought.*

When the *first sounded vowel* in a word is a *second-place* vowel, the outline is written in the *second position;* as, ⌐ *bake,* ⌐ *share,* ⌐ *load,* ⌐ *road,* ⌐ *code.*

14

When the *first sounded vowel* in a word is a *third-place* vowel, the outline is written in the *third position* ; as, |⁚⁚⁚ *deem,* |⁚⁚⁚ *dim,* ⌐| *lead,* ⌐| *lid,* ⌐ *keyed,* ⁚⁚⌐ *cool.*

24. The first upstroke or downstroke in the outline indicates the position, as shown in the foregoing examples.

It is not practicable to write a horizontal stroke through the line ; therefore, when an outline consists entirely of horizontal strokes, it is written in the *first* position if the first sounded vowel is a first-place vowel, and in the *second* position if the first sounded vowel is either a second- or a third-place vowel ; as, ⌒⁚⁚⁚ *mocking,* ⌒⌒ *making,* ⌒⁚ *meek,* ⁚⁚⁚ *cook.*

Exercise 8
Read and copy

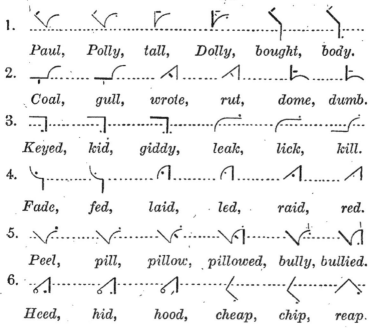

1. Paul, Polly, tall, Dolly, bought, body.

2. Coal, gull, wrote, rut, dome, dumb.

3. Keyed, kid, giddy, leak, lick, kill.

4. Fade, fed, laid, led, raid, red.

5. Peel, pill, pillow, pillowed, bully, bullied.

6. Heed, hid, hood, cheap, chip, reap.

Exercise 9

Read, copy, and transcribe

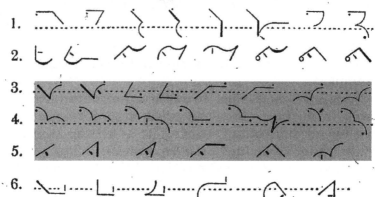

Exercise 10

Write in Shorthand

1. Patch, batch, Fanny, shop, shoddy, jolly.
2. Paid, page, bake, beck, jail, jelly.
3. Leap, lip, leave, live, lead, lid.
4. Nave, navy, enough, bale, bell, below.
5. May, make, name, namely, comb, money.
6. Feed, food, sheep, ship, loom, limb.

Grammalogues. 25. Frequently-occurring words are represented in shorthand by a single sign, as ＼ for *be*. These words are called *grammalogues* or letter-words, and the shorthand characters that represent them are called *logograms*, or word-letters. At the head of the following Exercises some logograms are given, which must be committed to memory. These characters are written *above*, *on*, or *through* the line, as, ⌐⌐⌐

Punctuation. 26. The period, or full stop, is represented by a small cross ; thus, × ; the dash thus, ⌐ ; the note of interrogation and the note of, exclamation ? and ! respectively. Other punctuation marks are written as usual. Two short lines underneath an outline indicate an initial capital.

GRAMMALOGUES

___ a, an, . the; ___ all, ＼ two, too; ___ of, ＼ to; ___ on, ι but; ___ (down) awe, ought, aught, ✓ (down) who; ___ (up) and, ╱ (up) should.

Exercise 11

Read, copy, and transcribe

1. [shorthand outlines]
2. [shorthand outlines]
3. [shorthand outlines]
4. [shorthand outlines]
5. [shorthand outlines]

Exercise 12

Write in Shorthand

(THE WORDS PRINTED IN ITALIC TYPE ARE GRAMMALOGUES.)

1. They *should* ask *the* Head *of the* Academy *to* change *the* date.
2. *Who* took *the* padlock off *the* gate *of the* paddock ?

2—(M).

3. Up *to the* date *of the* party she looked both rich *and* happy.

4. *The* head *of the* bank may leave *on* Monday.

5. They *ought* *to* change *the* date *on the* cheque *to the* fourth *of the* month.

Summary

1. FIRST-PLACE and SECOND-PLACE vowel-signs when occurring between two strokes are written after the first stroke ; THIRD-PLACE vowel-signs are written before the second stroke.

2. The position of an outline is governed by the first sounded vowel in the word.

3. A *grammalogue* is a frequently-occurring *word* represented by a single sign. The *sign* for a grammalogue is called a *logogram*.

4. The full stop is indicated by a small cross, × ; the dash by ⌐⌐ ; mark of interrogation and mark of exclamation by ? and ! respectively.

5. Two short lines underneath an outline indicate an initial capital.

CHAPTER IV

ALTERNATIVE SIGNS FOR *R* AND *H*

Consonant R. 27. The consonant *r* is provided with two different forms in order to facilitate the joining of strokes together, and also for the purpose of indicating an initial or a final vowel sound.

28. Initial *r* is written downward when preceded by a vowel sound ; as, ⌐ *oar*, ⌐ *array*, ⌐ *Arab.*

In other cases, the general rule is to write initial or final *r* upward when it is followed by a vowel sound, and downward when it is not followed by a vowel sound ; as, ⟋ *ray* but ⟍ *air ;* ⌄ *parry* but ⟍ *par ;* ⌐ *tarry* but ⌐ *tar ;* ⟋ *sherry* but ⟨ *share.*

29. Downward *r* is always written initially before *m* because of the easier joining.

Consonant H. 30. The upward form of *h* is most commonly used ; but the downward form is written when the letter stands alone or is immediately followed by ___ *k* or ___ *g ;* as, ⌐ *hay*, ⌐ *hake*, ⌐ *Haig.*

Exercise 13
Read, copy, and transcribe

1.
2.
3.
4.
5.

Exercise 14

Write in Shorthand

1. Arm, aroma, Orkney, arcade, arrow, ear.
2. Rob, rod, Rodney, Ruth, rage, roach.
3. Perry, Derry, Murray, furrow, morrow, ferry.
4. Deer, jeer, gear, fear, veer, leer.
5. Racy, writ, retail, revere, reverie, wreck.
6. Hook, hog, heath, hatch, hedge, hood.

GRAMMALOGUES

~ put; \ be, ~ to be; | it; ⌐ had, | do, ⌐ difference, different; / much, / which.

Exercise 15

Read, copy, and transcribe

Exercise 16

Write in Shorthand

1. They hope *to* reach Orkney *on the* fourth *of* May.
2. *The* red colour *on the* door *and the* yellow *on the* window *had a* poor effect.
3. He *ought to be* fair, *and* pay *the difference to* Reid *and* Hannah.

4. If they get *the* money *it should* make *much* difference *to the* firm.

5. They *had a* heavy mail *on* Monday.

6. Tom saw *the* head *of the* firm leave at four or so.

Summary

1. The consonant *r* initially is written downward if a vowel precedes, and upward if a vowel does not precede.
2. The consonant *r* finally is written upward if a vowel follows, and downward if no vowel follows.
3. Downward *r* is written before *m.*
4. The consonant *h* standing alone, or followed by *k* or *g,* is written downward; in other cases the upward form is written.

CHAPTER V

DIPHTHONGS

" A diphthong is a union of two vowel sounds in one syllable." (*Prof. Skeat.*)

Diphthongs. 31. There are four common diphthongs, namely, $\bar{\imath}$, *ow*, *oi*, and $\bar{u}$, as heard in the sentence *I now enjoy music.*

They are represented as follows—

$$\bar{I} \quad OW \quad OI \quad \bar{U}$$

32. The signs for $\bar{\imath}$ and *oi* are written in the first place ; the signs for *ow* and $\bar{u}$ are written in the third place ; thus, ___ *tie*, ___ *time*, ___ *toy*, ___ *toil* ; ___ *cow*, ___ *cowed* ; ___ *duty*, ___ *mule*.

Joined Diphthongs. 33. The diphthong signs may be joined to the consonant in many words ; thus, ___ *item*, ___ *idle*, ___ *ivy*, ___ *ice*, ___ *eyes*, ___ *ire*, ___ *isle* or *I'll*, ___ *I'm* (*I am*), ___ *nigh*, ___ *now*, ___ *bow*, ___ *avow*, ___ *dew*, ___ *Matthew*, ___ *issue*, ___ *owl*.

34. The semicircle representing $\bar{u}$ may be written (for convenience in joining ; thus, ___ *cue*, ___ *argue*, ___ *mew*, ___ *new*, ___ *value*. The sign for $\bar{\imath}$ is abbreviated when prefixed to *l* and *m*, and the sign for *ow* is abbreviated when affixed to *n*, as shown in the examples in paragraph 33.

Triphones. 35. A small tick attached to a diphthong-sign represents any vowel immediately following the diphthong ; thus, ___ *diary*, ___ *loyal*,

22

⅃ _vowel,_ ↳ _attenuate,_ ↗ _annual,_ ⌐ _annuity,_
◺ _riot,_ ⅃ _ingenuous._

These signs are called _triphones_ because they represent three vowels in one sign.

Abbreviated W. 36. The initial sound of _w_, before _k, g, m, r_ is represented by a right semicircle ; thus, ⌐ _wake,_ ⌐ _wig,_ ⌐ _womanly,_ ⌐ _wear,_ ⌐ _wary._

37. When _w_ is preceded by a vowel, the stroke ╱ must be written ; as, ╱ _awake,_ ╱ _awoke,_ ╱ _aware._

Exercise 17
Read, copy, and transcribe

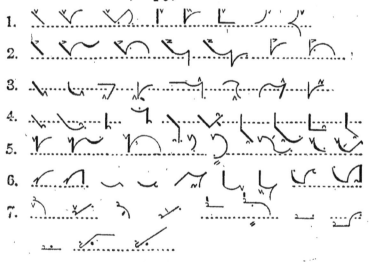

1.
2.
3.
4.
5.
6.
7.

Exercise 18
Write in Shorthand

1. Bite, tile, time, timely, ripe, ride, fire, fiery.
2. Coil, coiling, toyed, joy, enjoy, coinage, Doyle.
3. Rout, rowdy, cowed, pouch, vouch, loud.

4. View, review, dupe, tunic, fury, mule.
5. Item, eyes, nigh, deny, voyage, argue, arguing, genuine.
6. Wear, wary, weary, woke, awoke, war, warm.

GRAMMALOGUES

∧ *how,*   *why;*   *beyond,* ⌒ *you;* ∕ *large;*   *can,*
   — *come;*   *go,*   *give-n;*   *for;* ⌟ *have.*

Exercise 19

Read, copy, and transcribe

Exercise 20

Write in Shorthand

1. *How can you* attach *the* wire *to the* high chimney?
2. They were due *to* arrive at five, *but* were delayed *a* long time at Wick.
3. *You should* verify each item *on the* bill.
4. *Do you* like *the* new tyre *you have had* put *on the* car?
5. Few *of the* party knew *why you had to go to* Newquay *on the* tenth *of* July.
6. *A* week ago I saw Doyle, *but he had* no time *to give to* my work; he *had to* hurry *for the* boat.

Summary

1. The four diphthongs are *ī, ow, oi, ū.*
2. The diphthongs *ī* and *oi* are put in the *first* vowel-place ; and *ow* and *ū* in the *third* vowel-place.
3. A diphthong may be joined to a stroke where convenient.
4. A small tick attached to a diphthong sign indicates the addition of a vowel to the diphthong.
5. Initial *w* before *k, g, m, r,* is represented by a right semicircle.

CHAPTER VI

PHRASEOGRAPHY

Phrasing. 38. Phraseography is the writing of two or more words together without lifting the pen, the resulting outline being called a *phraseogram*. The best phraseograms are those which combine the qualities of *facility*, *lineality*, and *legibility*. A phraseogram should be easy to write ; it should not ascend too far above, nor descend too far below, the line ; and it must be legible when written. Subject to the observance of these conditions, the practice of phrase writing will greatly increase the writer's fluency and speed..

(*a*) The first word-form of a phraseogram must occupy the position in which it would be written if it stood alone. Thus, the phrase *How can they* would be represented by the outline ⌐ , commencing *on* the line, because *how*, if it stood alone, would be written on the line. Similarly, ⌐ *I have* commences *above* the line, because *I*, standing alone, would be written above the line.

(*b*) A first-position word-form may be slightly raised or lowered, however, to permit of a following stroke being written *above*, *on* or *through* the line ; as, ⌐ *I thank you* (and using the logogram ⌐ *with*), ⌐ *with much*, ⌐ *with which*, ⌐ *with each*.

26

(c) When joined to *k, m, l* (up). the sign __ˇ__ *may* be shortened ; thus, __ __ *I can*, __ __ *I am*, __ __ *I will.*

(d) With rare exceptions it is unnecessary to vocalize phraseograms. The word *he* standing alone, or at the beginning of a phrase, is written __ __ ; but in the middle of a phrase the word is represented by the logogram ¡ ; thus, __ __ *he may,* __ __ *if he may,* __ __ *he should know,* __ __ *if he should know.* For the sake of an easier joining the word *much* is some-times written in full in phrases ; as, __ __ *so much,* __ __ *how much ;* and *were* is written either __ __ or __ __ ; thus, __ __ *they were,* __ __ *you were,* __ __ *we were,* __ __ *if he were.* In phrases, the word *him* should have the dot vowel inserted ; thus, __ __ *of him,* __ __ *to him.*

Tick *the*. 39. The word *the* may be expressed by a light slanting *tick*, joined to a preceding character and written either downward (from right to left) or upward (from left to right).

(a) DOWNWARD : __ __ *of the,* __ __ *and the,* __ __ *should the,* __ __ *with the,* __ __ *by the,* __ __ *if the,* __ __ *have the.*

(b) UPWARD : __ __ *beyond the,* __ __ *what the,* __ __ *how the,* __ __ *at the,* __ __ *which the,* __ __ *was the.*

This tick for *the* must never be used initially.

NOTE— __ __ *on the* and __ __ *but the* should slope a little to secure a better angle.

PHRASES

I thank you		why have you
I think you should be		with you
I have the		so much
I have had		with much
I saw the		with which
I see		with each
I am		when they
I may be		what do you
I will		what was
I will be		what can be
you should		it would be
you should be		it should be
you can		it will be
you will		it was
you will be		which was
you may be		which were
you were		he should be
if you were		he will be
they were		if he
how can they		if he were
why do you		too much

GRAMMALOGUES

thank-ed, (think; though, (them;) was,
whose; / shall, wish; with, when;
what, would; O, oh, owe, he.

Exercise 21
Read, copy, and transcribe

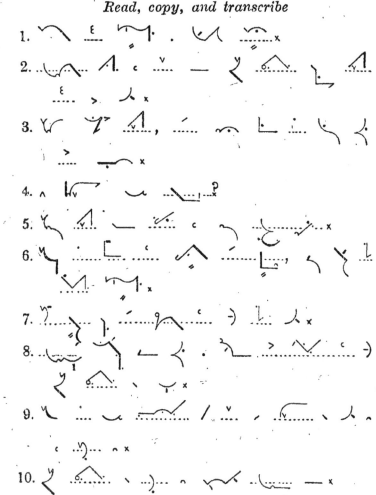

Exercise 22

Write in Shorthand

(Phraseograms in the following letterpress exercises are indicated by the hyphen.)

1. *Why-do-you* think he-*was* aware *of-the* likely failure *of-the* firm ?
2. I-*thank-you for-the* tube *of* colour, *which* I-*think should-be all*-right.
3. They deny they-were at-*the* Tower at-*the* time *of-the* fire.
4. I-*think-you* owe the Head *an* apology *for-the* way *you* hurried away *on*-Monday.
5. If-*he*-were aware *of-the* date, he-*would,* I-*think, have come with* us.
6. Kenneth Doyle, *whose* view *all of* us share, wrote *to* say he-*would* arrive at five.
7. I-*think too*-much time *was-given to-the* topic. *What-do-you think ?*

Summary

1. *Phraseography* is the name given to the principle of joining word-forms together. The outline thus obtained is called a *phraseogram.*
2. The following must be carefully noted—
    (*a*) Awkward joinings must be avoided.
    (*b*) The first word-form in a phraseogram must occupy its own position. A first-position word-form may, however, be raised or lowered to permit of a following stroke being written above, on or through the line.
3. The word *the* may be expressed by a light slanting tick joined to a preceding character and written either downward or upward. The tick for *the* is never used initially.

CHAPTER VII

CIRCLE *S* AND *Z*

Circle S and Z. 40. The consonants *S* and *Z* are represented not only by the strokes) and) but also by a small circle o Initially the circle represents the light sound of *s* only ; medially and finally it represents the sound of *s* or *z*. The sound of *z* initially must be represented by the stroke) as, ⟍ *zeal,* ⟍ *zero,* ⟍ *zenith.*

Left and Right Motion. 41. In this chapter, and in the following pages, the term *Left Motion* means the motion of the hand in writing the longhand letter *O* ⟲, the opposite motion being termed the *Right Motion* ⟳. The circle *s*, when standing alone, is written with the *left* motion.

42. The circle *s* is written (*a*) inside curves, (*b*) outside angles, and (*c*) with the *left* motion when joined to straight strokes not forming an angle ; thus,

(*a*) ⟍ *safes,* ⟍ *soothes,* ⟍ *essays,* ⟍ *sashes,* ⟍ *seems,* ⟍ *sense,* ⟍ *sings,* ⟍ *slays,* ⟍ *source,* ⟍ *fossil,* ⟍ *thistle,* ⟍ *Cecil,* ⟍ *muscle,* ⟍ *nestles,* ⟍ *designs,* ⟍ *lisps.*

(*b*) ⟍ *gasp,* ⟍ *rasp,* ⟍ *risk,* ⟍ *task,* ⟍ *Biscay,* ⟍ *justice,* ⟍ *hasp.*

(*c*) ⟍ *space,* ⟍ *seeds,* ⟍ *sages,* ⟍ *soaks,* ⟍ *sorrows,* ⟍ *Busby,* ⟍ *tacit,* ⟍ *cask,* ⟍ *razor,* ⟍ *wiser.*

31

43. Initial circle *s* is always read *first;* final circle *s* is always read *last;* and vowel signs are placed and read in relation to the stroke consonant, and not to the circle, as in the foregoing examples.

44. The circle *s* may be added to a stroke logogram, as, ⎯ *come,* ⎯ₒ *comes,* ⟍ *put,* ⟍ₒ *puts.*

Stroke L and Circle. 45. When the stroke *l* immediately precedes or follows a circle which is attached to a curve, it is written in the same direction as the circle; thus, 𝒢 *lesson,* ⎯⎯ *cancel,* ⧖ *vessel,* ⌒ *loser.*

46. A lightly-sounded vowel may be omitted, as in ⟋ *poison,* ⋀ₒ *refusal,* ⌒ *answer,* ⅃ *desire.*

Exercise 23

Read, copy, and transcribe

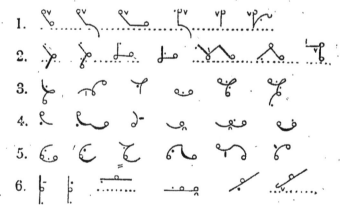

Exercise 24

Write in Shorthand

1. Lays, slays, oars, soars, face, facing.
2. Poison, poisonous, pacifies, voicing, rising, toilsome.
3. Dusky, excites, customs, justice, rusty, suffice.
4. Less, Leslie, shame, shameless, shamelessly, slums.
5. Excusing, refusing, spacing, basin, dozen, resigns.
6. Hope, hopeless, hopelessly, consul, pencil, fossils.

GRAMMALOGUES

usual-ly; *as, has,* *is, his;* *because;* *itself;* *those, thyself,* *this,* *thus.*

Exercise 25

Read, copy, and transcribe

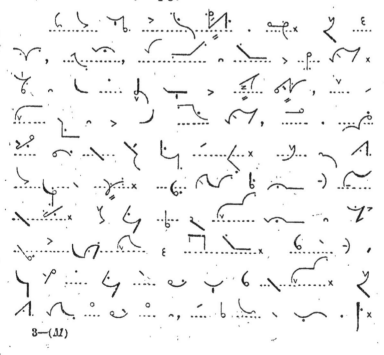

3—(M)

Exercise 26

Write in Shorthand

If Miss Nelson *wishes to* see-*the* works, she *can come to-this* office *on* Tuesday or Wednesday *of-this* week, *and*-I-*shall-be* happy *to* show *all-the* details she may desire *to* see. I-*think-it-is but* fair *to* say *this is-the* busy season *with* us, *and* I-*shall-have but a* few minutes *to* spare *to* Miss Nelson. My deputy *can* take charge *of-the* lady. I-will *thank-you* if-*you*-will *put-the* facts *to-the* lady *as* nicely *as you-can, because* she may *think* I-am *an* idle fellow *with-much* time at-my disposal. I-know *you*-will excuse *this* appeal, *and*-I hope *you*-will-*do what* I ask, *as* I *should-be* sorry *to* upset Miss Nelson, or *to* appear *to be* rude *when* she *comes.*

Summary

1. A small circle used initially represents *s* only; medially and finally it represents *s* or *z*.
2. The circle *s* is written outside angles, inside curves, and with the left motion to straight strokes not forming an angle.
3. An *initial* circle is always read *first;* a *final* circle is always read *last.*
4. The stroke *l*, immediately preceding or following a circle attached to a curve, is written in the same direction as the circle.
5. The circle *s* may be added to stroke logograms.

Stroke S and Z. 47. Wherever there is an initial or a final vowel *sound*, there must be a stroke consonant, to provide a place for the vowel *sign*. Therefore, the stroke *s* must be written when a vowel precedes initial *s*, or when a vowel follows final *s* or *z*; thus, ⟩ *ace*, ⟩ *say*; ⟩ *oose*, ⟩ *zoo*; ⟩ *asp*, but ⟩ *sap*; ⟩ *ask*, but ⟩ *sack*; ⟩ *racy*, but ⟩ *race*; ⟩ *busy*, but ⟩ *bees*.

48. Where the stroke *s* is written initially in the root word, it is retained in compounds and in derivatives formed by means of a prefix, thus, ⟩ *saw*, ⟩ *saw-bench*, ⟩ *assailed*, ⟩ *unassailed*, ⟩ *ease*, ⟩ *disease*.

The stroke is also written—

(a) In words like ⟩ *science*, ⟩ *sewer*, where a triphone immediately follows initial *s*.

(b) In words like ⟩ *cease*, ⟩ *saucer*, where initial *s* is immediately followed by a vowel and another *s* or *z*.

(c) In words like ⟩ *sinuous*, ⟩ *tortuous*, ⟩ *joyous*, where the final syllable *-ous* is immediately preceded by a diphthong.

Exercise 27

Read, copy, and transcribe

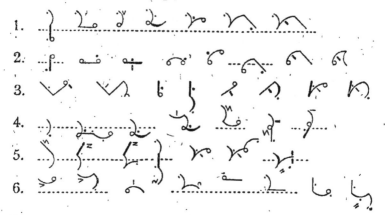

Exercise 28

Write in Shorthand

1. Asp, aside, assess, Assam, assailing, asylum, assayed.
2. Base, basso, juice, juicy, legs, legacy, coals, colza.
3. Spouse, espouse, seek, Essex, score, Oscar, Isaac.
4. Essays, essence, escapes, Eskimo, say, aces.
5. Siamese, sciatica, sighing, easy, uneasy, uneasily, uneasiness.
6. Sinuous, tortuous, vacuous, tenuous, ingenuous.

GRAMMALOGUES

⁀ me, ⌢ him; ◠ myself, ⌒ himself; ＼ special-ly,

＼ speak; ＼ subject-ed; �\ several.

Exercise 29

Read, copy, and transcribe

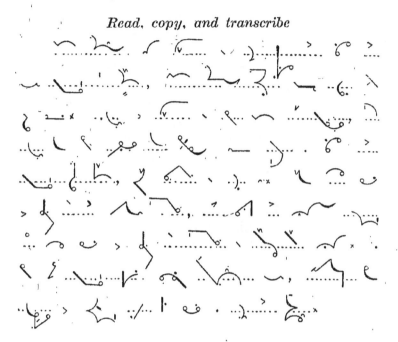

Exercise 30

Write in Shorthand

For *several special* reasons I *should* like *you to-come*
and see *me on* Wednesday *as* early *as you-can.* I
specially desire *you to-*write out-*the* names *of all-the*
firms *with-which-you have-had* business dealings since
you came *to* us. I-*shall* discuss *a* new policy *with-you,*
and-the names *for-which* I ask may-*be of* use. I-am
a bit upset at-*the* refusal *of* Askew *and* Benson *to-*take
those Eskimo rugs, *and-I should* like *to* know-*the*
reasons *for-the* refusal. I-*have several subjects* besides
these *of-which* I-*wish to speak to-you when* I-*see-you*
on Wednesday. Ask *to* see *me as* soon *as you* arrive.

Summary

The stroke *s* or
z must be
written :

1. When a vowel precèdes initial *s* or follows final *s* or *z*.
2. When initial *s* is immediately followed by a vowel and another *s* or *z*.
3. When initial *s* is immediately followed by a triphone.
4. When the final syllable *-ous* is preceded by a diphthong.
5. When the word is a compound like *sea-mew, saw-bench.*
6. When the word is a derivative like *unceasing, unassailed,* where the stroke would be written in the root word.

CHAPTER IX

LARGE CIRCLES *SW* AND *SS* OR *SZ*

SW Circle. 49. A large INITIAL circle, written with the same motion as the circle *s*, represents the double consonant *sw*, thus, ＿ℓ＿ *seat*, ＿ℓ＿ *sweet*, ⌀ *sum*, ⌀ *swum*. As a vowel cannot be written to a circle, the stroke *w* must be written in words like ⌀ *sway*, ⌀ *suasive*. The *sw* circle is used initially only.

SS Circle. 50. A large MEDIAL or FINAL circle, written with the same motion as circle *s*, represents *s-s*, having a light or heavy sound, with the intervening vowel *ĕ*; thus, ⌀ (*ses*) *necessity*; ⌀ (*sez*) *passes*; ⌀ (*zes*) *possessive*; ⌀ (*zez*) *causes*. When a vowel other than *ĕ* intervenes, it is indicated by placing the vowel-sign within the circle; thus, ⌀ *exist*, ⌀ *exhaust*, ⌀ *exercised*. Final *s* is added thus, ⌀ *exercises*. The large circle is also used to express the sounds of two *s*'s in consecutive syllables, as in ⌀ *mis-spell*.

Plurals and Possessives. 51. As ⌀ *Lucy*, ⌀ *policy*, ⌀ *jealousy*, etc., are written with the stroke *s*, the stroke *s* is retained in the derived words ⌀ *Lucy's*, ⌀ *policies*, ⌀ *jealousies*. (See also pars. 47 and 48.)

52. A few words ending in *s-s* are written with the circle and stroke, or the stroke and circle, in order to distinguish them from other words containing similar consonants, and in which the large

circle is employed ; thus, ⟩ *possess,* but ⌣ *pauses ;*
⌐ *access,* but ⌐ *axis ;* ⟋ *recess,* but ⟋ *races.*

Large Circles in Phraseography. 53. The *sw*
circle is used for the words *as we* in phrases like
ℓ *as we have,* ⌐ *as we can,* and for *as w-* in ℓ *as*
well as ; and the *ss* circle for the two *s's* in phrases
like ⟩ *in this city,* ⟨ *this is,* ⌐ *as is,* or *as has,*

○ *is as* or *is his.*

Exercise 31

Read, copy, and transcribe

1. ⟨image of shorthand characters⟩

2. ⟨image of shorthand characters⟩

3. ⟨image of shorthand characters⟩

4. ⟨image of shorthand characters⟩

5. ⟨image of shorthand characters⟩

6. ⟨image of shorthand characters⟩

7. ⟨image of shorthand characters⟩

Exercise 32

Write in Shorthand

1. Sweetly, sweetness, swig, swain, swing, swimmer.
2. Entices, reduces, revises, ounces, minces, laces.
3. Roses, peruses, terraces, essences, fences, romances.
4. Dazes, decisive, races, resist, misses, Mississippi.
5. Fallacy, fallacies, Morrissey, Morrissey's, curacy,
   curacies.
6. Thesis, emphasis, paralysis, Genesis, Nemesis, axis.

GRAMMALOGUES

⌣ in, any, ⌣ own ; ⟍ your, ⟍ year ; ⁄ arc,

⁄ our, hour ; ℗ ourselves, ⟨ themselves.

Exercise 33

Read, copy, and transcribe

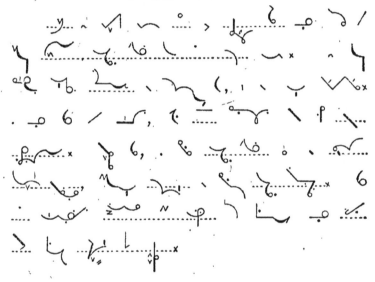

Exercise 34

Write in Shorthand

The invoices *and* bills *of* lading *for-the* valances *and* laces *are* ready *for* despatch, *and-the* cases *themselves are to*-leave *by-the* " Swiss Valley," sailing *on* Wednesday. *The* advices *should-be with our* customers *by-the* tenth *of-*March, *and-*they-will-*do all-*they *can to-*make *a* success *of-the* deal. They know-*the* business thoroughly, *and you-*may safely leave *it to-them. It-is* scarcely necessary *to* emphasize *what* they *themselves* know *already.*

Summary

1. A large initial circle represents *sw*.
2. A large medial or final circle represents the light or heavy sound of *s-s* with an intervening vowel.
3. Where a root word ends with stroke *s*, the plural, possessive, or third person singular is formed by the addition of the circle *s*.
4. Where a root word ends with a circle *s*, the plural, possessive, or the third person singular is formed by the use of the large circle *ses*.
5. A few words ending in *s-s* are written with the circle and stroke, or with the stroke and circle, to distinguish them from words in which the large circle is employed.
6. The *sw* circle is used in phrases like *as well as, as we know;* and the *ss* circle in phrases like *it is said, in this city.*

CHAPTER X

LOOP *ST* AND *STR*

Loop ST. 54. The combination *st*, as in *steam*, *mist*, *passed* (pa*st*) is represented by a loop made half the length of the stroke to which it is attached ; thus,
⌒∿ *seem*, ⌒∿ *steam*, ↶ *sown*, ↶ *stone*, ᴏ⸳ *sake*, ⸱⸱ *stake*, ⌒ₒ *miss*, ⌒∿ *mist*, ⌠° *lace*, ⌠° *laced*, ↘ₒ *pass*, ↘ *past*.

Like the circle *s*, the *st* loop is written with the Left motion to straight strokes and inside curves, as shown above. Like the circle *s*, too, the *st* loop is always read first at the beginning of the stroke and last at the end.

55. Since a final *vowel* sound requires a final *stroke*, in order to provide a place for the vowel-sign (par. 47), it follows that the *st* loop cannot be employed finally when a vowel follows *t ;* thus, ↘ *best*, but ↘ₒ *bestow ;* ↙ *rust*, but ↗ᵢ *rusty ;* ⸛ *honest*, but ⸛ *honesty*.

56. The *st* loop may also be employed finally for the heavy sound of *zd*, as in the words ↙⸗ *fused*, ↗⸗ *refused*, ⸗↘ *opposed*, ↓⸗ *disposed*. The word *caused* is written ⊓ₗ to distinguish it from ⊏ *cost*.

Loop STR. 57. A large loop, extending two-thirds of the length of the stroke to which it is attached, represents *str*. This *str* (ster) loop *is never written at the beginning of an outline*. Like the circle *s* and the *st* loop, the *str* loop is written with the Left

43

motion to straight strokes, and inside curves; thus, ⤳ *pass*, ⤳ *past*, ⤳ *pastor*, ⤳ *fast*, ⤳ *faster*.

58. The *st* and *str* loops may be used medially where a good joining results; thus, ⟆ *justify*, ⟆ *elastic*, ⟆ *masterpiece*.

59. The *st* loop cannot be employed when a vowel occurs between *s* and *t*, nor can the *str* loop be written when a strongly sounded vowel occurs between *st* and *r*, because where there is a vowel sound there must be a stroke consonant to provide a place for the vowel-sign (par. 47). Compare ⟆ *best* and ⟆ *beset*, ⟋ *rest* and ⟋ *receipt*, ⟆ *pastor*, ⟆ *pasture*, ⟆ *poster*, ⟆ *posture*.

60. The circle *s* is added to a final loop as follows— ⟆ *taste*, ⟆ *tastes*; ⟆ *lustre*, ⟆ *lustres*.

Exercise 35

Read, copy, and transcribe

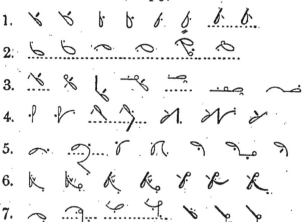

Exercise 36

Write in Shorthand

1. Stout, stoutly, stock, stockade, style, stylish.
2. Rust, rusts, nest, nests, waste, wastes.
3. Box, boxed, lapse, lapsed, refuse, refused.
4. Coaster, coasters, boaster, boasters, muster.
5. Stone, stole, stave, stem, stung, star.
6. Gassed, gazette, vest, visit, rust, russet.
7. Bolsters, barrister, waster, lustre, sinister, minister.

GRAMMALOGUES

first, *influence*, *influenced*, *next*, *most*, *language, owing*, *thing*, *young*, *Lord*, *we*.

Exercise 37

Read, copy, and transcribe

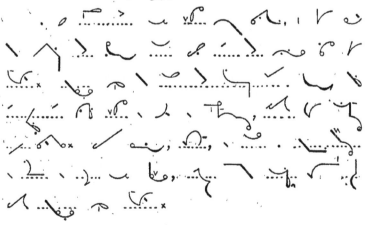

Exercise 38

Write in Shorthand

The language of-the young barrister in-the case was most stately, and it-must have influenced both judge and jury. It almost looked as-if-the case was lost at-the first, because of-the calm way in-which-the opposing counsel set out to state-the facts for-his side. But-the young barrister faced the test fairly, and-his language and style, though different, showed him to be a master of-law and logic. We-shall watch his career at-the bar, and-we-think he-must succeed because of-his abilities.

Revisionary Exercise (A)

Write in Shorthand

If-you-can put me up for a week in August, I-shall-be ready to-go and stay with-you. You-can-have as much walking as you-like. I-shall-be at-your disposal at almost any hour, and-as I-am a rare walker myself, I-think I-can say you-will-have all-the exercise you wish. You ought-to be a different fellow when I-leave, if-you-will-be influenced by-me. I-think I-can give-you a mile in six and beat you. I-have-had some talk with young Lord Robson several-times in-the past week, and he says you-can-do five miles an hour. Those-who saw you last autumn and-know what you-can-do, all say-the same thing. This-is all I-know as to-your form. But-we-shall-see for ourselves. I-think-you-will own I-am far beyond you in speed. It-will-be a case of-each for-himself and-the race to-the faster of-the two. Oh, I-know I-shall beat you, unless you-are faster this year. Those-who think poorly of-themselves only induce those-

who know *them to-think-the* same. I *speak for-myself, because* I-know *myself.* I-*can* say *a* deal on-*this subject, and*-I *usually do*-so. *You* ask *why* I-*have* stayed away so-long. *The* answer *is* business keeps *me* away. *When would-you* like *me to-come* ? *The* best of luck *to-you and to-the* rest *of-the* family ! *It*-will-*be* nice *to* see *them all, though* I-saw *most of-them a* month or-*two* ago.   (283 words)

Summary

1. A small loop represents *st ;* a large loop represents *str.*

2. The *st* loop may be used initially, medially or finally.

3. The *st* loop may be employed finally to represent the sound of *zd.*

4. The *str* loop may be used medially or finally, but not initially.

5. The *st* loop cannot be employed when a vowel occurs between *s* and *t*, nor can the loop be written immediately before a final vowel.

6. The *str* loop cannot be written when a strongly sounded vowel occurs between *st* and *r*.

CHAPTER XI

INITIAL HOOKS TO STRAIGHT STROKES AND CURVES

Double Consonants. 61. The liquids *r* and *l* frequently blend with other consonants so as to form a double consonant, as in the words *pray*, *blow*, *drink*, *glare*, *fry*, *fly*, or are separated from a preceding consonant by an obscure vowel only, as in *paper*, *maker*, *table*, *babel*. These consonant combinations are represented by prefixing a hook to the simple shorthand characters to indicate their union with *r* and *l*.

R Hook to Straight Strokes. 62. A small initial hook, written with the Right motion, adds *R* to straight strokes; thus,

p,	pr,	br,	tr,	dr,	chr,	jr,	kr,	gr.

L Hook to Straight Strokes. 63. A small initial hook, written with the Left motion, adds *L* to straight strokes; thus,

p,	pl,	bl,	tl,	dl,	chl,	jl,	kl,	gl.

R Hook to Curved Strokes. 64. A *small* initial hook, written inside the curve, adds *r* to a curved stroke; thus,

f,	fr,	vr,	thr,	THr,	shr,	zhr,	mr,	nr.

L Hook to Curved Strokes. 65. A *large* initial hook, written inside the curve, adds *l* to a curved stroke ; thus,

$$\smallsmile \quad \subset \quad \subset \quad \subset \quad \smile \text{ (upward)} \quad \frown \quad \smile$$

f, ~ *fl,* ~ *vl,* ~ *thl,* ~ *shl,* ~ *ml,* ~ *nl.*

66. The stroke ╱ *r* is not hooked initially, because the characters ⟋ and ⟋ are employed for *w* and *y.*

SHR and SHL. 67. The double consonant ⟋ *shr* is always written *downward,* and the double consonant ⟋ *shl* is always written *upward.*

Small Hook to NG. 68. The hooked form ⟋ represents *ng-kr* or *ng-gr,* as heard in the words ba*nkr,* fi*nger.*

69. The hooked forms should be called by their syllabic names ; as, ╲ *per,* ╲ *pel,* ⊂ *fer,* ⊂ *fel,* etc.

Vowels and Double Consonants. 70. Vowels are placed and read to the hooked forms as they are placed and read to the simple forms ; thus, ╲ *pie,* ╲ *ply,* ╲ *apply ;* ⟋ *lead,* ⟋ *leader,* ⟋ *leaderless ;* ⟍ *pity,* ⟍ *pretty ;* ⟍ *Peter,* ⟍ *Peterloo ;* ⟂ *tie,* ⟂ *try,* ⟂ *trifle,* ⟂ *trifler.*

Extended Use of L Hook. 71. In order to obtain easier forms the *l* hook is sometimes used in words in which the *l* properly belongs to the following syllable, and not to the stroke to which it is attached ; thus, ⟋ *deeply,* ⟋ *briefly,* ⟋ *briefless,* ⟋ *thinly,* ⟋ *enlivener,* ⟋ *peevishly.*

Exercise 39

Read, copy, and transcribe

Exercise 40

Write in Shorthand

1. Pry, pride, preach, preacher, bray, break, breaker.
2. Crow, croak, cricket, grew, group, grape, bigger.
3. Ply, plied, played, plum, place, replace, replaces.
4. Problem, enclose, enclosure, blow, blows, bluster.
5. Double, pedal, fiddle, model, fickle, glow, gloat.
6. Fred, afraid, tougher, other, otherwise, every, usher, pressure, inner.
7. Honour, honourable, flavour, flower, Fletcher, faithful, privilege, Marshall, specialize.

GRAMMALOGUES

~ *principle, principal-ly ;* ⟍ *liberty,* ⟍ *member, remember-ed,* ~ *number-ed ;* ⌐ *truth ;* ⌐ *Dr., doctor,* ⌐ *dear,* ⌐ *during ;* / *chair,* / *cheer,* / *larger ;* — *care.*

Exercise 41

Read, copy, and transcribe

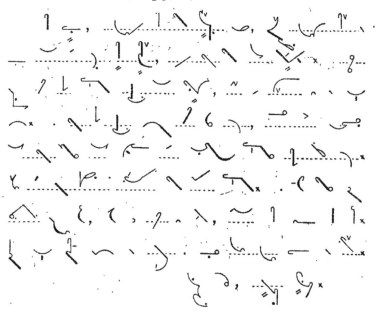

Exercise 42

Write in Shorthand

Dear-Sir,

Thank-you for-your favour *of-the first* of April, *and-for* mailing *me your* price-lists *and* samples of blue *and* black inks *and* glue *in-the several* sizes *of* bottles. I-*think-the* labels *are* better *and* brighter now. I-*shall give-the* samples *a* fair trial *during-the next* few weeks, *and*, if suitable, I-*may-be* able *to* stock *a large number of-the* smaller sizes. *As* I-*think-you* know, my *principal* business *is with* legal offices, *and*, *as you*-will agree, *it-is* essential *to* offer *them* only *first*-class inks.

Yours-truly,

Summary

1. A small initial hook written with the Right motion adds *r* to simple straight strokes except ╱

2. A small initial hook written with the Left motion adds *l* to simple straight strokes except ╱

3. The hooked signs should be called by their syllabic names.

4. A small initial hook to curves adds *r ;* a large initial hook to curves adds *l.*

5. *Shr* is always written downward, and *shl* is always written upward.

6. *Ng* with a small initial hook represents the sounds of *ng-kr*, *ng-gr.*

7. Hooked forms may be considered as representing syllables.

CHAPTER XII

ALTERNATIVE FORMS

Additional Signs for FR, VR, etc. 72. The strokes ↘ *r*, ⟩ *s*, are not hooked for the addition of *r* or *l*. They are, however, hooked to provide alternative forms for *fr, vr, fl, vl, thr, thr*; thus,

ᒐ ᒐ ᑊ ᑊ ᒐ ᒐ
fr,   *vr,*   *thr,*   *thr,*   *fl,*   *vl.*

The first form of each pair is called a *left* curve, because it is made with the Left motion; the second form of each pair is called a *right* curve, because it is made with the Right motion. There is only one form for *thl* (, namely, the left curve.

73. (*a*) When standing alone, the *left* curves for *fr, vr, thr*, are used if a vowel precedes, and the *right* curves if a vowel does not precede; thus,

⌇ *affray,* ↘ *fray,* ⌇ *ether,* ⌇ *three.*

(*b*) When joined to another stroke, the form is used which gives the easier joining, preference being given to the right forms; thus, ⌇ *Friday,*

↘ *virtue,* ↘ *frame,* ↘ *verbal,* ⟩ *thermal,*

⟩ *leather,* ⌇ *coffer,* ↗ *lover.* Generally, it will be found that the *left* curves join better with strokes written towards the *left,* and the *right* curves with strokes written towards the *right.*

FL and VL. 74. The right curves ᒐ *fl,* ᒐ *vl* are used only after *straight upstrokes* and the *horizontals*

— *k,* — *g,* ⌣ *n;* thus, ⌇ *cavil,* ⌇ *naval,*

53

⤷ *rifle*, ⤶ *weevil*. In all other cases the left curves ⌒ *fl*, ⌒ *vl* are used; thus, ⌒ *flow*, ⌒ *aflow*, ⌒ *flake*, ⌒ *flicker*, ⌒ *joyful*, ⤶ *arrival*.

Intervening Vowels. 75. (*a*) In order to obtain a briefer or an easier outline, an initially hooked form may be used even when a vowel separates *l* or *r* from the stroke consonant. Where necessary, an intervening dot vowel between a stroke and an initial hook may be indicated by writing a small circle, instead of a dot, either after or before the stroke; thus, ⌒ *barley*, ⌒ *challenge*, ⌐ *narrate*, ⤴ *sharply*; and an intervening dash vowel or diphthong may be indicated by striking the sign through the stroke consonant; thus, ⟋ *Burmah*, ⤴ *coarsely*, ⤳ *nullify*, ⌐ *lecture*.

(*b*) If the vowel-sign cannot easily be written through the stroke, it may be placed at the beginning or the end for a first-place or a third-place vowel respectively; thus, ⟋ *corner*, ⤴ *tolerable*, ⤵ *captures*.

(*c*) In words like ⤴ *perceive*, ⌐ *telegraphy*, ⟋ *mercury*, ⤴ *nervously*, the hooked form sufficiently represents the first syllable of the word. With the exception of ⤴ *nurse*, ⤴ *Turk*, ⌐ *dark*, and a few other words, the initially hooked strokes are not used in monosyllables where the consonants are separated by a vowel. Such words as ⟍ *pair*,

✓ *pale,* ⌐ *tare,* ⌐ *tore* are written with the separate strokes, so as to indicate the intervening vowel.

Exercise 43

Read, copy, and transcribe

1.

2.

3.

4.

5.

6.

7.

8.

Exercise 44

Write in Shorthand

1. Fray, three, Friday, frank, differ, endeavour.
2. Free, freely, thrifty, recover, waver, Waverley.
3. Flood, flask, flock, playful, grateful, effectively.
4. Baffle, trifle, shovel, removal, inflame.
5. Rival, roughly, hovel, cavalry, gravel.
6. Charming, courage, encourage, furnace, Norwich.

GRAMMALOGUES

people; *belief, believe-d;* *tell,* *'till;* *deliver-ed-y;* *largely;* *call,* *equal-ly;* *over,* *however;* *valuation.*

Exercise 45

Read, copy, and transcribe

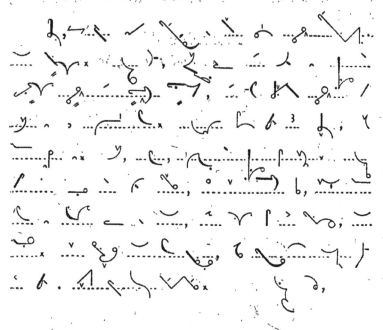

Exercise 46

Write in Shorthand

Have-you ever noticed *what* useful lessons *you-may-receive* through *a* shrewd look at-*the* faces *of-the* people *you-come* across *in* travelling? *You-will-see in-them* humour *and* gloom; generosity *and* miserable stinginess; pluck *and* nervous fear; wisdom *and* simplicity. *You-will-notice the* drinker *and-the* abstainer; *the* hopeful *and-the* fearful; *the* clever talker *and-the* bore; *the* flighty *and-the* modest; *the* pilferer *and-the* honest fellow; *the* loafer *and-the* worker. Five minutes *in a* tramway car may offer us many lessons if-*we care to*-take *them*.

Summary

1. (a) When standing alone, the left curves ⟍ *fr*,
⟍ *vr*, (*thr*, (THr are used if a vowel
precedes, and the right curves ⟍ *fr*, ⟍ *vr*,
) *thr*,) THr, if a vowel does not precede.

(b) When joined to another stroke either curve is
used in order to secure an easier joining.

2. The right curves ⟍ *fl*, ⟍ *vl* are used after
straight upstrokes, and after the horizontals
— *k*, — *g*; and ⌣ *n* ; in all other cases the
left curves ⟍ *fl*, ⟍ *vl* are used.

3. (a) An intervening dot vowel between a stroke
and an initial hook is shown by writing a
small circle for the dot vowel, either after
or before the stroke.

(b) An intervening dash vowel, or a diphthong,
is shown by intersecting the sign for the
vowel or diphthong.

CHAPTER XIII

CIRCLE OR LOOP PRECEDING INITIAL HOOK

S before Straight Strokes Hooked for R. 76. Initial *s*, or *sw*, or *st*, preceding a straight stroke hooked for *r*, is expressed by writing the circle or loop on the same side as the *r* hook, that is, with the Right motion; thus, ⟍ *pry*, ⟍ *spry*; ⟋ *tray*, ⟋ *stray*; ⌐ *crew*, ⌐ *screw*; ⌐ *eater*, ⌐ *sweeter*; ⌐ *utter*, ⌐ *stutter*; ⌐ *ochre*, ⌐ *stoker*.

S before other Hooked Strokes. 77. In other cases *s* is written inside the initial hook, so that both circle and hook are clearly shown; thus, ⟍ *offer*, ⟍ *suffer*, ⟍ *sever*, ⟍ *deceiver*, ⌐ *soother*, ⌐ *sinner*, ⟍ *prisoner*, ⟍ *plies*, ⟍ *supplies*, ⟍ *possible*, ⟍ *pedestal*, ⌐ *settle*, ⌐ *satchel*, ⌐ *sickle*, ⟍ *bicycle*, ⌐ *exclaim*, ⌐ *evil*, ⌐ *civil*, ⟍ *prosper*, ⟍ *offspring*, ⌐ *destroy*, ⌐ *extra*, ⌐ *mystery*, ⌐ *nostrum*, ⌐ *lisper*, ⌐ *reciter*, ⌐ *wiseacre*.

(*a*) Where *l* hook cannot be clearly shown in the middle of a word, the stroke *l* is written; thus, ⟍ *forcible*, ⟍ *unsaddle*, ⌐ *musical*.

(*b*) When *skr* or *sgr* follows *t* or *d*, the circle is written with the Left motion; thus, ⌐ *tacker*, ⌐ *Tasker*; ⌐ *degree*, ⌐ *disagree*; ⌐ *digress*, *disgrace.* When *skr* occurs after *p* or *b*, the hook *r* may be omitted; thus, *prescribe,* *subscriber.*

Exercise 47

Read, copy, and transcribe

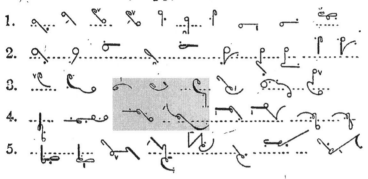

1.

2.

3.

4.

5.

Exercise 48

Write in Shorthand

1. Set, setter, settle, stab, stabber, sable, sweet, sweeter, sweetly, seek, seeker, sickle.
2. Supreme, sublime, cider, sidle, sacred, seclude.
3. Traceable, disclosure, plausible, classical, distressed, extremity, Tasker, task.
4. Suffers, simmers, sinners, peacefully, explosive, expels, risible, rasper.
5. Disgraces, discloses, prescribes, crossways.

GRAMMALOGUES

from;   *very;*   *there, their;*   *more,* *remark-ed,*   *mere, Mr.;*   *nor,*   *near;* *surprise,*   *surprised;*   *sure;*   *pleasure.*

PHRASE

they are.

Exercise 49

Read, copy, and transcribe

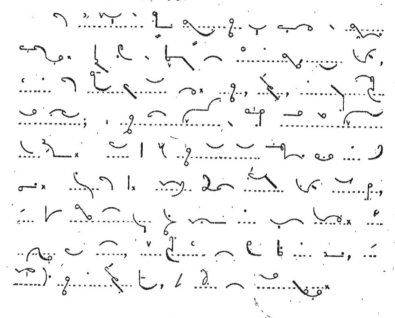

Exercise 50

Write in Shorthand

We-are surprised to know *from-your* favour *of-the* sixth of August *of-the* extremely long delay *in-the* delivery *of-the* Surrey *and* Gloucestershire books. So far *as-we-can* discover, *there-is*-no very clear reason *for-the* delay. *We-have* looked *into-the* case, *as* you*-may-be-sure, and it-is* still *a* mystery. *Mr.* Strong, *our* dispatch clerk, expressly disclaims *any* blame, *but,* if-possible, he-will take *more care with-the* books still *to-come.* He-will personally supervise *the* addressing *of-the* parcels. By-*the* way, *we* hope *to-have-the* new Uxbridge book ready *very* soon. *It-will-be in-the* same style *as our* classical library.

Summary

1. The circles *s* and *sw* and the loop *st* are prefixed
   to the straight strokes hooked for *r* by writing
   the circle or loop with the Right motion.
2. The circle *s* is prefixed to all other initially hooked
   strokes by writing the circle inside the hook, so
   that both the circle and hook are clearly shown.
3. The circle in words like *tusker* and *disgrace* is
   written with the Left motion; but when *skr*
   follows *p* or *b*, the *r* is omitted.

CHAPTER XIV

N AND F HOOKS

N Hook. 78. A small final hook, struck by the Right motion ↩ adds *n* to all straight strokes; thus. ⟋ *Ben.* ⌐ *tone,* ⟋ *chain,* ⁀ *coin,* ⟋ *rain,* ⟋ *hone.*

79. The hook which represents *r* at the beginning of a straight stroke, and that which represents *n* at the end, are both struck by the Right motion; thus, ⟍ *brain,* ⌐ *train,* ⊂⊃ *crane.*

80. A small final hook, written inside the curve, adds *n* to all curved strokes.; thus, ⟍ *fain,* ⌐ *thin,* ⟋ *assign,* ⟋ *shine,* ⌒ *moon,* ⟋ *lean.*

F-V Hook. 81. A small final hook, struck by the LeFt motion ↩, adds *f* or *v* to all straight strokes; thus, ⟍ *buff,* ⌐ *tough,* ⌐ *chafe,* ⁀ *cave,* ⟋ *rave,* ⟋ *hive.*

82. The hook which represents *l* at the beginning of a straight stroke, and that which represents *f* or *v* at the end, are both struck by the LeFt motion; thus, ⟍ *bluff,* ⊂⊃ *cliff,* ⊂⊃ *glove.*

83. There is no *f* or *v* hook to curves; therefore the stroke *f* or *v* must always be employed if *f* or *v* follows a curved stroke. The following pairs of words illustrate this: ⟍ *fine,* ⟍ *five;* ⟍ *line,* ⟍ *live;* ⟍ *nine,* ⟍ *knife;* ⌒ *moon,* ⟍ *move.*

84. A final hook cannot be employed when the word ends with a vowel sound, because a final vowel

requires a final stroke (par. 47). Compare ⟍ *pen*
and ⟍ *penny;* ⟍ *puff* and ⟍ *puffy;* ⟍ *fun*
and ⟍ *funny;* ⟿ *men* and ⟾ *many.*

LN and SH N. 85. The hooked forms *ln* and *sh n*
when joined to another stroke may be written
upward or downward; thus, ⟋ *gallon,* ⟋ *melon;*
⟋ *fallen,* ⟋ *aniline;* ⟋ *situation,* ⟋ *extenuation.*

Hooks used Medially. 86. The *n* and *f* hooks may
be employed medially when they join easily and
clearly with the following stroke; thus, ⟋ *plenty,*
⟋ *agent,* ⟋ *suddenness,* ⟋ *punish,* ⟋ *painful,*
⟋ *defence,* ⟋ *divide,* ⟋ *refer,* ⟋ *graphic.* If
these outlines are compared with the following, it
will be observed that a stroke is often used medially
in preference to a hook in order to secure more facile
outlines, or for purposes of distinction: ⟋ *brandy,*
⟋ *agency,* ⟋ *suddenly,* ⟋ *pronounce,*
⟋ *painless,* ⟋ *reviewer,* ⟋ *gravity.*

Syllable -NER. 87. The hook *n* and downward *r*
are used for the representation of the final syllable
-ner when following a straight upstroke; in all other
cases, the syllable is represented by the sign ⟿;
thus, ⟍ *opener,* ⟋ *joiner,* ⟿ *keener,* ⟋ *liner;*
but ⟋ *runner,* ⟿ *winner,* ⟋ *yawner.*

N and F Hooks in Phraseography. 88. The *n* hook is sometimes used in phraseography for the words *been, than, on,* and *own,* and the *f-v* hook for the words *have* and *of;* thus, ⟍ *I have been,* ⅃ *I had been,* ⟍ *better than,* ⟋ *carried on,* ⟩ *their own,* ⟋₂ *our own,* ⟋ *which have,* ⌐ *out of.*

Exercise 51

Read, copy, and transcribe

1.

2.

3.

4.

5.

Exercise 52

Write in Shorthand

1. Open, opening, tune, tuning, dine, dining, strain.
2. Begin, beginning, run, runner, win, winner, join.
3. Fan, fancy, fin, finish, vain, vanish, mean, meanness, noun, renown.
4. Pave, paving, prove, provide, provoke, chaff, chaffinch, refer, referring, preserve.
5. Pen, penny, deaf, defy, fun, funny, men, many.

GRAMMALOGUES

⟍ *been;* ⌡ *general-ly;* ⌐ *within;* ⟨ *southern;* ⟋ *northern;* ⟍ *behalf;* ⌊ *advantage,* ⌐ *difficult.*

Exercise 53

Read, copy, and transcribe

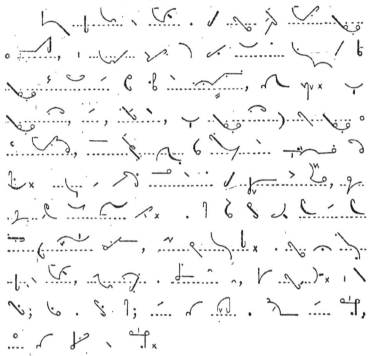

Exercise 54

Write in Shorthand

Local authorities, *as* borough *and* urban councils, *generally* derive *their* main revenue *from-the* rates they levy. They-may, *of*-course, receive profits *from any* business carried-*on* by-*them* *within-the* borough. *Over and* above *all-this* they receive allowances *from-the* state. Either men or women may appeal *to-the* authorities, *and*-they *very* often do, if-they *think* they-*have-been* unfairly assessed. *But it*-will-*be difficult for-them to* obtain relief unless they-*are* able *to*-prove *their* case, *and* satisfy-*the* authorities *as to a* supposed *over*charge.

Summary

1. A small final hook struck by the Right motion adds *n* to straight strokes.
2. A small final hook struck by the LeFt motion adds *f* or *v* to straight strokes.
3. A small final hook adds *n* to curves.
4. There is no *f* or *v* hook to curves.
5. When a word ends with a vowel a final stroke must be used.
6. When joined to other strokes, *ln* and *sh n* may be written either upward or downward.
7. Hooks *n, f* or *v* may be used medially where an easy and legible joining is secured.
8. The final syllable *-ner* is represented by ⌣ when following any stroke except the straight upstrokes.
9. In phraseography, the *n* hook is sometimes used to represent the words *been, than, on,* and *own,* and the *f-v* hook for the words *have* and *of.*

CHAPTER XV

CIRCLES AND LOOPS TO FINAL HOOKS

Straight Strokes followed by NS, etc. 89. The sound of *s* or *ses*, *st* or *str* is added to the hook *n* attached to a straight stroke by writing the circle or loop on the same side as the hook, that is, with the Right motion, as ⌡ *Dan,* ⌡ *dance,* ⌡ *dances,* ⌡ *danced,* ⌡ *Dunster;* ⟍ *pen,* ⟍ *pens,* ⟋⟍ *expense,* ⟋⟍ *expenses;* ⟍ *spin,* ⟍ *spins,* ⟍ *spinster,* ⟍ *spinsters;* ⌐ *glen,* ⌐ *glens,* ⌐ *glances,* ⌐ *glanced;* ⌶ *dispense,* ⌶ *dispenses,* ⌶ *dispensed.*

Curves followed by NS, etc. 90. (*a*) The small circle (representing the sound of *z*) is added to the hook *n* attached to curves by writing the circle inside the hook; thus, ⟍ *fine,* ⟍ *fines;* ⟍ *vines,* ⟍ *frowns,* ⌐ *thrones,* ⟋ *shines,* ⟍ *balloons,* ⟍ *earns,* ⟍ *zones,* ⌒ *mines,* ⌒ *nines,* ⌒ *lawns.* The effect of the preceding rule is that the hook *n* and the small circle attached to a curve represent in all cases the *heavy* sound of *nz,* as in the words *fens* (nz), *vans* (nz), *Athens* (nz), *zones* (nz), *shines* (nz), *shrines* (nz), *moans* (nz), *nouns* (nz), *loans* (nz), *earns* (nz).

(*b*) Where the light sound of *ns* follows a curve, as in the word *fence*, it is expressed by ◡ ; thus, ⟍ *fence,* ⟍ *evince,* ⌒ *lance,* ⌒ *mince,* ⟍ *thence,* ⌒ *nonce.* The effect of this rule is that the construction of outlines is regular in all related words of this class, so that the transcription of the forms is facilitated ; thus, ⟍ *fence,* ⟍ *fences,* ⟍ *fenced,* ⟍ *fencing ;* ⌒ *mince,* ⌒ *minces,* ⌒ *minced,* ⌒ *mincer,* ⌒ *mincing ;* ⟍ *evince,* ⟍ *evinces,* ⟍ *evinced,* ⟍ *evincing.*

Circle S added to F-V Hooks. 91. The circle *s* is added to the hook *f* or *v* by writing the circle inside the hook ; thus, ⟍ *puff,* ⟍ *puffs,* ⌐ *caves,* ⟋ *waves,* ⌐ *heaves,* ⟍ *operatives,* ⟍ *observes,* ⟍ *archives,* ⟋ *sheriffs.*

Medial NS or NZ. 92. When *ns* or *nz* occur medially both letters must be shown, as in the words ⟍ *pensive,* ⌐ *density,* ⌐ *chancel,* ⌐ *Johnson,* ⌐ *cancer,* ⌐ *cleanser,* ⟍ *fencer,* ▨ *immensity,* ⌐ *rancid,* ⌐ *ransack,* ⌐ *wincer,* ⌒ *lonesome,* ⌒ *ransom,* ⌒ *winsome,* ⌒ *hansom.*

Exercise 55

Read, copy, and transcribe

1.

2.

3.

4.

5.

6.

Exercise 56

Write in Shorthand

1. Pence, expense, sixpence, sixpences, dispense, dispenses, dispensed.
2. Button, buttons, train, trains, entrance, entrances, entranced, disappearance, disappearances.
3. Shun, shuns, ocean, oceans, mean, means, linen, linens, saloon, saloons.
4. Reprieve, reprieves, native, natives, chief, chiefs, observe, observes.
5. Fence, offence, offences, immense, immensity, allowance, allowances, prominence.

GRAMMALOGUES

balance ;   *circumstance ;*   *deliverance ;*   *signify-ied-icant ;*   *significance ;*   *opinion.*

Exercise 57

Read, copy, and transcribe

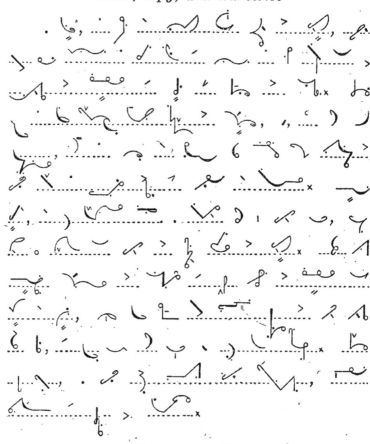

Exercise 58

Write in Shorthand

If I annoy *you in-the deliverance of-*my *opinion,
as-the* chances *are* I-may, *put it* down *to a* reading
man's reverence *for* books, *and-his* diligence *in-the*
pursuit *of a* course *which* lightens many *an hour
for-him. Think of-*these *significant* facts, *and your*
frowns may vanish. If-*you have a* love *of* books,

you-will feel no loneliness if *and when* men forget *you.* *You-can* dispense *with-them in-the circum-stances* ; *for-you*-will-*have within your*self, through-*the* brains *of-your* authors, many better men *to*-replace them. *The balance of advantage in-the* change *is* likely *to be in-your* favour. *You*-will grasp-*the significance of-this remark,* I-am-*sure ; for-the* man who derives *pleasure from* reading books makes *for-himself* reserves *of* strength *to-call*-upon against *the* time *of*-trouble or stress.

Summary

1. The sound of *s* or *ses*, *st* or *str* is added to hook *n* attached to straight strokes by writing the circle or loop on the same side as the hook.
2. Circle *s* is added to straight strokes hooked for *f* or *v*, and to curves hooked for *n*, by writing the circle inside the hook.
3. The light sound of *ns* after a curve is expressed by the sign ‿ₚ *ns*.
4. The heavy sound of *nz* after a curve is expressed by the circle *s* written inside the hook *n*.
5. When *ns* or *nz* occur medially both letters must be shown.

CHAPTER XVI

THE *SHUN* HOOK

The Termination -SHUN.   93. The termination *shun* or *zhun*, variously spelt -*tion*, -*sion*, -*cian*, -*tian*, -*sian*, etc., is represented by a large hook, to which circle *s* may be added as required, as, ⤴ *notion*, ⤴ *notions*, ⌐ *caution*, ⌐ *cautions*.

94. The *shun* hook is written inside curves; thus, ⤵ *fashion*, ⤵ *fashions*, ⟋ᗞ *motion*, ⤴ *nation*, ⤴ *nations*.

95. (*a*) When added to a straight stroke with an initial attachment (circle, loop, or hook) the hook is written on the side *opposite* to the initial attachment, in order to preserve the straightness of the stroke; thus, ⊥ *citation*, ⤳ *sections*, ⟍ᗞ *oppression*, ⤳ *Grecian*.

(*b*) The *shun* hook is written with the Right motion after the form ╲ , light or heavy, and with the Left motion after the forms ⌐ ⌐ , in order that the *k* or *g* may be kept straight; thus, ⤳ *affection*, ⤳ *vacation*, ⌐ *selection*, ⌐ *selections*; and

96. On the side opposite to the last vowel when following a straight stroke *without* an initial attachment, in order to indicate where the last vowel occurs; thus, ⤵ *passion*, ⤵ *option*, ⌐ *action*, ⌐ *cautions*, ⤵ *occasion*; but

72

(a) On the right side of $|$ *t*, $|$ *d*, $/$ *j*, because
it is known that the last vowel always occurs after
these letters, and there is no need to indicate the fact,
and also because the writing of the hook on the right-
hand side of these letters carries the hand forward
in readiness for the next word ; thus, ⟍ *rotation*,
⟍ *notation*, ⟍ *gradation*, ⟍ *logicians*.

Exercise 59

Read, copy, and transcribe

1.
2.
3.
4.
5.
6.

Exercise 60

Write in Shorthand

1. Erasion, invasions, division, elevation, mansion.
2. Solution, desolation, relations, stipulations.
3. Exception, impression, celebration, recitation,
   discussion, exclusion.
4. Specification, infection, navigation, relegation.
5. Occupation, Russian, occasion, education, obliga-
   tion, lubrication.
6. Deputation, adaptation, imitation, presentation.

Shun following Circles S and NS. 97. When *shun* follows the circle *s* or circle *ns*, it is expressed by a small hook written on the opposite side to the circle and with the same motion; thus, ↓ *decision*, ┴ *dispensation*.

(*a*) A third-place vowel between the circle and the *shun* hook is expressed by the vowel-sign being written outside the hook; thus, ↘ *position*, ↘ *physician*, ⌐ *transition*. The circle *s* may be added thus, ↘ *positions*, ⌐ *transitions*.

(*b*) When a second-place vowel is to be read between the circle and *shun* it need not be indicated; thus, ↘ *possession*, ─e *accession*, ℃ *sensation*. First-place vowels do not occur between the circle and *shun*.

Shun Hook Medially. 98. The *shun* hook may be used medially; thus, ↓ *additional*, ⌐ *actionable*, ↙ *devotional*, ↘ *positional*, ⌐ *transitional*.

Words ending in -uation and -uition. 99. When a diphthong and a vowel occur immediately before *shun*, the stroke *sh* and the hook *n* must be written thus, ⌐ *extenuation*, but ⌐ *extension*; ⌐ *intuition*, but ⌐ *notation*. This does not apply to such words as ─e *accentuation*, ⋁ *perpetuation*, where, in order to avoid a lengthy outline, the large hook is used.

Exercise 61

Read, copy, and transcribe

1. [shorthand outlines]

2. [shorthand outlines]

3. [shorthand outlines]

4. [shorthand outlines]

Exercise 62

Write in Shorthand

1. Proposition, propositions, precision, procession, processions.
2. Disposition, indisposition, accusation, accusations, vexation.
3. Mission, missions, missionary, commission, commissions, commissionaire, exception, exceptional.
4. Discretion, discretionary, affection, affectionate.

GRAMMALOGUES

[shorthand] *subjective,* [shorthand] *subjection ;* [shorthand] *signification :*
[shorthand] *information ;* [shorthand] *satisfaction,* [shorthand] *justification,*
[shorthand] *generalization.*

Exercise 63

Read, copy, and transcribe

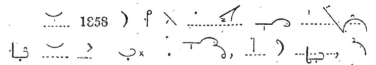

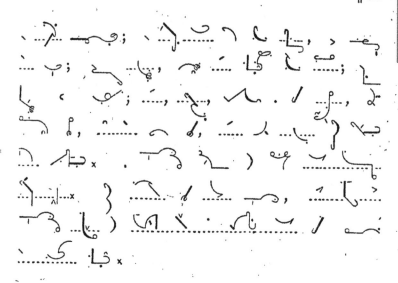

Exercise 64

Write in Shorthand

Lord Macaulay *was* blessed *with-the* possession *of* rare powers *of*-memory. *His* accumulation *of* facts *was* immense. He-*was almost in a* state *of subjection to-his* memory, *and a subjective* examination *of-the information in-his* possession at *any*-time *would* have-been a revelation even *to-himself*. *The* retention *and* repetition *of* figures, *the* manipulation *of* facts *in* discussion, *the* selection *and* citation *of* authorities caused *him* no hesitation. He-*was to-have-been a* barrister, *but-the* legal profession *had* no fascination *for-him*. Macaulay took *a* share *in-the* promotion *of* education, *but-his* reputation rests mainly *on-his* famous essays. *His* criticisms brought *him into* opposition *with several* fashionable authors, *and-his* expositions occasionally produced bitterness *in* opposite factions.

Summary

The hook -*shun* is written—

To curves	Inside the curve.
To straight strokes with initial attachment	On the side opposite to the initial attachment.
To *k* and *g* following the curves ⟍ ⟍ ⌒ (up)	With the Left or Right motion as required to keep the *k* or *g* straight.
To straight strokes other than *l, d* or *j* without initial attachment	On the side opposite to the last vowel.
To *t, d* and *j* without initial attachment	On the right side.
Following the circles *s* or *ns*	On the side opposite to the circle.
Finally	In *punctuation* and a few similarly long words.
Medially	Like the other hooks.

CHAPTER XVII
THE ASPIRATE

Upward H. 100. The upward form of *h* is employed in the great majority of cases, because it joins more readily with other strokes and abbreviations; as,

⌒ *hope,* ⌒ *head,* ⌒ *hatch,* ⌒ *hedge,* ⌒ *hush,* ⌒ *honey,* ⌒ *hung,* ⌒ *hero,* ⌒ *hearth,* ⌒ *hose,* ⌒ *husk,* ⌒ *hisses,* ⌒ *haste,* ⌒ *hove,* ⌒ *hen,* ⌒ *Henry,* ⌒ *hackle,* ⌒ *hawker,* ⌒ *hammer,* ⌒ *upheave,* ⌒ *behead,* ⌒ *adhesive,* ⌒ *Jehovah,* ⌒ *overhaul,* ⌒ *enhance,* ⌒ *rehearse.*

Downward H. 101. The downward form of *h* is used

(a) When *h* stands alone, as in / *hay,* / *high,* and in compounds and derivatives like ⌒ *haystack,* ⌒ *higher,* ⌒ *highly;*

(b) When *h* is followed by — *k* or — *g*; as, ⌒ *hawk,* ⌒ *hog;*

(c) When *h* follows upward *l* or a horizontal stroke; as, ⌒ *Lahore,* ⌒ *coherence,* ⌒ *mahogany,* ⌒ *unhook.*

Following S, etc. 102. (a) In a few words like ⌒ *Soho* and ⌒ *Sheehy,* the circle of *h* is written inside the curve; and in such words as ⌒ *Fitzhugh,* and ⌒ *racehorse,* where *s* and *h* occur medially, the circle is enlarged for the representation of *s*.

78

(b) When h follows another stroke, it must be written so that it cannot be misread for *s ch* or *sr;* thus, ⤳ *cohere,* but ⤳ *exchequer;* ⤳ *abhor,* but ⤳ *observer.*

Tick H. 103. (a) When preceding strokes ⌒ *m,* ⌒ *l,* ⟍ *r,* initial h is represented by a short tick, written in the direction of downward *h*; thus, ⤳ *home,* ⤳ *healthy,* ⤳ *harm.*

(b) The tick h may be employed medially in phrasing, but not in words; thus, ⤳ *for whom,* ⤳ *of her,* ⤳ *to her;* but ⤳ *inhuman,* ⤳ *overhaul.*

Dot H. 104. Where a stroke form, of h is not convenient in the middle of a word, h is represented by placing a light dot before the vowel which is to be aspirated; thus, ⤳ *apprehensive,* ⟍ *perhaps,* ⤳ *vehicle,* ⤳ *hogshead,* ⤳ *uphill,* ⤳ *downhill,* ⤳ *manhood.*

Exercise 65

Read, copy, and transcribe

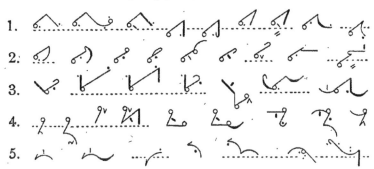

Exercise 66

Write in Shorthand

1. Head, hitch, huge, hyphen, hurry, hurries.
2. Host, hóne, heave, hovel, haggle, hence, hover, boyhood, prohibition, cohesive.
3. Hack, hackney, hawk, Hawkins, hoax, cohere, high, higher.
4. Home, hall, hallow, hire, neighbourhood, freehold.

PHRASES

Dear Sir, yours truly, every circumstance, all circumstances, you will remember, I believe, I will tell you, I am surprised.

Exercise 67

Read, copy, and transcribe

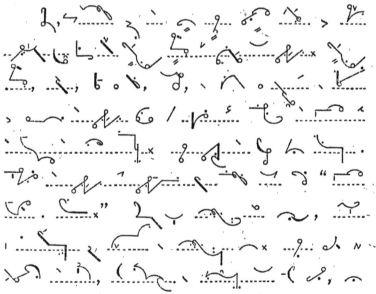

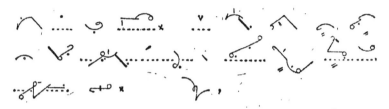

Exercise 68

Write in Shorthand

Dear-Sir,—*The* heavy mahogany table *for-your* new home, " Hillside," Woodhouse Lane, *is* ready *for delivery* at *any*-time *when-we* hear *from-you*. *We* hope *to-have-the* hangings fixed *to*-morrow, *and-the* curtains hung by Wednesday *next*. *The* new hammocks *and* hassocks *are almost* ready, *and-they-will-be delivered next* week. *Our* van may-*be in-your* neighbourhood *on*-Monday, *in-which*-case *you shall-have-the* hall *chairs and-the* whole *of-the* small household *things* then. *But for a* mishap at *our* Harley Works, *you would-have* had-*the* hair cushions *for-the* settee before *this*. *We* hope, *however*, *to*-receive *them on*-Friday, *and to-deliver them with-the* other *things on*-Monday. *Yours*-truly,

Summary

1. The upward form of *h* is most commonly used.
2. The downward form is written when *h* is the only stroke in the word and in compounds and derivatives like *hayrick*, *high-flown*; also before *k* or *g*.
3. The tick *h* is written initially to ⌒ ⌒ ⟍ The word HoMeLieR forms a useful mnemonic.
4. The dot *h* is used as an alternative to the stroke in the middle of a word.

6—(*M*)

CHAPTER XVIII
UPWARD AND DOWNWARD *R*

In order to present a complete statement of the rules for the writing of the alternative forms of *r*, the directions given to the student in par. 27 are repeated here.

Vowel preceding R. 105. When initial *r* is preceded by a vowel, the downward form is used; thus, ⌐ *air,* ⌐ *airy,* ⌐ *erase,* ⌐ *ire,* ⌐ *Irish,* ⌐ *orb.*

Vowel following R. 106. In other cases, the general rule is to write initial or final *r* upward when it is followed by a vowel, and downward when it is not followed by a vowel; thus, ⌐ *rob,* ⌐ *borrow;* ⌐ *rainy,* ⌐ *narrow;* ⌐ *carry,* ⌐ *car;* ⌐ *furrow,* ⌐ *fur;* ⌐ *sorry,* ⌐ *soar;* ⌐ *story,* ⌐ *store;* ⌐ *ware,* ⌐ *wary;* ⌐ *siren,* ⌐ *stern.*

107. Initial *r* followed by *m* is always written downward, because of the easier outline thus obtained; as, ⌐ *roam,* ⌐ *ram.*

108. Facility of outline is of the utmost importance, however, and accordingly either form of *r* is written, and vowel indication ignored, in order to secure a facile form. The upward form is written, therefore, in ⌐ *irate,* ⌐ *arch,* ⌐ *urge,* ⌐ *earth,* ⌐ *oracle,* and similar words where *r* is immediately followed by | *t,* | *d,* / *ch,* / *j,* (*th* or ⌐ *kl,* ⌐ *gl,* ⌐ *w.*

109. Generally, the upward form is preferable after two downstrokes; as, ⌐ *prepare,* ⌐ *trampler,*

82

Shakespeare, because the hand is thereby carried back to the line of writing. But the downward form is better in _____ *pinafore,* ⤳ *shuffler,* ⟍ *persevere,* etc., because of the easier joining with the preceding *f* or *v.*

110. After a single straight upstroke, the upward form is easier, because it avoids an angle ; thus, ⟋ *roar,* ⤳ *aware,* ⟋ *yore ;* but the suffix *-er* must be written with downward *r* in ⟋ ⟍ *roarer,* ⟋ ⟍ *rarer,* because a treble-length straight upstroke would not be easily readable.

111. The upward form is obviously better in _____ *officer,* ⤳ *nicer,* ⟋ *closer,* ⟋ *razor,* where *r* immediately follows a curve and circle like ⟍ₒ or ⟍ₒ , or a straight horizontal or upstroke circled for *s.*

R Finally Hooked. 112. When *r* follows another stroke and is hooked finally, it is generally written upward ; thus, ∨∕ *spurn,* ∨∕ *fern,* ∨∕ *portion.*

Medial R. 113. Medial *r* is generally written upward ; as in _____ *park,* _____ *parsnip,* ⤳ *terrify,* _____ *mark,* ⟋ *roared ;* but the downward form is retained in some derivative words, as, _____ *powerful,* ⟍ *barely,* ⤵ *disarrange ;* and the use of the alternative forms provides a distinction in pairs of words such as _____ *clerk,* _____ *cleric.*

Exercise 69

Read, copy, and transcribe

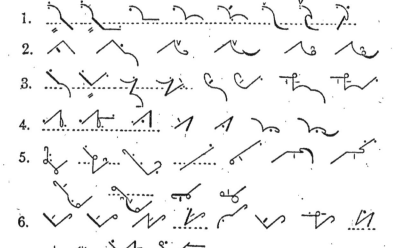

Exercise 70

Write in Shorthand

1. Ear, era, erase, argue, oral, Eric, early.
2. Retire, retrace, review, reviewing, rose, roses, rank.
3. Paris, diary, gallery, victory, assurance, memory.
4. Answer, censor, cruiser, origin, turn, Lucerne.
5. Perth, veracity, parade, terrible, forty, firm.

PHRASES AND CONTRACTIONS

by all, by all means; at all, at all costs; in our, in our opinion; everything, something; anything, nothing.

Exercise 71

Read, copy, and transcribe

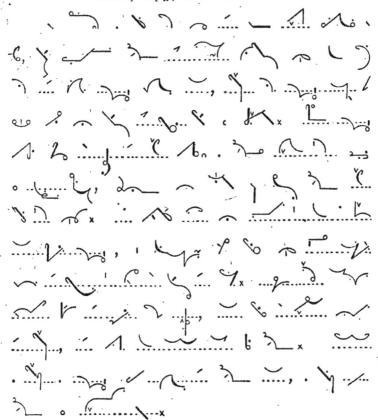

Exercise 72

Write in Shorthand

The food eaten by man bears *something* like-*the* same relation *to-his* power *of* working *as-the* coal thrown *into-the* furnace bears *to-the* engine *which* drives *the* rotary press, 'or draws *the* train. *The* power *in-our* arms or *in-our* brains *is* rightly said *to be* produced *in-our* stomach, *and it-is from-the* same organ *we* derive *the* force necessary *to*-rouse us *to* severe exertion *in-the* earning *of-the* wage or salary *we* receive *for our* services.   *Something of-the* value *of-our* work rests upon-*the* strength producing value *of-our* food. At-*all*-costs, *and* by-*all*-means, *we should* take measures *to* ensure-*the* food value *of* everything *we* eat.

Summary

Initial *r*

> Written downward when preceded by a vowel, and initially before *m ;* as ᘒ *erase,* ⟍ *room.*

Initial or Final *r*

> Written upward when followed by a vowel, and downward when not followed by a vowel, as ⟋ *race,* ⟍ *parry,* ⟍ *air,* ⟍ *par.*

Medial *r*

> Generally written upward ; but downward in some derivatives.

When hooked and following another stroke

> Generally written upward ; as, ⟍ *burn,* ⟍ *mourn.*

For an easier outline

> Written either upward or downward irrespective of vowels ; as, ⟋ *earth,* ⟍ *answer,* ⟍ *deplore,* ⟍ *debar.*

CHAPTER XIX

UPWARD AND DOWNWARD L AND SH

Upward L. 114. The stroke *l*, whether initial or final, is most commonly written upward; as in ⌒ₒ *lapse*, ∨ *spell*, ⌒ *load*, ⌐ *delay*, ⌐ *allege*, ⌐ *jelly*, ⌒ *lake*, ⌐ *coal*, ⌒ *loaf*, ∨ *fellow*, ⌒ *loathe*, ⌐ *Othello*, ⌒ *Lacey*, ⌐ *assail*, ⌐ *sale*, ⌐ *stale*, ⌐ *leisure*, ⌐ *shallow*.

L preceding or following Curve and Circle. 115. When *l* immediately precedes or follows a circle which is attached to a curve, it is written in the same direction as the circle; thus, ⌐ *lesson*, ⌐ *nasal*, ⌐ *elusive*, ⌐ *vessel*, ⌐ *losing*, ⌐ *Kingsley*, ⌐ *lissom*.

L after N and NG. 116. After the strokes ⌣ *n* and ⌣ *ng*, final *l* is written downward so as to avoid a change of motion; as in ⌐ *only*, ⌐ *wrongly*, ⌐ *manly*; and the downward form is retained in derivatives; as, ⌐ *manliness*, ⌐ *enlisting*.

L and Vowel Indication. 117. For the purpose of vowel indication, initial *l* is written downward when preceded by a vowel and followed immediately by a horizontal, not hooked or circled initially; thus, ⌐ *alike* but ⌐ *like*; ⌐ *alone* but ⌐ *loan*; ⌐ *along* but ⌐ *long*; ⌐ *elm* but ⌐ *lame*.

87

118. Also for the purpose of vowel indication, final *l* is written upward after ⌐ *f*, ⌐ *v*, ᴏ— *sk*, or a straight upstroke when a vowel follows *l*, and downward when no vowel follows *l*; thus, ⌐ *follow* but ⌐ *fall*; ⌐ *valley* but ⌐ *vale*; ᴏ⌐ *scaly* but ⌐ *scale*; ⌐ *ruly* but ⌐ *rule*.

Medial L. 119. Medial *l* is generally written upward; but either form is used for an easier joining; thus, ⌐ *unload* but ⌐ *unlock*; ⌐ *vulgar* but ⌐ *overlook*; ⌐ *facility* but ⌐ *film*.

Upward and Downward Sh. 120. (*a*) The curve ⌐ *sh*, joined to another curve, generally follows the motion of that curve; thus, ⌐ *fish*, ⌐ *smash*, ⌐ *lash*; but it is written *downward* after the curve ⌐ *n*; thus, ⌐ *gnash*. When joined to a straight stroke, *sh* is generally written downward; thus, ⌐ *push*, ⌐ *cherish*, ⌐ *shake*, ⌐ *sherry*; but it is written *upward* after the heavy stroke | *d*, as in ⌐ *dash*.

(*b*) After a straight down stroke with an initial attachment, *sh* is generally written on the opposite side to such attachment; thus, ⌐ *spacious*, ⌐ *blush*, ⌐ *brush*. In other cases the form is used which gives the easier joining; as in ⌐ *sugar*, ⌐ *shackle*, ⌐ *chauffeur*, ⌐ *shovel*.

Exercise 73

Read, copy, and transcribe

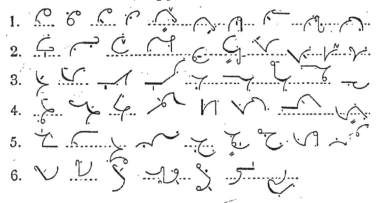

Exercise 74

Write in Shorthand

1. Lie, lies, sly, slice, slices, steel, stolen, swallow.
2. Alps, Alaska, loth, loafer, lore, locker, latch.
3. Alack, lack, allocation, location, license, Allison.
4. Bale, billow, towel, Filey, veal, villa, dwell.
5. Canals, denial, frowningly, vessel, profusely.
6. Unlucky, lucky, pulling, spelling, sculling.
7. Plush, splash, crush, atrocious, waspish.

PHRASES

as is; is as; this is; last year; at first; just now.

Exercise 75

Read, copy, and transcribe

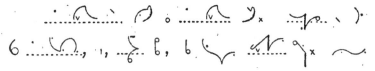

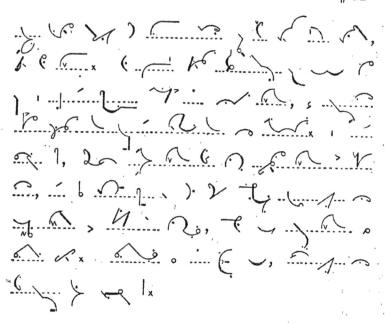

Exercise 76

Write in Shorthand

Dear-Sir,

The volumes *of-the* French Revolution *for-which-you* ask *in-your* favour *of-the* first July *shall-be delivered to-you* early *to*-morrow. *We-are* just-now out-*of* stock *of-the* "Life *of* Lord Lumley," last-*year's* best seller, *and we-are* unable *to* say *when-we-shall* receive copies. *We-have* a daily *delivery from-the* wholesalers, *however, and you*-may-rely upon *our* mailing-*the* volume *to-you as*-soon-*as* it reaches us.   *We-are* taking-*the liberty of* enclosing *for-your* approval "Naval Lessons *of-the* War," by Philip Bailey.   Please return *this with-the next* parcel if-*it* makes no appeal *to-you*.   *Yours*-truly,

Summary

1. The upward form of *l* is most commonly written.
2. When immediately preceding or following a circle which is attached to a curve, *l* follows the direction of the circle.
3. Final *l* is written downward after *n* and *ng*, and derivatives of words similar to *manly*.
4. When preceded by a vowel and followed immediately by a horizontal, initial *l* is written downward.
5. After ⌣ *f*, ⌣ *v*, ⌒ *sk*, or a straight upstroke, final *l* is written upward when followed by a vowel, and downward when not followed by a vowel.
6. Medial *l* is generally written upward.
7. Stroke *sh*, following a straight downstroke having an initial attachment, is written opposite to the initial attachment. In other cases the form is used which gives the better joining.

CHAPTER XX
COMPOUND CONSONANTS

Initial W. 121. A *large* initial hook adds *w* to *k* — and — *g*; thus, —꜀ *keen*, ꜀ *queen*, ꜀ *Gwynn.*

Initial WH. 122. A *small* initial hook to *l* represents *w*, and a *large* initial hook to *l* represents *wh*; thus, ⎛ *ell*, ⎛ *well*, ⎛ *whale.*

Strokes L and R Thickened. 123. Downward *l* is thickened for the addition of *r* preceded by any lightly sounded vowel, and downward *r* is thickened for the addition of *-er* only; thus, ⟍ *vale*, ⟍ *valour*; ⟍ *hire*, ⟍ *hirer.*

Addition of P or B to M. 124. The curve ⌒ *m* is thickened for the addition of *p* or *b*; thus, ⌒ *hem*, ⌒ *hemp*, ⌒ *moss*, ⌒ *emboss.*

Aspirated W. 125. The aspirate is added to ⟋ *w* by enlarging the hook; thus, ⟋ *weasel*, ⟋ *whistle*, ⟋ *aware*, ⟋ *where.*

Stroke L after KW. 126. After ⌒ *kw*, *l* is written upward when followed by a vowel, and downward when not followed by a vowel; thus, ⌐ *squally*, ⌐ *squall.*

Vowel preceding W. 127. The initial hooks in *wl* and *whl* are read *first*. Therefore, if a vowel precedes *w*, the stroke form of *w* or *wh* must be written, and not the hook; thus, ⟋ *while*, ⟋ *awhile.*

92

Use of LR and RR Signs. 128. The form of *l* or *r* which is used in the root word is. retained in the derivative ; thus, 〰 *boil,* 〰 *boiler.* 〰 *mill,* 〰 *miller ;* 〰 *full,* 〰 *fuller ;* 〰 *snare,* 〰 *snarer.* The use of 〰 *rer* is strictly confined to derivatives of words written with downward *r.*

Vowel after Final R. 129. The thickened forms 〰 *lr,* 〰 *rr* must not be written finally if a vowel follows *r ;* compare 〰 *fuller* with 〰 *foolery ;* 〰 *valour* with 〰 *valorous.*

Hooked Form of MP. 130. An initial or final hook may be attached to the sign 〰 ; as in 〰 *scamper,* 〰 *hempen,* 〰 *ambition.* The sign 〰 is not used when *pr, br, pl* or *bl* immediately follows *m.* Compare 〰 *empress* with 〰 *emperor ;* 〰 *embrace* with 〰 *embower ;* 〰 *imply* with 〰 *impel ;* 〰 *emblem* with 〰 *embolden.*

Exercise 77

Read, copy, and transcribe

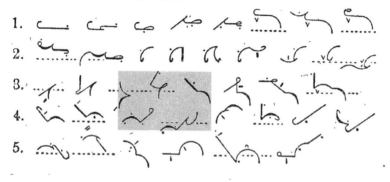

Exercise 78

Write in Shorthand

1. Quake, earthquake, square, liquid, liquidation, require, Maguire.
2. Wall, wallflower, welfare, will, willing, unwilling, while, awhile, jump, romp.
3. Fairer, scorer, scaler, nowhere, whisper, whimper.
4. Imprison, umbrella, taller, similar, failure.

GRAMMALOGUES

✓ *whether;* ⌒ *impossible;* ⌒ *important-ance,*
⌒ *improve-d-ment.*

Exercise 79

Read, copy, and transcribe.

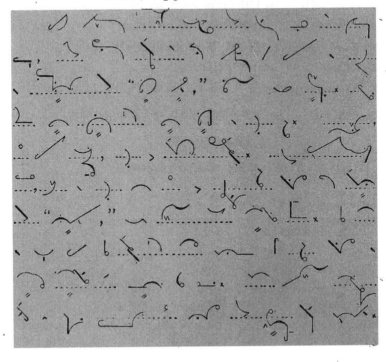

Exercise 80

Write in Shorthand

I-*have*-no *wish* to impose my views upon-*the* ambassador, or *to* embarrass *him* by asking *for impossible improvements ;* but *it-is* important I *should* impress upon *him the* chancellor's *opinion* *in-the* case *of-those* lumber vessels. *You*-will-see *how* imperative *it-is* I *should* see-*the* ambassador, if-*we-are* to-*have any* improvement *in-our* relations just-now. I-desire *to* discover *whether-the* whaler's story *is* true, or-*the* idle tale *of a* wilful imposter. I-*shall* occupy only *a* quarter *of an hour,* and-I-am-*sure the* ambassador will agree *the importance of-the* case *is* well worth-*the* time.

Summary

1. Table of compound consonants—

Character	Name	Letters	As in
⌒	kwā	QU	**qu**ick, re**qu**est
⌣	gwā	GU	**gu**ava, lin**gu**al
ſ (up)	wel	WL	**w**ail, un**well**
ſ (up)	hwel	WHL	**wh**ale, mean**while**
⌐ (down)	ler	LR	fee**ler**, scho**lar**ly
⌐ (down)	rer	RR	poo**rer**, sha**rer**
⌒	{emp} {emb}	MP, MB	ca**mp**, **emb**alm
⌣	hwā	WH	**wh**ere, every**wh**ere

2. After ⌒ *kw* stroke *l* is written upward when followed by a vowel, and downward when not followed by a vowel.

3. The initial hooks to *l* are always read first.

4. When the downward forms of *l* or *r* are written in root words, the thickened forms ⌒ *lr*, ⌝ *rr* are written in the derived words.

5. The thickened forms ⌒ *lr*, ⌝ *rr* must not be used when a vowel follows *r*.

6. The sign ⌒ is not used when *m* is immediately followed by *pr*, *br*, *pl* or *bl*.

CHAPTER XXI

VOWEL INDICATION

Vowels Implied. 131. A careful reading of the rules governing the use of the circles, loops, and hooks will have led the student to realize (*a*) that when a word begins or ends with a consonant, that consonant is to be written with the briefest form ; as, ⟨shorthand⟩ *soup*, ⟨shorthand⟩ *place*, ⟨shorthand⟩ *spinsters*, ⟨shorthand⟩ *dances*, ⟨shorthand⟩ *craves*, unl ss there is a rule to the contrary, as in the words ⟨shorthand⟩ *Siam* and ⟨shorthand⟩ *joyous*; and (*b*) that when a word begins or ends with a vowel sound, the first or last consonant, as the case may be, must be represented by a stroke in order to accommodate the vowel-sign.

It will be seen from the foregoing that in very many words an initial or a final vowel may be *implied* by the outline of the word, without the use of the vowel-sign. The following illustrations will serve as additional examples of the implication of initial or final vowels.

INITIAL VOWEL IMPLIED

asleep,   *assume,*   *arising,*   *arrives,*   *along.*

alike,   *aware,*   *awake,*   *awhile,*   *awoke.*

INITIAL CONSONANT IMPLIED

sleep,   *sum,*   *rising,*   *raves,*   *long.*

like,   *wear,*   *wake,*   *while,*   *woke.*

FINAL VOWEL IMPLIED

lessee,   tasty,   penny,   defy,   robbery.

sorry,   worry,   follow,   scaly,   yellow.

FINAL CONSONANT IMPLIED

less,   taste,   pen,   deaf,   repair.

sore,   wore,   fall,   scale,   yell.

In many of the words given in the following exercises an initial or a final vowel is suggested by the outline employed.

Exercise 81

Read, copy, and transcribe

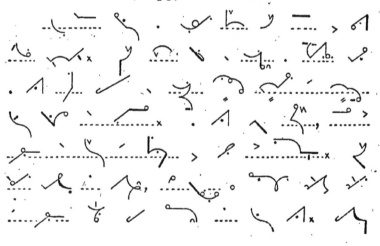

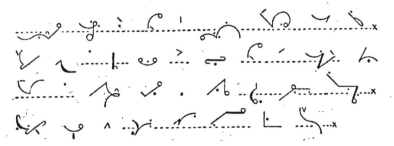

Exercise 82

Write in Shorthand

The judge *in-his* charge *to-the* jury said : *This*
poor boy's injury *is very* severe, *and-*if *what-he* states
is right, *it-was* due *to-the* absence *of a* hooter *on-the*
car *which* Robinson drove along-*the* arcade at *a very*
fast rate, *his* speed, if-*we-can* take-*the* story *of-the*
police *as* correct, *being* at-least forty miles *an hour,*
far *too* fast *in* so busy *a* thoroughfare. *The* boy
says *the* car came *on with a* rush, no alarm *was given,*
he-*was* struck *and-*thrown *with a* force so terrific
*as to-*break *his* right leg. If-*you think his* story *is*
right, *you-*will *give him* damages. If-*you* assume *his*
story *is* wrong, *and-*if *it* appears *to-you the* injury
was caused by *his own* lack *of* vigilance, *you-*will
refuse *him the* damages *for-which* he asks. *You-*
must *carefully* weigh both-*the* boy's case *and-the*
case *as* set out by Robinson *and* decide *on-the* facts
*as-*they appear *to-you.*

Revisionary Exercise (B)

Dear Dr. Fry,

By-*all-*means, apply *to-my people to-tell-you of-*my
travels *during-the* past three *years.* I-*believe it-*will-
be *difficult for-you to-believe* all-they-will-*tell-you,*
because-it-is almost *beyond belief.* They-will-*tell-you*
a very attractive story, *all-the more* striking *because*

of-its truth. If-*you*-leave *your call till* ne*xt* month, *there*-may-*be more to-tell-you, and-the* news items may-*be equal to anything you have* read. Every-day brings before-*me circumstances* unknown *to-me* before, *and* every *circumstance is* singular *in itself. It-is very difficult for-me to be surprised at anything* now. I-am-*surprised* at *nothing* at-*all, nor do* I-*think there-is anything to surprise me, because* my-life *during-the* past few *years has* brought *me* so-many *surprises from all* quarters. I-*have-been delivered from* troubles *when deliverance would* appear *to-have-been impossible, and when an* improvement *of-circumstances* looked *too difficult to be* possible. *You*-will-see-*the significance of-this when you* know *something of what* I-*have-been* through, *though-the* tale *can-be* no-*more* than *a mere generalization* or *general* review. Still, *it*-will-*be as near-the* facts *as* possible *in-the circumstances.* I-will-*tell-you and Mr.* Oliver *more when* I-see-*you, and it*-will-*be an advantage and an* immense *satisfaction to-me to-tell-you* both. *You*-will-then *be* at *liberty to* ask *for any number of* details, *and,* as-far-*as* I-am-able *to-remember them,* I-will *give them, to-you.* I-*can* see *myself in-your* easy-chair *in-the larger of-your two* rooms at home, *with* my journal *on*-my knee *and-the cheerful* listeners facing *me* while I-talk *of-the* days *of*-my *subjection and-of-the* dreary *subjective* examinations I gave *myself in justification of*-my actions. *In*-my *opinion, you*-will say-*the* tale *is significant, and, in signification of-the* happenings *in-the northern and southern* climes, far *beyond anything you* know. I-must leave-*the balance of-the* tale, *however, till* I-*can go over it with-you.* I-*have* some *information, largely* personal *to-you, which* I-must *tell-you* at-*all*-costs before long. I-trust *the information* will *give-you as-much-pleasure as* I-*think-it*-will. *Anyway it*-will enable *you to-*set *a right* *valuation* upon-*the* rest *of*-my story.   Please *remember me to-the* children at home, *and to-the* older *and larger* children   also.   I-*shall-be* home   again   *within* six months.   I-*shall* hope to see-*the principal members of-the* local literary club *within a* few days *of*-my return.   Ever *yours,* Arthur Clyde.   (468 words)

Summary

1. An initial vowel requires the use of an initial stroke, in order to give a place for the vowel-sign : a final vowel requires the use of a final stroke, for the same reason.

2. An initial or a final vowel may frequently be indicated by the form written for the initial or final consonant.

3. Words beginning with the sound of a consonant have that consonant represented in the briefest form unless there is a rule to the contrary, as in the case of the word *Siam.*

4. Similarly, words ending with the sound of a consonant, or group of consonants, have the consonant or group represented in the briefest form.

CHAPTER XXII

THE HALVING PRINCIPLE (Section 1)

General Rule. 132. Halving a stroke in length indicates the addition of *t* or *d*. In words of one syllable, however, unless the stroke is finally hooked, or has a joined diphthong, a light stroke is halved for *t* only, and a heavy stroke for *d* only.

Halving for either T or D. 133. (*a*) In words of more than one syllable, a stroke may be halved for either *t* or *d*; thus, ⌒ *rabbit*, ⌒ *rapid*; ⌐⌐ *credit*, ⌐ *debit*; ⎯ *honoured*, ⎯ *applied*.

(*b*) A stroke having a final hook or a joined diphthong may be halved for either *t* or *d*; thus, ⤬ *pave*, ⤬ *paved*; ⌡ *ten*, ⌡ *tent* or *tend*; ⌒ *men*, ⌒ *meant* or *mend*; ⌐ *few*, ⌐ *feud*; ⤬ *prow*, ⤬ *proud*.

Halving for T only, or for D only. 134. (*a*) In words of one syllable, light strokes, without a final hook or a joined diphthong, are halved for *t* only; thus, ⤬ *play*, ⤬ *plate*, but ⤬ *played*; ⌐ *thaw*, ⌐ *thought*, but ⌐ *thawed*.

(*b*) In words of one syllable, heavy strokes, without a final hook or a joined diphthong, are halved for *d* only; thus, ⤬ *bray*, ⤬ *brayed*, but ⤬ *bright*; ⌐ *gray*, ⌐ *grade*, but ⌐ *greet*.

Vocalizing Half-length Forms. 135. (*a*) Vowel-signs to half-length forms are read next to the primary stroke; thus, ⌐ *fie*, ⌐ *fight*; ⌐ *off*, ⌐ *oft*; ⌐ *seek*, ⌐ *sect*; ⌐ *seeker*, ⌐ *secret*.

Circle S following Half-length Forms. 136. Circle *s* at the end of a half-length form is read after the *t* or *d* indicated by the halving; thus, _ *coat,* _ *coats;* ⌐ *mount,* ⌐ *mounts;* ⌐ *rent,* ⌐ *rents;* ⌐ *rift,* ⌐ *rifts.*

Half-length H. 137. Half-length *h,* when not joined to another stroke, is always written upward; as, ⌐ *height,* ⌐ *heights;* ⌐ *hunt,* ⌐ *hunts;* ⌐ *haft,* ⌐ *hafts.*

Halving Principle not Employed. 138. The halving principle is not employed—

(*a*) In words of more than one syllable when a vowel follows final *t* or *d,* because a final vowel requires a final stroke; as, ⌐ *pit,* but ⌐ *pity;* ⌐ *greed,* but ⌐ *greedy;*

(*b*) When a triphone immediately precedes *t* or *d;* as, ⌐ *fight* but ⌐ *fiat,* ⌐ *died* but ⌐ *diadem;*

(*c*) Where a more distinctive outline is obtained by the use of the stroke *t* or *d;* as, ⌐ *secret,* but ⌐ *sacred;* ⌐ *unavoidable,* but ⌐ *inevitable;* ⌐ *hotly,* but ⌐ *hotel;*

(*d*) Where the half-length *r* [╱] would stand alone, or with final circle *s* only [⌐] added; therefore, in such words as ⌐ *right,* ⌐ *rights,* the stroke *t* must be written. The reason for this is to prevent clashing between *rt* and the sign for *and* or *should,* and between *rts* and the sign for *and-is.* Such words as ⌐ *rents,* ⌐ *rifts,* are safely written with a half-length form.

Position of Half-length Forms. 139. Upward or downward half-length characters must not be written through the line for the indication of vowels. Where the first upstroke or the first downstroke in an outline is a half-length, the outline is written so that the half-length stroke appears over the line for the indication of a first-place vowel, and on the line for the indication of a second or a third-place vowel; thus, ‿‿ *optical,* ⤵ *vertical,* ⤸ *lightly,* ⤸ *lately,* ⟋ *witness,* ⟋ *military,* ⌐ *netted,* ⌡ *tint.*

Exercise 83

Read, copy, and transcribe

Exercise 84

Write in Shorthand

1. Tie, tight, trite, Coe, coat, coats, Kate, skate.
2. Weigh, weight, weighty, fry, fright, frights.
3. Gray, grade, grades, graded, met, metal.
4. Label, labelled, open, opened, land, lands, lent.
5. Tight, tied, tidy, wit, witty, pat, patty.
6. Heat, heats, hunt, hunts, raid, raids.

GRAMMALOGUES

quite, ___ could ; ___ accord-ing, ___ cared :

guard, ___ great ; ___ called, ___ equalled, cold ;

___ gold ; ___ that, ‹ without, ___ wished.

Exercise 85

Read, copy, and transcribe

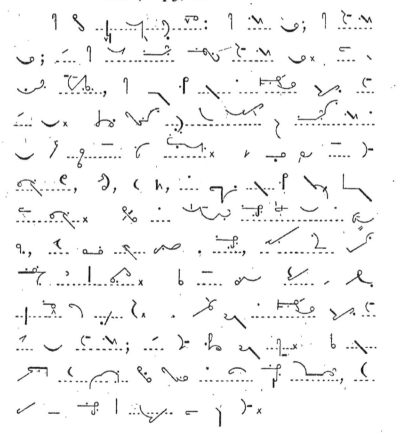

Exercise 86

Write in Shorthand

It-has-been maintained *that* certainty does-not admit *of* degrees *of any* kind ; *that-there-can-be* no shade *of difference in-the* intensity *of-our* certainty. *But* let us see.   A man may-*be* certain *that-he* settled *his* debt *with-his* tailor *on-the* 10th *of* October, *and-in gold*, or *that-he* paid *his* local rates *on* demand. *But is-this* certainty *equalled* by-*the* certainty *with-which* he knows *that* three *and* four make seven, or *that* heat will melt butter?   *Is there* not *a great difference ?*

Summary

1. Halving a stroke indicates the addition of *t* or *d*.
2. Unless it is finally hooked, or has an attached diphthong, a light stroke in words of one syllable is halved for *t* only, and a heavy stroke for *d* only.
3. Vowel-signs to halved forms are read next to the primary stroke.
4. Half-length *h*, when not joined to another stroke, is always written upward ; half-length upward *r* must not be written alone, or with a final circle *s* only added.
5. The halving principle is not applied when a word ends with a vowel, when *t* or *d* is immediately preceded by a triphone, and in a few other cases where the fuller form is necessary to secure distinction of outline.
6. Half-length forms should not be written through the line for vowel indication.

CHAPTER XXIII

THE HALVING PRINCIPLE (SECTION 2)

Strokes M, N, L, R. 140. (a) The four strokes ⌒ ⌣ ⌐ ⟍ which are halved to express the addition of *t*, are also halved and thickened to indicate the addition of *d*; thus, ⌒ *md*, ⌣ *nd*, ⌐ *ld* (down), ⟍ *rd*, as in the words ⌒ *mate*, ⌒ *made*; ⋏ *aimed*, ⌐ *timid*; ⌣ *neat*, ⌣ *need*, ⌣ *end*; ⟋ *old*, ⟍ *aired*.

(b) The half-length form ⌐ *ld*, standing alone, is used only for words beginning with a vowel; as, ⌐ *ailed*, ⟋ *old*; so that words like ⟍ *sold*, ⟍ *styled*, ⟋ *holed*, must be written with the full strokes.

(c) When a vowel occurs between *l-d* or between *r-d*, both consonants must be written in full. Compare ⟍ *pallid* with ⟍ *paled*; ⟍ *married* with ⟍ *marred*; ⟍ *sorrowed* with ⟍ *sword*; ⟍ *hurried* with ⟍ *hoard*.

(d) The signs ⌐ ⟍ cannot be halved to represent the syllables -*lerd*, -*rerd* respectively, because the forms ⌐ ⟍ are used for representing *ld*, *rd*, as explained above.

(e) The strokes ⌒ *mp*, *mb*, ⌣ *ng* cannot be halved for the addition of either *t* or *d*, unless they are hooked initially or finally; thus, ⌐ *impute*, ⌐ *imbued*, ⟍ *belonged*; but ⟍ *hampered*, ⟍ *rampart*, ⟍ *lingered*, ⟍ *impugned*.

107

RT and LT. 141. (*a*) The signs for *rt* and *lt* are generally written upward; thus, ⌣ *part*, ⌄ *pelt*, ⌣ *fort*, ⌣ *fault*; but ⌐ *lt* is written downward after ⌣ *n* and ⌣ *ng*, as in ⌣ *inlet*, ⌣ *ringlet*; and it is written downward after ⌒ *w* if no vowel follows *l*; thus, ⌐ *dwelt*, but ⌐ *twilight*.

(*b*) The light sign ⁄ may be used for *rd* when it is not convenient to write ⌐; thus, ⌐ *lard*, ⌐ *coloured*, ⌐ *cordage*, ⌐ *preferred*.

(*c*) After the *shun* hook,) *st* may be written downward or upward; thus, ⌐ *protectionist*, ⌐ *progressionist*.

Joining of Strokes of Unequal Length. 142. (*a*) The halving principle may be applied to words like ⌐ *afford*, ⌐ *named*, where the difference of thickness shows the inequality of length; but in other cases two strokes of unequal length must not be joined unless there is an angle at the point of junction. Words like ⌐ *cooked*, ⌐ *looked*, ⌐ *propped*, ⌐ *minute*, ⌐ *fact*, must, therefore, be written with full-length strokes.

(*b*) Half-sized *t* or *d* is always disjoined when immediately following the strokes *t* or *d*; thus, ⌐ *attitude*, ⌐ *treated*, ⌐ *dreaded*, ⌐ *credited*. The half-sized stroke is also disjoined in some other cases, as ⌐ *aptness*, ⌐ *tightness*, ⌐ *hesitatingly*.

Past Tenses. 143. In past tenses *-ted* or *-ded* is always indicated by half-length *t* or *d* respectively; thus, ⌐ *parted*, ⌐ *braided*, ⌐ *coated*, ⌐ *graded*.

The Halving Principle in Phraseography. 144. The halving principle is employed in phraseography as follows—

(a) For the word *it*, as in ⌣ *if it*, ⌣ *if it is;* (b) *not*, as in ⁓ *I am not*, ⁓ *you may not*, ⁓ *I will not;* (c) *word* and *would* by ╱ as in ⌣ *this word*, ⌣ *we would be;* and (d) in phrases like ⌐ *at all times*, ⌣ *able to make.*

Exercise 87

Read, copy, and transcribe

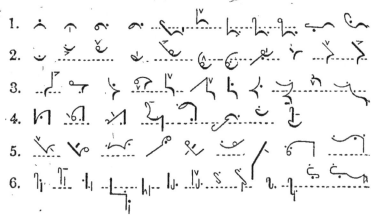

Exercise 88

Write in Shorthand

1. Amid, signed, doled, dazzled, sailed, heard.
2. Collide, colt, borrowed, bored, thronged.
3. Impede, dreamed, scampered, conquered.
4. Quilt, quilled, sunlight, answered, glared.
5. Chatted, treated, pathetic, flared, deadness.
6. Liken, likened, exported, shunted, trended.

GRAMMALOGUES

‾‾ cannot; ⌐ gentleman, ⌐ gentlemen; ⌐ particular,
⌐ opportunity; ⌐ child; ⌐ build-ing; ⌐ told;
⌐ tried, ⌐ trade, toward, ⌐ towards; ‾‾ hand, ⌐ under.

Exercise 89

Read, copy, and transcribe

Exercise 90

Write in Shorthand

Quite early *in* man's attempt *to* penetrate *into-the*
great secrets *of-the* earth, *when-he* *tried* *to*-find *its*
hidden treasures *of gold and* diamonds *for-the* purposes *of-trade,* he learned one *important* fact, namely,

thut-it grows hotter *as you* descend. *This-is* evident, also, *from-the* hot springs found *in different* parts *of-the* world, *and* still *more* evident *from-the* volcanoes *which, when* violently active, pour out molten rock until *it* covers *the* country around *to a* thickness *of-*many feet. *A great* authority *on-the subject has* asserted *that-there-are* slight earth tremors every quarter *of an hour. The hand of-*man seems weak indeed *when-we-think of-the* wondrous power *of-*these mighty forces.

Summary

1. The four strokes ⌒ ⌣ ⌐ ⟍ are halved and thickened for the addition of *d.*

2. The thickened forms ⌐⌐ are not used if a vowel comes between *l-d, r-d.*

3. *Ler* and *rer* are never halved ; *mp* and *ng* may be halved when initially or finally hooked.

4. *Rt* is generally written upward ; *lt* is written upward, except after *n, ng ;* after *w, lt* is written downward if no vowel follows *l.*

5. The upward form ⟋ may be used medially and finally for *rd.*

6. The half-length ⟩ *st* may be written downward or upward after *shun.*

7. Two strokes of unequal length must not be joined unless there is an angle at the point of junction, or unless, in the case of curves, the difference of thickness clearly shows the inequality of length.

8. Half-sized *t* or *d* is always disjoined when immediately following the strokes *t* or *d.*

9. In past tenses *-ted* or *-ded* is always indicated by half-length *t* or *d* respectively.

10. The halving principle is used in phraseography to represent *it, not, word, would.*

CHAPTER XXIV

THE DOUBLING PRINCIPLE

The General Rule. 145. With the few exceptions named below, the addition of the syllable -*tr* or -*dr*, or -*THr*, or, in common words -*ture*, is indicated by doubling the length of the preceding stroke ; thus, ⟋ *fie*, ⟍ *fighter* ; ⌡ *ten*, ⌐ *tender* ; ⌣ *nigh*, ⌣ *neither* ; ⌐ *track*, ⌐ *tractor* ; ⌐ *seek*, ⌐ *sector* ; ⌐ *Dow*, ⌐ *doubter* ; ⌐ *won*, ⌐ *wonder* ; ⌐ *grave*, ⌐ *grafter* ; ⌐ *impugn*, ⌐ *impounder* ; ⌐ *centre*, ⌐ *central* ; ⌐ *enter*, ⌐ *enteric* ; ⌐ *pick*, ⌐ *picture* ; ⌐ *few*, ⌐ *future*, ⌐ *nay*, ⌐ *nature* ; ⌐ *natural*.

Doubling of Straight Strokes. 146. The doubling principle must not be applied to a straight stroke unless it follows a circle or stroke consonant, or has a final hook, or an attached diphthong. Compare ⌐ *skater* with ⌐ *cater* ; ⟍ *captor* with ⌐ *potter*; ⌐ *wonder* with ⌐ *wader* ; ⌐ *doubter* with ⌐ *daughter* ; ⌐ *tutor* with ⌐ *tether*.

Strokes MP and NG. 147. The character ⌐ *mp-mb*, when not initially hooked, is doubled for the addition of -*er*, and the character ⌣ *ng* for the addition of -*kr*, -*gr* ; thus, ⌐ *bump*, ⌐ *bumper* ; ⌐ *vamp*, ⌐ *vamper* ; ⌣ *inker*, ⌐ *linger*, ⌐ *Ingersoll*.

112

Alternatives for MPR, MBR. 148. There are therefore alternative forms for *mpr*, *mbr*, the double-length form ⌒ and the hooked form ⌒ The hooked form is used when *mpr*, *mbr* immediately follows an upstroke or ⎯ *k*; in all other cases the double-length form is used ; thus, ⌒ *umber*, but ⌒ *slumber;* ⌐ *tamper*, but ⌐ *hamper;* ⌐ *chamber,* but ⌐ *cumber.*

Alternatives for NG-KR, NG-GR. 149. There are alternative forms for *ng-kr*, *ng-gr*, the double-length ⌣ and the hooked form ⌣ The double-length form is used initially and when following a circle or an upstroke. In all other cases, the hooked form is written ; thus, ⌣ *anchorage*, but ⌣ *bunkering;* ⌣ *sinker*, but ⌣ *drinker;* ⌣ *hunger,* but ⌣ *pinker;* ⌣ *rancour*, but ⌣ *canker.*

Stroke L. 150. The stroke *l*, standing alone, or with only a final circle attached, is doubled for *-tr* only ; thus, ⌐ *letter*, ⌐ *letters;* ⌐ *alter*, ⌐ *alters;* but ⌐ *leader*, ⌐ *leather.*

Circle S and Double-length Strokes. 151. Circle *s* at the end of a double-length form is read after the syllable indicated by doubling ; thus, ⌐ *voters,* ⌐ *renders,* ⌐ *rafters,* ⌐ *rectors,* ⌐ *pictures.*

C—(M)

Past Tenses. 152. When the present tense of a verb of more than one syllable is written with either a double-length character or a hooked form, the past tense is written with the halving principle; thus,

⟍ *ponder,* ⟍ *pondered;* ⎯⎯ *canter,* ⟍ *cantered;*

⟋ *winter,* ⟋ *wintered;* ⎯⎯ *matter,* ⎯⎯ *mattered;*

⟋ *malinger,* ⟋ *malingered;* ⎯⎯ *conquer,*

⎯⎯ *conquered.*

Doubling Principle not employed. 153. The doubling principle is not employed—

(*a*) When a vowel follows final -*tr*, -*dr*, etc., because a final vowel requires a final stroke for the vowel sign; as, ⟍ *flatter,* but ⟍ *flattery;* ⟋ *winter,* but ⟋ *wintry;* ⟍ *feather,* but ⟍ *feathery;* ⎯⎯ *anger,* but ⎯⎯ *angry.*

(*b*) In words like ⟍ *panther,* ⟍ *Arthur,* where the *thr* is a light sound.

Position of Double-length Strokes. 154. (*a*) All double-length downstrokes are written through the line; as, ⟍ *painter,* ⟍ *fetter,* | *tender.*

(*b*) Double-length horizontals are written either above the line or on the line, according to the first vowel heard in the word; thus, ⎯⎯ *matter,* ⌐ *mother,* ⌣ *enter,* ⎯⎯ *neither.*

(*c*) Double-length upstrokes are written *above,* or *on,* or *through* the line, according to the first vowel heard in the word; thus, ⟋ *loiter,* ⟋ *render,* ⟋ *hinder.*

The Doubling Principle in Phraseography. 155. The doubling principle is employed in phraseography for the indication of the words *their, there;* thus, ____ *in,* ____ *in their;* ____ *I know,* ____ *I know there is;* ____ *take,* ____ *take their way;* ____ *I can be,* ____ *I can be there;* ____ *has to be,* ____ *has to be there;* ____ *upon,* ____ *upon their.*

Exercise 91

Read, copy, and transcribe

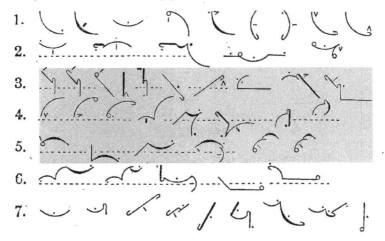

Exercise 92

Write in Shorthand

1. Flatter, thither, aster, voters, enters, neuter.
2. Fender, lavender, shedder, feeders, godfathers.
3. Central, centralization, dysenteric, eccentric.
4. Bidder, spider, plotter, sector, painter, winter.

5. Louder, Lowther, builder, cylinder, chambermaid, sinker, hunger, hungered, whimper, conquer.
6. Mutter, muttered, wander, wandered, temper, tempered, alter, altered, shatter, shattered.
7. Pander, pantry, seconder, secondary, voter, votary, cinder, cindery, enter, entry.

GRAMMALOGUES

chaired, cheered; sent; third, short; spirit; yard, word; rather, writer; wonderful-ly; therefore; school, schooled.

Exercise 93

Read, copy, and transcribe

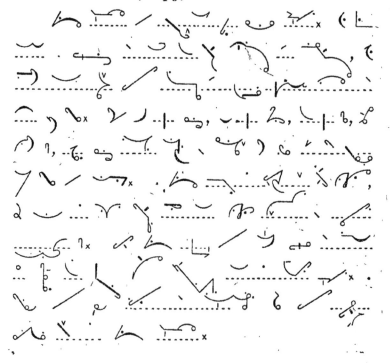

Exercise 94

Write in Shorthand

We-have to *hand* to-day, *under* last Wednesday's date, another copy *of-the wonderful* catalogue issued by Crowder *and* Sanderson.   *Their* motor cycle department *rather* appeals *to-the* boys *in-this school, and-we-have, therefore, sent word that-we should* like *several* extra copies *of-the* catalogue.   *The* new leather belt, just *over a yard in* length, *for* use *with a* water-proof coat, seems *wonderfully* cheap.   *There-is,* also, *a rather* attractive lamp, *with* silvered reflector, suitable *for any* holder, *and-this should* take well *with-the* boys.   These *people are* enterprising.   *They-are* inventors *as*-well-*as* dealers, *and-therefore we should-be-*able-*to* rely upon-*their* motor fittings *being* absolutely up *to* date.

Summary

-tr, -dr or *-*TH*r*, or, in common words, *-ture* is added	by doubling the length of the preceding stroke.
-er is added to the curve ⌒, and *-kr* or *-gr* is added to the curve ⌣	by doubling the length of the curve.
there or *their* in a phrase is expressed	by doubling the length of the preceding stroke.

Past tenses of verbs of more than one syllable.	are written with the halving principle.
The Doubling Principle is not applied	when a final vowel immediately follows -tr, -dr, etc.
The double-length form ⌒ -mpr or -mbr	is written (a) initially ; (b) after a circle or loop ; (c) after a downstroke.
The hooked form ⌢ -mpr or -mbr	is written in all other cases.
The double-length form ⌣ ng-kr or ng-gr.	is written initially and when following a circle or an upstroke.
The hooked form ⌣ ng-kr or ng-gr.	is written in all other cases.

CHAPTER XXV

DIPHONIC OR TWO-VOWEL SIGNS

In many words two vowels occur consecutively, each being separately pronounced. To represent these, special signs have been provided called *diphones* (from the Greek *di* = double, and *phōnē* = a sound).

Use of Diphones. 156. In most instances, the first of the two consecutive vowels is the more important, and therefore the diphonic sign is written in the vowel-place which the first vowel would take if this occurred alone. The method of using the *diphones* is explained in the following rules.

157. The *diphone ɩ* is written as follows—

(*a*) In the first vowel-place to represent the vowel *ah* or *ă* and any vowel immediately following; thus, ⌁ sahib, ⌁ Judaism.

(*b*) In the second vowel-place to represent *ā* or *ĕ*, and any vowel immediately following; thus, ⌁ layer, ⌁ laity, ⌁ betrayal, ⌁ surveyor;

(*c*) In the third vowel-place to represent *ē* or *ĭ* and any vowel immediately following; thus, ⌁ real, ⌁ reality, ⌁ re-enter, ⌁ amiable, ⌁ meander, ⌁ geography, ⌁ geographical, ⌁ champion, ⌁ heaviest, ⌁ burying, ⌁ glorious, ⌁ creator, ⌁ creation, ⌁ serial, ⌁ serious.

119

158. The *diphone* ⟂ is written as follows—

(*a*) In the first vowel-place to represent *aw* and any vowel immediately following; thus, ⟋ *flawy*, ⟋ *drawer*, ⟋ *drawings*, ⟋ *cawing*;

(*b*) In the second vowel-place to represent *ō* and any vowel immediately following; thus, ⟋ *showy*, ⟋ *bestowal*, ⟋ *poet*, ⟋ *poetical*, ⟋ *coercion*, ⟋ *coincide*, ⟋ *coincident*, ⟋ *heroic*.

(*c*) In the third vowel-place to represent *ōō* and any vowel immediately following; thus, ⟋ *bruin*, ⟋ *brewery*, ⟋ *Louisa*, ⟋ *Lewis*, ⟋ *truant*, ⟋ *Druid*, ⟋ *Druidical*, ⟋ *shoeing*, ⟋ *hallooing*.

Extended Use of Angular Sign. 159. The angular sign ⟋ is also used to represent the consecutive vowels in the small class of words like ⟋ *Spaniard*, ⟋ *million*, ⟋ *bullion*, ⟋ *question*.

Exercise 95

Read, copy, and transcribe

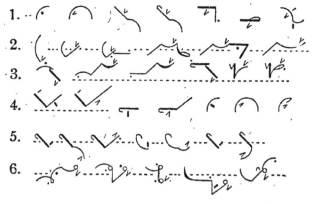

Exercise 96

Write in Shorthand

1. Slay, slayer, bay, bayonet, air, aerometer.
2. Pay, payable, betray, betrayer, obey, abeyance.
3. Re, real, really, reinforce, readdress, readmission.
4. Billow, billowy, blow, blower, co, coincide.
5. Hero, heroic, snow, snowy, slow, slowest.
6. Cruel, brewing, jewel, ruinous, ruination.

Exercise 97

Read, copy, and transcribe

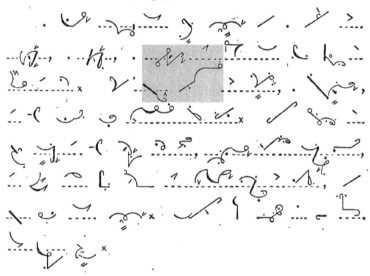

Exercise 98

Write in Shorthand

Dear Mr. Brewer,

It-is to be regretted that-the arrangement with-the band of-the Cleopatra has fallen through, but I-shall-be-able-to re-arrange-the programme and it-will-not affect-the gaiety of-the members of-the

Lyceum *on*-Monday.   *We-have-had* *to*-reappoint *the* late manager *of-the* local theatre *as* Master *of* Cere-monies, *because-he* knows *the* ceremonial *to be* observed, *and-we-shall-have* to reassemble-*the* *members* *of-the* chorus, *and* readmit *those-who* retired last June.   I-am worrying-*the* decorators, *and* *doing* my utmost *to*-make these slowest *of* slow *people* finish *their* work.

Very-truly-*yours*,

Summary

Place	Value of the Diphone ∕	Place	Value of the Diphone ⁊
1	*ah* or *ă* + any vowel	1	*aw* + any vowel
2	*ā* or *ĕ* ditto	2	*ō* ditto
3	*ē* or *ĭ* ditto	3	*ōō* ditto

The angular sign ∕ is also used to represent the consecutive vowels in such words as mill*i*on.

CHAPTER XXVI

MEDIAL SEMICIRCLE

As explained in a previous chapter, a right semicircle is used initially as an abbreviation for *w* before the strokes *k, g, m* (and *mp*) and the two forms of *r*. The medial use of a semicircle is explained in the present chapter.

Left and Right Semicircles. 160. (*a*) A *left* semicircle is written in the middle of a word to represent the sounds *wah, wā, wē,* or their corresponding short sounds.

(*b*) A *right* semicircle is written in the middle of a word to represent the sounds *waw, wō, wōo,* or their corresponding short sounds.

161. The following diagram shows the places of the semicircles, and the sounds they represent.

Place	Left Semicircle ᴄ	Place	Right Semicircle ᴐ
1	represents *w* + *ah* or *ă*	1	represents *w* + *aw* or *ŏ*
2	,, ,, + *ā* ,, *ĕ*	2	,, ,, + *ō* ,, *ŭ*
3	,, ,, + *ē* ,, *ĭ*	3	,, ,, + *ōo* ,,*ŏo*

162. The medial semicircle is, therefore, simply an abbreviation for *w* followed by a vowel. The sign is usefully written in words like ⌐ *boudoir,* ⌐ *assuage,* ⌐ *sea-weed ;* ⌐ *seaward,* ⌐ *Wordsworth,* ⌐ *lamb's-wool,* i.e. where the *w* is not essential to the outline.

123

Exercise 99

Read, copy, and transcribe

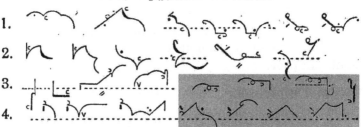

1.
2.
3.
4.

Exercise 100

Write in Shorthand

1. Sealing-wax, twenty, twentieth, Cromwell, Bothwell.
2. Dwindle, dwindled, wherewith, *there*with, bewilder, bewildered.
3. Breakwater, blameworthy, seaworthy, Wandsworth, Cornwallis.
4. Wick, wicked, wickedly, weaken, weakness.

Exercise 101

Read, copy, and transcribe

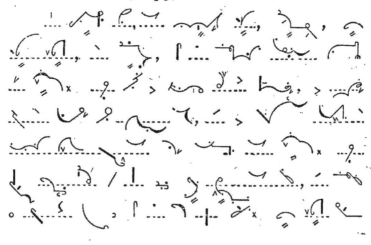

Exercise 102

Write in Shorthand

Dear-Sirs,

We-thank-you for-your-letter of-last week and we-are asking Messrs. Cromwell and Warbeck, of Wentworth, to-look into-the matter forthwith. We hope that-the flow of-water into-the workings may dwindle away with-the advent of-the dry weather, and-that-the trouble may cease of-itself. In-any-case, you-may-rely upon-us to-do all-that-we-can to stop-the nuisance in-question. We-have already told our engineer, Mr. Walter Welson, to-make close enquiry into-the matter, and-we-thank-you again for-the kindly way in-which-you have warned us of-the possible loss both to-ourselves and to-you.

Yours-truly.

Summary

1. A semicircle is employed medially as an alternative to the stroke w.
2. A medial *left* semicircle represents wah, wā, wē, or the corresponding short sounds.
3. A medial *right* semicircle represents waw, wō, wōō, or the corresponding short sounds.

CHAPTER XXVII
PREFIXES

Initial Com- or Con-. 163. Initial *com-* (or *comm-*) or *con-* (or *conn-*) is expressed by a light dot written at the beginning of the following stroke ; thus, ⟍ *combine,* ⟍ *commence,* ⟍ *congratulate,* ⟍ *connection.* In a few words clearer outlines are obtained by writing the prefixes fully ; thus, ⟍ *commotion,* ⟍ *commission,* ⟍ *commiserate,* ⟍ *consul,* ⟍ *connote.*

In words beginning with the prefix *com-* or *con-*, represented by a dot, the position of the outline is governed by the first vowel after the prefix.

Medial Com-, etc. 164. Medial *com-, con-, cum-,* or *cog-*, either in a word or in a phrase, is indicated by disjoining the form immediately following the *com-,* etc. ; thus, ⟍ *becomingly,* ⟍ *welcoming,* ⟍ *incompetent,* ⟍ *uncontrolled,* ⟍ *circumference,* ⟍ *recognize,* ⟍ *in compliance,* ⟍ *by consent,* ⟍ *1 am compelled.* This method may be used after a dash logogram when this is written upward, but not when it is written downward ; compare ⟍ *on the committee,* ⟍ *of the committee ;* ⟍ *should commence* and ⟍ *to commence.*

Accom-. 165. *Accom-* (or *accommo-*) is represented by — *k,* joined or disjoined ; thus, ⟍ *accommodation,* ⟍ *accompany.*

Intro-. 166. *Intro-* is expressed by ⟍ *ntr ;* thus, ⟍ *introduce,* ⟍ *introspection.*

Magna-, etc. 167. *Magna-*, *magne-* or *magni-* is expressed by a disjoined ⌒ *m;* thus, ⌒⌐ *mag-nanimity,* ⌐ *magnetize,* ⌐ *magnify.*

Trans-. 168. *Trans-* may be contracted by omitting the *n;* thus, ⌐ *transfer,* ⌐ *transmit,* ⌐ *transgression;* but sometimes the full outline is preferable, as, ⌐ *transcend,* ⌐ *transit.*

Self- and Self-con- or Self-com-. 169. (*a*) *Self-* is represented by a disjoined circle *s* written close to the following stroke in the second vowel-place ; thus, ⌐ *self-defence,* ⌐ *self-made.*

(*b*) *Self-con-* or *self-com-* is indicated by a disjoined circle *s* written in the position of the *con-* dot ; thus, ⌐ *self-control,* ⌐ *self-complacency.*

In- before Str, Skr and H (up). 170. *In-* before the circled strokes ⌐ ⌐ ⌐ is expressed by a small hook written in the same direction as the circle ; thus, ⌐ *instrument,* ⌐ *inscriber,* ⌐ *inhabit.*

Negative Words. 171. (*a*) The small hook for *in-* is never used in negative words, that is, where *in-* signifies *not.* In such cases *in-* must be written with the stroke *n;* thus, ⌐ *hospitable,* ⌐ *inhospitable;* ⌐ *suppressible,* ⌐ *insup-pressible;* ⌐ *humanity,* ⌐ *inhumanity.*

(b) Words which have the prefix *il-*, *im-*, *in-*, *ir-*, *un-*, are written in accordance with the following rules, so as to provide the necessary distinction between positive and negative words, and other pairs of words where distinction is required—

(c) By writing the downward *r* or *l* when the rules for writing initial *r* or *l* permit of this being done; thus, ⟋ *resolute,* ⟍ *irresolute;* ⟋ *resistible,* ⟍ *irresistible;* ⟍ *limitable,* ⟍ *illimitable.*

(d) By repeating the *l, m, n* or *r* in cases where a distinction cannot otherwise be obtained; thus, ⌐ *legal,* ⌐ *illegal;* ⌐ *mortal,* ⌐ *immortal;* ⌐ *noxious,* ⌐ *innoxious;* ⟋ *necessary,* ⟋ *unnecessary;* ⟋ *redeemable,* ⟋ *irredeemable;* ⟋ *radiance,* ⟋ *irradiance.*

Logograms. 172. Logograms, joined or disjoined, may be used as prefixes or suffixes; thus, ⟋ *almost,* ⟋ *understand,* ⟋ *undermine,* ⟋ *unimportant.*

Exercise 103

Read, copy, and transcribe

1.

2.

3.

4.

5.

6.

Exercise 104

Write in Shorthand

1. Competent, combat, common, compensate, compound, compact, compare.
2. Conductor, conflict, constant, convulsion, conserve, conscientious, contango.
3. Commissioners, incomplete, recognized, un-congenial, reconsider, incumbent.
4. *We*-were compelled, accompanying, accomplices, introducing, introduces.
5. Magnificent, magnifier, magnificence, transmission, translated, transmitter.
6. Self-possession, self-congratulation, instructor, inherent, inhumanly, insuperable.
7. Illiberal, immaterial, innocuous, unknown, reparable, irreparable, reclaimable, irreclaim-able, *under*stood, *under*sell, *trade*-mark.

GRAMMALOGUES

selfish-ness ;   *inscribe-d* ;   *inscription* ;

instruction ;   *instructive.*

Exercise 105

Read, copy, and transcribe

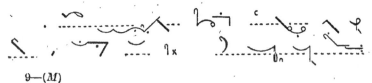

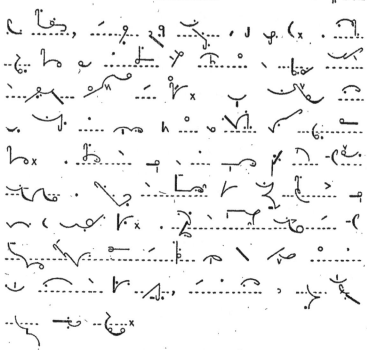

Exercise 106

Write in Shorthand

We-thank-you for-your communication *and instruc-tion* regarding-*the* lightning conductors *for-the* new Conservative Club *in* Conway Road.　*The* slight mis-conception *has*-now *been* removed, *and your* recom-mendations *shall-be* carefully considered.　*We-are having-the* corner-stones *inscribed this* week, *and-we-have*-no-doubt *that-you*-will-find-*the* inscription will satisfy *you*.　*We* suggest *for-your* consideration *that-it-would-be instructive and* useful *to-have a* trans-lation *of-the* Latin *inscription* printed *and* circulated before-*the* opening ceremony.　*You*-will-not consider us *selfish* if-*we* arrange *for a* photograph *of-the* ceremony showing *our* name *as* contractors *for-the* work.

Summary

PREFIX	REPRESENTED BY
Initial *con-*, *com-*	A light dot.
Medial *con-*, *com-*	Disjoining the form immediately following the *con-*, etc.
Accom-	The stroke — *k* joined or disjoined.
Intro-	The double-length ⌣ *ntr.*
Magna-, etc.	Disjoined ⌢ *m.*
Trans-	The sign for *trs*, or by the full form.
Self-	A disjoined circle *s* written in the second vowel-place.
Self-con-	A disjoined circle *s* written in the place of the *con-* dot.
In- before certain circled straight strokes	A small hook written with the Right motion.
Il-, *ir-*	Downward *l* or *r*, or by the repetition of the initial consonant.
im-, *in-*, *un-*	Repeating the ⌢ *m* or ⌣ *n.*
Logograms	May be used as prefixes or suffixes.

CHAPTER XXVIII
SUFFIXES AND TERMINATIONS

-Ing. 173. The stroke ‿ is generally employed in the representation of *-ing*. Where this stroke cannot be written, or, where, if written, an awkward joining would result, a light dot is used to represent the suffix *-ing*. The dot *-ing* is written—

(*a*) After light straight downstrokes and downward *r*, as ╲ *paying,* ⌐ *tying,* ╱ *etching,* ⟋ *hoeing,* ⟍ *hearing,* ╳ *spluttering.*

(*b*) After circle *ns*, after *k* and *g* hooked for *f* or *v*, and after an upstroke finally hooked ; as, ⟍ *prancing,* ⌐ *coughing,* ⟋ *waning.*

(*c*) After a half-length or a double-length stroke where no angle would be obtained by the use of the stroke ‿ , as ╲ *brooding,* ╲ *fidgeting,* ⌒ *matting,* ╲ *fielding,* ⌒ *muttering.*

(*d*) Generally after a contracted logogram ; as, ╲ *remembering,* ‿ *coming,* ╲ *thanking* ; but the stroke ‿ is employed in ⟋ *wishing,* ‿ *calling,* ‿ *having,* ⟋ *surprising.*

(*e*) The dot *-ing* cannot be used medially ; therefore the stroke *ng* is written in *-ingly* ; thus, ╲ *admiring,* but ⟋ *admiringly* ; ⟋ *deserving,* but ⟋ *deservingly.*

132

(*f*) Wherever -*ing* would be represented by a dot, -*ings* is indicated by a dash; thus, / *etchings*, *scrapings*, *plottings*, *windings*, *rinsings*.

-Ality, etc. 174. - *Ality, -ility, -arity, -ority, -elty,* and similar terminations are expressed by disjoining the stroke immediately preceding the termination; thus, *formality*, *barbarity*, *novelty*, *frivolity*, *feasibility*, *majority*.

-Logical-ly. 175. - *Logical* and -*logically* are expressed by a disjoined / *j*; thus, *genealogical-ly*, *mythological-ly*.

-Ment. 176. - *Ment* is, as a rule, expressed by *mnt*; thus, *sentiment*, *agreement*. If this sign does not join easily, however, the contracted form ᴗ may be used; thus, *imprisonment*, *commencement*, *refinement*, *preferment.*

-Mental-ly-ity. 177. - *Mental, -mentally,* and -*mentality* are expressed by a disjoined *mnt*; thus, *fundamental-ly*, *instrumental-ly-ity.*

-Ly. 178. - *Ly* is expressed by / *l*, joined or disjoined; thus, *chiefly*, *friendly*; or the hook *l* is employed; thus, *deeply*, *positively.*

-Ship. 179. - *Ship* is expressed by a joined or disjoined / *sh*; thus, *friendship*, *citizenship*, *scholarship*, *leadership.*

-Fulness and -lessness or -lousness. 180. (a)
-*Fulness* is expressed by a disjoined ⌣ *fs;* thus,
⌣ *usefulness,* ⌐ *carefulness,* ⌐ *gratefulness.*

(b) -*Lessness* and -*lousness* are expressed by a
disjoined ⌒ *ls;* thus, ⌒ *heedlessness,* ⌒ *hope-
lessness,* ⌒ *sedulousness.*

-Ward, -wart, -wort; -yard. 181. -*Ward, -wart* or
-*wort,* and -*yard* are expressed by a half-sized *w* and
y respectively, as in the words, ⌐ *backward,*
⌐ *stalwart,* ⌐ *brickyard.*

Compound Words. 182. Compounds of *here, there,
where,* etc., are written as follows—

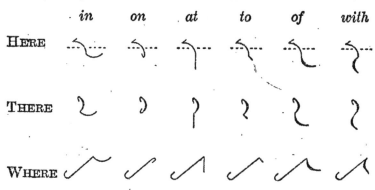

	in	on	at	to	of	with
HERE						
THERE						
WHERE						

Exercise 107

Read, copy, and transcribe

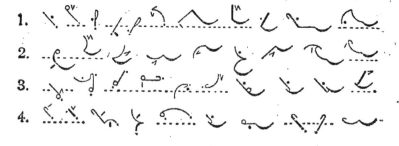

1.
2.
3.
4.

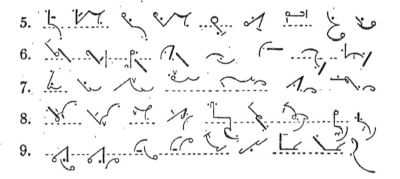

Exercise 108

Write in Shorthand

1. Sapping, tying, teaching, fearing, webbing, wading, lodging, shaking, flogging, loving, scathing, sowing, rushing, slaying, roaring.
2. Dispensing, enhancing, craving, surrounding, ballooning, opposing, menacing, puffing, disjoining, caning, concerning.
3. Pleating, obtruding, permitting, scaffolding, flitting, smothering, dissecting, smelting, sauntering, *speaking*, castings.
4. Solubility, singularity, fatality, novelties, etymological, accompaniment, effacement, sentimentally, vainly, frankly, exhaustively.
5. *Chair*manship, clerkship, playfulness, credulousness, in*difference*, hereby, *there*about, whereunto.

PHRASES

you will be able to, *we are able to;*
at the same time, *at some time,*
for some time; *this was,* *that was;*
according to the.

Exercise 109

Read, copy, and transcribe

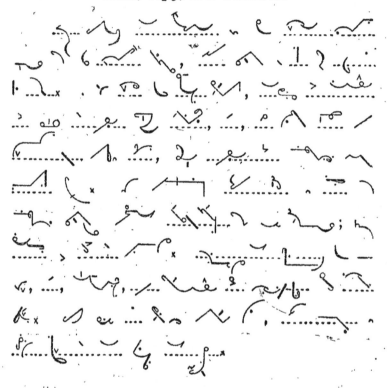

Exercise 110

Write in Shorthand

I-am-sorry *to* interfere *with-the* arrangements *for-the* announcement *of-the* concert season, *but* at-the-same-time I-am compelled *to* say *that* I-*think-the* form proposed *is*-not likely *to-have-the* effect *of* introducing new *members to-the* society. I-fear-*the* psychological effect *of-the wording of-the* circular, *which-is more* like *a* command or *instruction* than *an* invitation. I-*think it*-will provoke *a* feeling *of* resentment *in-the*-minds *of-those* whom *you-are* addressing, *and* at-*the*-same-time convey *a* false impression. I-am conscious *of* no *selfishness in* communicating *with-you* on-*the* matter, *because-it-is quite* immaterial *to-me whether-the member*ship *is large* or small ; *but, as-the* instructor *and* conductor *of-the* choir, I-must, *in* self-defence, warn *the* committee against *a* possible misconstruction *of-their* circular. I-*think-you*-will-*be*-able-*to* induce *them to* change *it.* I-*have-been* wanting *to* see-*you for*-sometime, *and*-if-*you*-will *call* some-time *during-the* coming week I-*shall-be*-glad *of a* little conversation *with-you.*

Revisionary Exercise (C)

I-*cannot quite under*stand *how you*-came *to* act *as you* did *in-the* court *to*-day, *nor how you could put-the* case against *that child with*-such *particular* force, missing no *opportunity that-you*-were able-*to* seize *to*-make-*the* poor *child* appear guilty *of-the* theft. *You*-may say *that, without-the* evidence *of-the gentleman whose* purse *was*-taken, *and without-the* statements *of-the* other *gentlemen who* said they saw-*the child* put her *hand* into-*the* old *gentleman's* pocket, there-*would* certainly *have-been* no case *for-the* jury. *But,* surely, *according-to-the* evidence *of-the guard called* by-*the* defence, *there-was more*-than *a* doubt *that-the* prisoner *was-the child* seen by-*the gentlemen who* testified. *The guard told a* straightforward tale, *and, though-you tried to* shake *his* evidence *you* failed *to do*-so, except *towards-the* end, *when-he* admitted he-saw *a gold* coin drop apparently *from-the child's* hands *to-the* ground. I-*think-you*-were *a* little *short with-the guard, and* I-*was* glad *when-the* people *in-the* court *cheered his* final reply. They *chaired him, too,* at-*the* end *of-the* case, *under* protest by-*him and-his* friends. I-*do-not believe-the* poor *child* came out-*of-the*

yard, as stated by-one-*of-your* witnesses, *and*-indeed
I-did-not *believe a word of-that* witness's evidence.
It-was given, in a bad *spirit, in a* tone *which sent a*
shiver through everyone *in-the* court, I-know *that*
at-least *a third of-his* story about-*the school and-the
wonderful instruction* he *had* received *there was*
untrue, I-know *this because* I-went *to-the school
myself and you*-will-find my name *inscribed on-the*
roll *of* honour hanging *in-the large* hall. *It-is*-not
wonderful, therefore, that I-*have a* doubt *of-that* man's
word. It-would-be rather more wonderful if I-*believed
his* story. I-*think that-he-is a selfish,* vindictive
fellow, *and it*-will-*be instructive to* follow *his* future.
*Any*way, I-*shall* set about *an* appeal *for-the child,*
whom I-*believe to be* absolutely innocent *of-the* crime
alleged against her.   (373 words)

Summary

Suffix	Represented by
-ing	The stroke ‿ where convenient ; otherwise by a light dot.
-ings	The stroke ‿ͻ where convenient ; otherwise by a light dash.
-ality, etc.	Disjoining the stroke immediately preceding the termination.
-logical-ly /	Disjoining the stroke / *j.*
-ment	The sign ⁀ *mnt*, where convenient ; otherwise by ‿ *nt.*

-mental-ly-ity	Disjoined ⌐ *mnt.*
-ly	The stroke ⌐ *l*, or by a form hooked for *l*.
-ship	The stroke ⌐ *sh.*
-lessness or *-lousness*	Disjoined ⌐ *ls.*
-fulness	Disjoined ⌐ *fs.*
-ward, etc., and *yard*	Half-sized *w* and *y* respectively.

Compounds	Generally formed by joining the outlines for the separate words.

CHAPTER XXIX

CONTRACTIONS

Omission of Consonants. 183. (*a*) Where *p* is very slightly sounded, it may be omitted, as in ⟍ *prompt,* ⌊ *tempt,* ⟍ *assumption,* ⟍ *exemption;* but the *p* is represented in words like ⟍ *trumpet,* ⟍ *trumpeter,* where it is clearly sounded.

(*b*) *K* or *G* is omitted between *ng* and *t,* or between *ng* and *sh,* when no vowel occurs immediately after *k* or *g;* thus, ⟍ *adjun(c)t,* ⟍ *extin(c)tion.* In ⟍ *trinket,* ⟍ *blanket,* and similar words, in which a vowel follows the consonant, the *k* or *g* is retained. The *k* is also retained in past tenses, as ⌣ *inked,* ⟍ *winked,* ⟍ *banked,* ⟍ *linked.*

(*c*) Medial *t,* immediately following circle *s,* may be omitted in many words; thus, ⟍ *postman,* ⟍ *honestly,* ⌊ *tasteful,* ⟍ *mistake,* ⟍ *mistaken,* ⟍ *institute;* and in phrases like ⟍ *most important,* ⟍ *there must be,* ⟍ *your last letter.* In some words, however, the full form is quite as facile as the contracted form; thus, ⌊ *drastic,* ⟍ *elastic,* ⟍ *plastic.*

140

Exercise 111

Read, copy, and transcribe

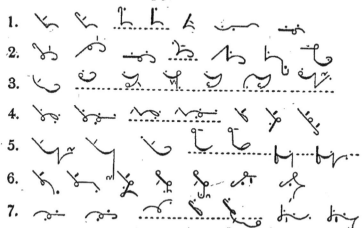

Exercise 112

Write in Shorthand

1. Presume, presumptive, bump, bumped, tempt, tempter.

2. Temptation, contempt, contemptible, cramp, cramped, thump, thumped.

3. Consumption, consumptive, stamp, stamped, swamped, resumptive.

4. Indistinct, distinction, extinct, manifest, manifestly, adjustments.

5. Rest, restless, list, listless, dishonest, dishonestly, waste-pipe.

6. Text, textbook, trust, trustworthy, postcard, Post Office.

Exercise 113

Read, copy, and transcribe

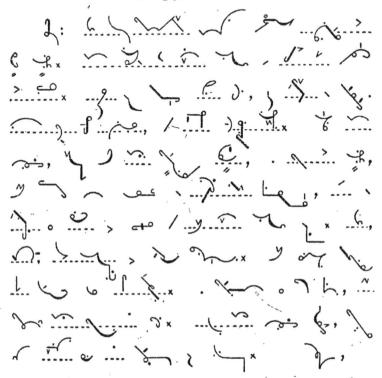

Exercise 114

Write in Shorthand

We-are-much-obliged *for-your*-letter *and* estimate *for-the* elastic web. *But surely there*-must-*be* some mistake *in-your* figures. Please-refer *to-your*-last-letter *to* us, dated 26th October, *in-which-you*-gave us *a* distinctly better price. Manifestly, *the* post-ponement *of-the*-order *for a* week *cannot* possibly *have*-made so *great a* difference *in-the*-price. *We* realize *that-the* web *is-the* best-finish, *as-it-is most-important it-should-be*, *but-you*-must-try *to-improve* upon *your* estimate, or *you-cannot* hope *to*-receive *the* order. *You*-must-*be* estimating, *we-think*, *on-the* assumption *that-the* web *is to be* silk finished. *That-is*-not so, *as you*-will-see *on* referring *to-our* last-letter. If-*there-is-to be a* resumption *of* business between-us, *your* estimate will-*have to be* reconsidered. *All-we* ask *for is a* web *with-the* best-finish, *but* not silk, *and of a* tasteful design. *What-can you* offer *to* tempt us *to* pass *the* order *to-you* ?

Other General Contractions.

184. Contractions for a number of words in common use are formed by the omission of a medial or final consonant or syllable. These contracted words, together with the classes of words contracted on the principles explained in the present chapter, constitute what may be termed General Contractions. A prefix or suffix may be attached to a contracted outline, and in this way the list of contractions may easily be extended ; thus,

⅄ *respect*, ⅄ *disrespect*, ⅄ *disrespectful*, ⅄ *respective*, ⅄ *respectively*. The halving principle may be applied to contracted forms for past tenses ; thus, ⅂ *endanger*, ⅂ *endangered* ; but in many cases the same form may safely be employed for both present and past tenses ; thus, ⅄ *respect-ed*, ⅃ *suspect-ed*. Contracted outlines are generally written on the line.

Omission of N

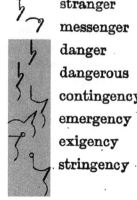

passenger	appointment
stranger	attainment
messenger	contentment
danger	assignment
dangerous	entertainment
contingency	enlightenment
emergency	abandonment
exigency	ironmonger
stringency	oneself

Omission of R

demonstrate	monstrous
remonstrate	manuscript
remonstrance	henceforward
ministry	thenceforward

Omission of -ect

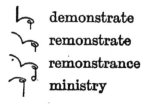

expect-ed	imperfect-ion-ly
inspect-ed-ion	suspect-ed
prospect	object-ed
respect-ed	project-ed
retrospect	architect-ure-al

Omission of kt before -ive

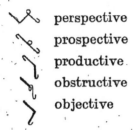

perspective	
prospective	
productive	
obstructive	
objective	

destructive	
destructively	
retrospective	
irrespective	
irrespectively	

Omission of K before -shun

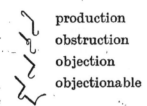

production	
obstruction	
objection	
objectionable	

destruction	
jurisdiction	
introduction	
retrospection	

Exercise 115
Write in Shorthand

The *appointment of a stranger as Passenger* Superintendent *is a* dis*appointment to-the* local candidates *for-the* position. *There-is a* rumour *of a demonstration of-*protest against *what-have-been called the monstrous* methods *of-the administration in-this-*matter. *There-is, however, great danger in a* form *of remonstrance that-*may provoke *a dangerous* outburst *in-*place *of-the-*present *contentment, and, with great respect to-the* leaders, *we-*fail *to* see *any prospect of-their* attaining *their object* if-they *demonstrate in-the* way suggested. *It-is always the* un*expected* and un*suspected contingency that-is* likely *to* happen, *and-we* expect-the present *emergency* will prove no exception *to-the* rule. *The introduction of a* policy *of obstruction* or *destruction,* or even *of* interference *with* reasonable *jurisdiction,* may-*be productive of* discontentment all-round. *It-is to be* hoped every means will-*be* sought *for-the attainment of-the objective.*

10—*(I)*

Exercise 116

Write in Shorthand

We-fear *there-is*-no *prospect* of success *for-those-who* raise *objection* *to-the* *appointment, and,* quite *irrespective* *of-the* merits *of-the* *respective* parties, *we-would* urge-*the abandonment of obstructive* measures *and-the entertainment of-the* suggested resort *to*-threats. Further *enlightenment is* necessary if matters *are to* proceed smoothly *henceforward.* *It-is* pleasant *to*-turn *from this-subject to-the* attractions *of-the* country-side, where *there-are* numerous *objects of entertainment and instruction for all who* care *to*-look *for-them.* *The* jerry builder *has*-not-yet begun *his destructive* work, *and-the monstrous things which* he *calls architecture, but which* cause dis*appointment and*-grief *to-the* genuine *architect, have*-not-yet appeared *to*-ruin-*the prospect.* *The* unspoiled beauty *of* nature still remains *to* compel *our respectful* admiration, *and to remonstrate in* silence against *those whose object is to*-make money, even *though it* involves *the destruction of-the-most* glorious *prospect.*

Exercise 117

Write in Shorthand

(a) Please-send *a messenger to-the passenger* office *and* ask if-*there-is any danger of-the* train *being* late at Macclesfield. *The* present *emergency has* arisen through-*the* death *of-the* man *in*-charge *of-the* post-office, *and-the abandonment of-the stranger's* claim might bring-about-*the very contingency we-are* striving *to*-avoid. *We-had-the* same *emergency on-the appointment of-the* postmaster three-*years*-ago, *and-the entertainment* then arranged *had to be* abandoned *because-it-was* felt *that-it-would-be dangerous to* proceed. *The abandonment* caused dis*appointment*, *of*-course, *but* *contentment* followed *enlightenment as-to-the* cause *and* eventually *the attainment of-the* orginal *object was* secured.

, (*b*) *The demonstration* against *the administration* *of-the* local funds *was, in-our-opinion, a monstrous* mistake, *and-we-shall remonstrate as* vigorously *as-* *we-can.* *The monstrosity in-the* shape *of an* effigy *of-the chair*man *of-the administrative* committee *was* *of-the-most objectionable* nature, *and-*only served *to* *demonstrate the* poor taste *of-those-who* designed *it.* I *should-have to-*write *a* long *manuscript* if I desired *to-*express my resentment properly, *and-*even then my *remonstrance would-not-be too* strong. I *should* like *to* assist *in-the administration of-*personal punishment upon-*the* men at-*the* head *of-this monstrous* business. *It-is* pleasant *to* know *that* no-one *from-the* *ministry was* concerned *in-the-*matter.

, (*c*) *As-to-the architect's project for-the* alteration *of-the* club premises, I *rather suspect that-his* idea *of-the architectural* possibilities *is imperfect and-*incorrect. *With great respect to-him,* because *of-the* *imperfection of-*my acquaintance *with architecture,* I *respectfully* suggest *that-he-should* take counsel *with* someone *whose architectural* ability *would* entitle *him to-*express *an opinion.* I *quite expect-the architect* will consider *me* dis*respectful, and-*I-am upset at-*the prospect of a* disagreement *with him.* My *object* *is to* secure *an inspection of-the* premises *as* they-*are,* *and* I-*believe-that* un*expected and,* indeed, un*suspected* possibilities may develop *as a* result. *There-can-be* no dis*respect in* suggesting *that a retrospective* view *of-the* case, so-*as-to* secure *a* proper *perspective, should-be* under*taken.* *This-is* exactly *what* I suggested sometime-ago, *but it-was* considered *an* interference *with-the administration, and* no steps were taken.

Exercise 118

Write in Shorthand

Irrespective entirely *of-the different* views *of-the respective* parties *to-the* discussion, I-am compelled *to* consider-*the* possible results *of-the obstructive* course taken by-*the* council. *There-can-be* no-doubt *that-the objective would-be more* easily attained if-these *merely destructive* methods were abandoned. They *can* only *be productive of-*mischief *in-the* case *of prospective* candidates *for* admission *to-the* society, *and-this whether we* consider-*the* matter *prospectively* or *retrospec*tively. *A retrospective* examination will show *what-has* occurred *in-the* past, *in* similar *circumstances, and a prospective* consideration will show *what-is* likely *to* occur *in-the* future, if-*the respective* parties *are* allowed *to* follow *their-own merely obstructive* ideas. Each will-*be destructive of-the* other, *and-*will certainly act *destructively,* no matter *what* each may say. They *should-be* instructed *to* consider, *respectively and* collectively, *the* effects *of-the* present methods *and* advised *to-*refuse *them.*

Exercise 119

Write in Shorthand

The objection to-the obstruction in-the new bill *is-*not simply *a* personal matter. *The obstruction is objectionable on-several* grounds. *First, because it-*will certainly lead *to a destruction of-the* opposition *which-has-been* so carefully arranged, *and,* secondly, *because-the-*matter *is* one *which* falls *under* another *jurisdiction. The introduction of* various methods *of-production and* reproduction *has* no bearing *on-the* question, *as-the* least *retrospection would-have* shown *beyond* doubt. *It-*may sound disrespectful, *but* my-*own* view *is that-the architect and-his* friends, *who-are,*

I-*suspect, the* authors *of-the* bill, *are* simply unaware *of-the* real *circumstances of-the* case, *and-have*-not *given-the project the* consideration *it* deserves.

Summary

General contractions are formed by the omission of

p in words where the *p* is only lightly sounded.

k or *g* between *ng-t* and between *ng-sh*.

t between circle *s* and a following consonant.

n in words like *passenger,* *emergency,* etc.

r in words like *remonstrate,* *demonstration.*

-ect in words like *expect-ed,* etc.

-kt in words like *productive,* etc.

Derivatives are formed from contracted outlines by attaching a prefix or a suffix, as in, *respect,* *disrespect,* *respectively.*

CHAPTER XXX

FIGURES, ETC.

Figures. 185. Figures *one* to *seven*, and the figure *nine* are represented by shorthand outlines. All other numbers, except round numbers, are represented in the ordinary way by the Arabic numerals. In dealing with round numbers the following abbreviations are used :

⌣ *hundred* or *hundredth*, as in 4 400 ;

(or (*thousand* or *thousandth*, as in 3 (3,000 ;

⌐ *hundred thousand*, as in 4 400,000 ;

⌒ *million*, or *millionth*, as in 3 3,000,000 ;

⌒ *hundred million*, as in 7 700,000,000 ;

\ *billion* (a million of millions), as in 4 \ *four billion.*

The principal monetary units are expressed as follows : ⌐ *pounds*, as in 2 £200, 6 (£6,000, 5 £5,000,000 ; ⌐ *dollar*, ⌐ *dollars*, as in 15 ($15,000 ; ⌐ *francs*, as in 4 400 fr. ; ⌐ *rupees*, as in 2 Rs. 2,000,000.

Accent, etc. 186. (*a*) Accent may be shown by writing a small cross close to the vowel of the accented syllable ; thus, ⌐ *ar'rows*, ⌐ *arose'*, ⌐ *renew'*.

150

(*b*) Emphasis is marked by drawing one or more lines underneath ; a single line under a single word must be made wave-like, ⌣ , to distinguish it from ⎯ *k*.

(*c*) The sign 𝔰 indicates that the preceding remark is to be taken humorously.

Proper Names, etc. 187. In the few cases where it is necessary to indicate exactly the vowel following a diphthong, the separate signs should be used and not the triphone as explained in paragraph 35 ; thus, ⤵. *Bryan*, ⤵. *Bryon*, ⌐ *Myatt*, ⌐ *Myott*, ⌐ *Wyatt*. Similarly, if it is necessary to indicate exactly the second of two consecutive vowels, the separate signs should be used and not the diphone ; thus, ⌐ *Leah*, but ⌐ *Leo* ; ⌐ *genii*, ⌣ *nuclei*, ⌐ *radii*. The necessity for the use of these separate vowel-signs will be found to arise but seldom.

Scotch, Welsh, and Irish Consonants and Vowels. 188. The Scotch guttural *ch*, and the Irish *gh* are written thus, ⌐ *ch*, as in ⌐ *loch*, ⌐ *Loughrea*, ⌐ *Clogher*. The Welsh *ll* by ⌐ *ll* ; thus, ⌐ *Llan*.

Foreign Consonants and Vowels. 189. The German guttural *ch* is written thus, ⌐ *ch*, as in ⌐ *ich*, ⌐ *dach* ; French nasal ⌐ , as in ⌐ *soupçon* ; French and German vowels ⌐ *jeune*, ⌐ *Goethe*, ⌐ *dû*.

Exercise 120

Write in Shorthand

*The Chair*man, *in* moving-*the* adoption *of-the* report *and* accounts, dealing *first with-the* accounts *of-the* local holding company, said *it-would-be* noted *that-the* amount paid up *on-the* shares *was* increased by F.42,560, or £3,546 ; *this-was to*-keep pace *with-the* increase *in* capital costs *of-the* property, including extensions *during* recent *years.* Sundry creditors at £3,507 included £2,583 *for* Java income-tax reserve (*of-which* £1,666 appearing *to-the* debit *of-* profit *and* loss account *was* additional *for-the-year*), besides bonus due *to-the* staff *and*-some *trade* items. *The* outlay *on* capital account £3,714, included £2,746 *for a* new drying installation, smoke house, etc., *the balance being for* upkeep *of-the* immature area. They-*had* now *a* monthly capacity *of* 15,000 lb. sheet, *the* policy *of-the* board *being to* increase *their* output *of-this* quality *to* 50 per-cent *of-the* estate's whole output.

Their cash assets *in*-London *and* Java amounted *to* £16,712, *an* increase *of nearly* £5,000. *The* crop *was* 449,000 lb., *as* compared *with-the* restricted crop *of* 230,473 lb. *in-the* preceding *year, and* against *an* estimate *of* 394,000 lb., despite *the* fact *that for-the* last *two*-months *of-the-year* they-were *on a* re- stricted basis. *The* average net selling price *was a* fraction *under* 1s. 1d., against 1s. 4·35d. last-*year.* *Thanks, however, to a* reduction *from* 1s. 1·80d. *to* 8·92d., *in-the* total costs, *the* net profit per pound *was* 4·02d., or 1½d. above-*the* previous *year.* *It-* *was largely owing to-this* reduction *in* costs *that*-they- *had* made *a* net profit *of* £8,843, *over* 12 per-cent *on-the* issued capital. He thought-*the* shareholders *would* agree *that-this-was a* pleasing result.

CHAPTER XXXI

NOTE-TAKING, TRANSCRIPTION, ETC.

Note-Taking. 190. The inexperienced writer may sometimes find difficulty in turning over the leaves of his note-book. The following method may be usefully adopted—While writing on the upper half of the leaf, introduce the second finger of the left hand between it and the next leaf, keeping the leaf which is being written on steady by the first finger and thumb. While writing on the lower part of the page shift the leaf by degrees, till it is about half-way up the book, and, at a convenient moment, lift up the first finger and thumb, when the leaf will turn over almost of itself. This is the best plan when writing on a desk or table. When writing with the book on the knee, the first finger should be introduced instead of the second, and the leaf be moved up only about two inches. The finger should be introduced at the first pause the speaker makes, or at any other convenient opportunity that presents itself. Another method is to take hold of the bottom left-hand corner of the leaf with the finger and thumb, and on the bottom line being reached the leaf is lifted and turned over. Some reporters prefer a reporting book the leaves of which turn over like those of a printed book. When such a book is used there is less difficulty in turning over the leaves with the left hand. Whichever form of book is used, the writer should confine himself to *one side* of the paper till the end of the book is reached, and then turn the book round and write on the blank side of the paper, proceeding as before.

11—(R)   153

Unvocalized Outlines.   191. The essentials of accurate note-taking are rapid writing and facile reading,
and it is to these objects that the following chapters
are directed, special methods being developed for the
formation of brief and legible outlines. The student
is already familiar with a method of forming contracted outlines. He will find in succeeding pages
further applications of that method, and also a
method of abbreviation by Intersection, which
gives distinctive forms for well-known combinations of words. Phraseography is also greatly
extended, and compact outlines are provided for
many technical and general phrases. Vocalization being a great hindrance to speed, Phonography
from its beginning is so constructed that the
necessity for the insertion of vowels is reduced to
a minimum. By means of the principle of writing
words in position, unvocalized outlines which are
common to two or more words are as readily
distinguished as are musical notes by means of the
difference of place assigned to them on the stave.

Position-writing.   192. In speed practice, which
should, of course, be pursued concurrently with the
careful study of the advanced style as hereafter
developed, the rules of position-writing should be
carefully observed. After a short time this will
become automatic. Even unique outlines that may
appear to be independent of position are rendered
still more legible by being written in accordance with the position-writing rules. At first
a few vowels may be inserted, in order to
promote clearness and to enable the writer to
acquire the power of vocalizing quickly when
necessary. But efforts should be made from the
outset to write the outlines clearly and in position,

and to make these, rather than vocalization, the factors on which reliance is placed for accurate reading. When a fair speed in writing has been reached the student should avail himself of opportunities of reporting public speakers, vocalizing but little even when there is ample time, so that the ability to dispense with vowels may be cultivated.

Practising the Rules. 193. Since perfect familiarity with the rules is essential to rapid writing, the aspirant for speed is advised to vary his dictation practice by writing from dictation the exercises which appear in ordinary type in the pages of the *Manual* or first part of the *Instructor*. Pitman's shorthand is a connected system, and the most elementary rules have been formulated with the needs of the fast writer in view all the time. There is an orderly development throughout the whole system, so that the advanced principles of abbreviation cannot be properly understood and instantaneously applied unless the elementary rules are understood and can be applied without hesitation. Practice in the writing of the exercises which illustrate the various rules has upon the shorthand student much the same effect as practising the scales has upon the advanced student of music. The more thoroughly the scales are studied and practised, the more easily will the musician play the most intricate passages in any musical composition. Similarly, the more familiar the speed writer is with the exercises given in illustration of the fundamental rules of the system, by means of repeated practice in writing exercises from dictation, the more easily and quickly will he become a fast and accurate writer of any matter he may be called upon to take in shorthand. It is well known that

the most accomplished pianists are the most persistent
and regular in their practice of difficult scales.
The shorthand writer cannot do better than follow
their example and apply their methods to his own
subject.

Knowledge of Outlines. 194. The reading of
printed shorthand in the advanced style is as important as writing practice, and should be practised
daily. It gradually gives an extensive knowledge
of outlines, and the power of reading unvocalized
shorthand, as well as trains the student in the selection of the best outlines, and also considerably
expedites the arrival of the time when the omission
of practically all vowels may be ventured upon.
When unvocalized shorthand can be read with
facility, speed and self-reliance will be greatly·
increased. The student in reading his notes should
observe whether he has omitted essential vowels or
inserted unnecessary ones. The latter is as important
as the former, because the loss of time occasioned by
the insertion of unnecessary vowels may render the
writer unable to keep pace with the speaker. An
outline which has caused difficulty in writing or
reading should be written in position several times,
the word being repeated aloud simultaneously with
the writing.

Knowledge of Contracted Forms. 195. It is impossible to lay too much stress upon the importance
of an absolutely perfect knowledge of the grammalogues and contractions. It will be found that any
ordinary piece of matter consists of about sixty per
cent—and sometimes more—of words which are
included in the lists of grammalogues and contractions given in this book. Easily written signs have
been given to those words for the very reason that

they are words in common use, and the student
should know them with such thoroughness that he
can write them at almost any speed at which they
can be dictated. This familiar knowledge can only
be obtained by repeated practice in writing from
dictation the exercises which have been compiled
for the purpose. The student cannot know these
special word-forms too well. Fluency in writing and
neatness in the formation of the forms will increase
in proportion as his knowledge grows, and the
general style of his shorthand notes will be improved
as a result.

Method of Practice. 196. To a great extent the
student must judge for himself as to his method of
practice, but the following is recommended—Begin
by taking down from dictation, well within your
powers, for periods of five minutes, and with the
insertion of none but necessary vowels. After half-
an-hour's practice, read back to the dictator a
passage chosen by yourself, and also one other, the
choice of which should be left to him. Resume
practice at an increased speed of ten words
per minute, the same method of reading being
pursued at the end of each half-hour. Continue
the same speeds each evening until the higher
becomes moderately easy, both in writing and
reading. Then begin at the higher speed, and at
the end of half-an-hour increase it by ten words a
minute. Read a portion of the notes which were
taken a day or two previously, to test your powers
unaided by memory. Aim at keeping not more
than two or three words behind the reader. After
a time you should occasionally practise writing
ten or a dozen words behind the reader, so as to
acquire the power of doing so in emergencies. Ear

and hand should work practically simultaneously
in order to secure the best results.   When a wrong
outline has been written, ignore the fact and go
on.   You may correct it afterwards at your leisure.
If several outlines are wrongly written, reduce the
speed.   The policy of hastening slowly was never
more justified than it is in learning to take a note.

Regular Practice.   197. At first, particular attention should be given to the outlines, but imperceptibly
the writing will become instinctive by practice,
which should be regular and systematic.   Practice
of an hour a day is better than two, or even three,
hours every second day.   Practice in writing, and
practice in reading both printed shorthand and your
own notes will quickly give you confidence, which
has its root in conscious ability to do the work
required.

Varied Dictation.   198. The subject-matter taken
down should be as varied as possible so that the
writer's vocabulary may be extended, but special
regard should be had to the object for which the art
is being acquired.   As to the size of the shorthand,
that which is natural to the individual is the best
for him ; but the writing should not be cramped.   A
free style is necessary and should be cultivated.   It
will add greatly to the legibility of the notes if the
large circles, loops and hooks are exaggerated in
size.   The pen should be held with only moderate
pressure, and the whole hand, poised lightly on
the little finger, should move with it.   The
common tendency to write sprawling outlines
when writing at a high speed is distinctly bad.   The
immediate cause is mental stress, partly induced
by anxiety lest a word should be omitted.   It is
obviously preferable to omit a few outlines rather

than to risk the legibility of many. If the possibility
of an occasional omission is not a source of fear, and
if there is confidence in the ability to record, at all
events the essential words of the speaker, the best
chance is secured of recording everything. Even if
something important has been left out, confidence
must be maintained, or the rest of the note will
suffer.

Concentration. 199. Concentration upon the work
in hand is necessary even when the art of note-
taking has been acquired, for unless the general trend
of the discourse is followed, together with the
grammatical construction of the sentences, the
transcript, owing to looseness of speech met with
everywhere, will sometimes be indifferent and possibly
misleading. Special attention should be paid to the
speaker's tone of voice and any peculiarities of
speech or manner which may render his meaning
clear, though he may not express himself properly.
Any habit persevered in becomes automatic,
and the mechanical writing of the shorthand
characters is fortunately no exception to the rule.
When experience has been gained, attention can
be concentrated almost entirely on the matter ;
but as in writing an important letter in longhand
some portion of the attention, slight, but nevertheless valuable, is devoted to the calligraphy
and punctuation, so should this be the case in
writing shorthand.

Punctuation in Note-taking. 200. Full stops should
always be written if at all possible because of the
great assistance it gives the note-taker in the transcription of his notes. Dashes should also be inserted
where possible in order to indicate where the speaker
drops the principal sentence and goes off at a tangent,

and where he resumes it, if ever. The commas at
the beginning and end of a parenthetical observation should be shown by a short space, the principal
instance being where the noun and verb are separated as in the following sentence : ꙙ" The soldier,
being tired after the long day's march, quickly
fell asleep." In such a simple case as this it is
hardly necessary, but with long and involved
sentences, it is of great assistance in analyzing
their construction to be able at once to locate
the verb, which will very often be the second or
third word after the second space. The following
are examples : " The speaker, having discussed
at length the arguments advanced by his opponent
in the various speeches he had delivered during
the week, earnestly urged his hearers not to be
influenced by specious promises "; and " We,
acting on behalf of the executive, who were of
one opinion as to the necessity of prompt action
in the matter, immediately issued a writ against
the offender and succeeded in gaining substantial
damages." As a corollary, it is obvious that a
space should be left only where it has a definite
meaning—a small space for a parenthesis or
important comma, and a somewhat larger one
for a full stop, if the stop cannot be written.

Reporting Technical Matter. 201. Where an engagement is expected for the reporting of highly
technical addresses, or for a meeting at which
speeches or discussions on highly technical matter
have to be reported, it is obviously advisable that
the shorthand writer should prepare himself before-
hand as well as possible. If he does not already
possess a fairly good knowledge of the subject-matter
of the lecture or subject of discussion dealt with at

which he is to exercise his professional skill, he should read up the subject so as to become more or less familiar with the terms which are likely to be used in connection with the engagement he has taken. Unless some such means are taken, it is likely that the shorthand writer's work will be unsatisfactory, both to himself and his clients. *Pitman's Shorthand Writers' Phrase Books and Guides* have been compiled with the object of furnishing assistance in the application of Phonography to technical matters, and *Technical Reporting* gives valuable advice and suggestions for those wishing to be successful in this special branch of the shorthand-writing profession.

Summary

1. Exercise yourself in the use of a note-book.
2. Practise the reading of unvocalized shorthand.
3. Always write in position.
4. Practise the illustrative exercises from dictation.
5. Enlarge your knowledge of outlines by reading printed shorthand.
6. Read at least a portion of every note you take.
7. Vary your dictation matter as much as possible.
8. Pay attention to the subject-matter dictated or spoken.
9. Always indicate the end of a sentence.
10. Acquire a perfect knowledge of the contracted forms.
11. Read up the subject before undertaking a report of technical matter.
12. Practise note-taking every day.

CHAPTER XXXII

ESSENTIAL VOWELS

Vocalized Outlines. 202. There are certain word-outlines which should be vocalized to some extent. The following directions, therefore, should be carefully noted—

(*a*) In single stroke outlines having an initial and a final vowel, the final vowel should be inserted; thus, ⎯ *echo*, ⎯ *arrow*, ⎯ *area*, ⎯ *era*.

(*b*) An outline should be written in position notwithstanding that it has an initially or a finally joined diphthong-sign; thus, ⎯ *Isaac*, ⎯ *item*, ⎯ *review*, ⎯ *institute*, ⎯ *future*, ⎯ *ague*, ⎯ *renew*.

(*c*) Where an upward or a downward *r* or *l* does not indicate a preceding or a following vowel, the vowel-sign should be inserted; thus, ⎯ *aright*, ⎯ *erode*, ⎯ *irritable*, ⎯ *oracle*, ⎯ *aroma*; ⎯ *jolly*, ⎯ *jelly*, ⎯ *gilly*; ⎯ *billow*, ⎯ *early*.

(*d*) Generally speaking, vowels should be inserted—

(1) Where words of the same part of speech have similar outlines and the same position;

(2) Where a word is unfamiliar, or unfamiliar in the special sense in which it is used; and

(3) Where an outline has been written incorrectly, badly, or in the wrong position, in which case the insertion of a vowel is the quickest way of making the outline legible.

(e) It is also advisable to vocalize as fully as possible :—

(1) Where the subject-matter is unknown ; and

(2) Where the language is poetical, unusual, or florid, because in these instances the context is not as helpful as in other cases.

The following lists contain some of the more common words in which the vowels indicated by italic should be inserted in order to facilitate transcription ; but after a little experience in shorthand writing the student will instinctively recognize other outlines in which distinguishing vowels should be inserted.

(1) *Insertion of an initial vowel*

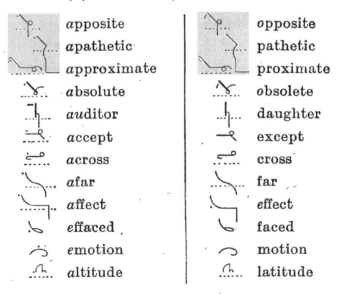

*a*pposite	*o*pposite
*a*pathetic	*pathetic*
*a*pproximate	proximate
*a*bsolute	obsolete
*a*uditor	daughter
*a*ccept	except
*a*cross	cross
*a*far	far
*a*ffect	effect
*e*ffaced	faced
*e*motion	motion
*a*ltitude	latitude

(2) *Insertion of a medial vowel*

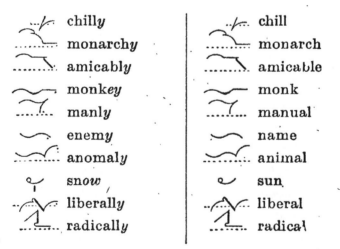

adápt		adopt
extricate		extract
commissionaire		commissioner
exaltation		exultation
voluble		valuable
amazing		amusing
innovation		invasion
lost		last
layman		laymen
sulphite		sulphate
humanly		humanely

(3) *Insertion of a final vowel*

chilly		chill
monarchy		monarch
amicably		amicable
monkey		monk
manly		manual
enemy		name
anomaly		animal
snow		sun
liberally		liberal
radically		radical

Exercise 121

Read, copy and transcribe

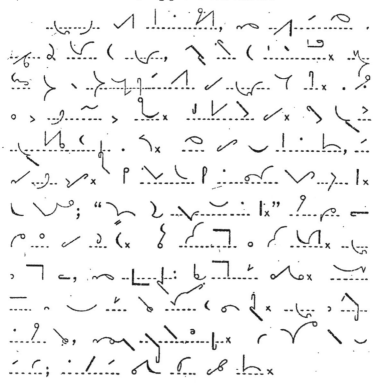

Exercise 122

Write in Shorthand

(*In this and in the following exercise the vowels marked in italic should be inserted. Marked in divisions of thirty words each.*)

We should-neither accept any theories nor adopt any views, however voluble the advocates of-such-may-be, except we-are convinced that-they-are authorized, and-have-been tested | and attested by-those upon whose veracity we-can rely, or unless our reason approves of-them and-we-have ample proof that-though they-may have some defects, | their adoption will-be valuable to us in-the-main, that-we-may employ them to-the benefit of-ourselves and others, and-that-they-will-be readily recalled on | occasions of necessity.   No matter how *a*pposite the arguments may appear which-are *a*dduced to-move us from an *o*pposite opinion, we should-be as *a*damant in-the face of | any demand upon-the feelings, which-our reason does-not sanction.   Thus, any *a*ttempt to-tempt us to foolish actions will-only *e*nd in-the failure of-the tempter.   We- | have-been end*o*wed with mental faculties far and *a*way above those with-which-the lower *a*nimals are end*u*ed, in order that-we-may protect ourselves from-our enem*i*es, and may | add to-our happiness.   It-is a fact, however, that-such-is-the *e*ffect of-persuasion upon some persons of weak will that-they become as mere wax in-the | hands of-those-who-would lure them to ruin. With-such people it-seems only necessary for a fluent rogue to *a*dvance an alluring prospect of an *a*ffluent position at- | little cost, and-they fall at-once, without a defence, into-the trap set for-them.   Is-not-this-the secret of almost every successful fraud we-have-heard or | read of in-any-nation ?   (275 words)

Exercise 123

Write in Shorthand

There-are, *a*las, too-many persons who-make-it their vocation or *a*vocation in life to dupe others less able than themselves.   They-have-no feelings of honour, or *e*lse | would-not prey on-the failings of-those around.   They despise veracity, and-their greed for gold amounts almost to voracity.   In order to obtain wealth they-make light of- | every obstacle, and are slow to *a*dmit themselves beaten.   They-are *a*verse to honest labour, and-yet they spare no pains to become versed in-the cunning arts necessary to | extract money from-their victims, and to extricate themselves from-the consequences of-their illegal actions.   They devise a plot, and, under-the semblance of *a*dvice, they *o*perate on-the | greed and-credulity of ignorant persons, and-having thrown them off their guard, lead them into foolish *a*dventures.   Truly " A fool and-his money are easily parted."   We should-not | attach too-much importance to a scheme because-it-is introduced with a flourish of fair words, nor should-we touch any speculative *a*ffair without first subjecting it to an | accurate examination. If-we could only examine the *a*nnual returns of failures and analyze their-causes, we should-find that many are *a*ttributable to an *u*tter absence of judgment in- | the conduct of business, and an over confidence in-the n*i*cety and honesty of-others.　　　　(225 words)

Summary

Vowels should be inserted—

(*a*) In single stroke outlines where a vowel is not indicated by position ;

(*b*) In cases where a vowel is not indicated by an initial or a final stroke ;

(*c*) In pairs of words occupying the same position but having a varying vowel ;

(*d*) Where the language is of an unusual character.

CHAPTER XXXIII
SPECIAL CONTRACTIONS

Formation of Contractions. 203. In the Special
Contractions dealt with in this chapter, the student
is introduced to further methods of contracting
outlines. The importance of having such contractions is shown by the fact that in ordinary language
only a very limited number of words are used. Of
these words at least 60 to 70 per cent are of frequent
occurrence, and are, therefore, included in the grammalogues and contractions of Pitman's Shorthand.
An essential point in forming contracted outlines
is to choose forms that are distinctive and legible at
sight. With this end in view the special contractions
are formed according to the following rules—

(*a*) By employing the first two or three
strokes of the full outline, as in ⋁⋀ *perform,*
ʃ *advertisement,* ⌐ᒾ *expediency,* ╱ *regular,*
⌒⌒ *unanimity,* ᒼ⌐ *henceforth.* (See sections
1-3.)

(*b*) By medial omission, as in ⅃ *intelligence,*
⌒ *sympathetic,* ⅌ *satisfactory,* ⌣ *influential,*
⌒⌒ *amalgamation.* (See section 4.)

(*c*) By using logograms, as in ⌐ *thankful,*
⌒ *something,* ⟍ *remarkable.* (See section 5.)

(*d*) By intersection, as in ⼖ *enlarge,* ⼦ *never-*
theless, ⼂ *notwithstanding.* (See section 5.)

168

Adjectives and Adverbs. 204. As a general rule the same contracted form may represent either an adjective or an adverb, but where a distinction is necessary the adverb should be represented either by writing a joined or disjoined *l*, or by writing the form for the adverb in full ; thus, ⌐ *irregular,* ⌐ *irregularly ;* ⌐ *substantial,* ⌐ *substantially.*

Contractions and -ing. 205. Dot -*ing* is generally used after contractions. In a few words such as ⌐ *distinguishing,* ⌐ *relinquishing,* and ⌐ *extinguishing,* where the stroke is clearly better, the stroke is used.

Arrangement of Lists. 206. The lists of contractions which follow are arranged according to the principles explained above, and the student should make himself thoroughly familiar with them. The portion of a word which is not represented in the contracted outline is shown in parenthesis. This arrangement will help the student to memorize the contracted forms. Thus, ⌐ *pec* is the contraction for *peculiar-ity,* ⌐ *perf* for *perform-ed,* ⌐ *perfs* for *performance,* ⌐ *Feb.* for *February,* ⌐ *fam* for *familiar-ity,* and so on. The exercises which follow each list should be written from dictation until they can be taken down with ease and rapidity, and read back from the shorthand notes without hesitation.

12—(R)

SPECIAL CONTRACTIONS: SECTION 1

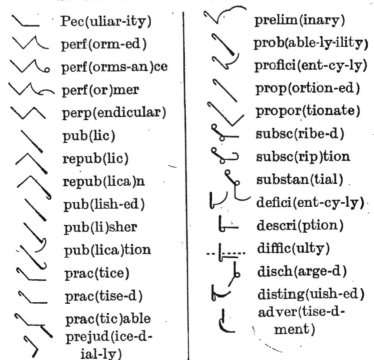

	Pec(uliar-ity)		prelim(inary)
	perf(orm-ed)		prob(able-ly-ility)
	perf(orms-an)ce		profici(ent-cy-ly)
	perf(or)mer		prop(ortion-ed)
	perp(endicular)		propor(tionate)
	pub(lic)		subsc(ribe-d)
	repub(lic)		subsc(rip)tion
	repub(lica)n		substan(tial)
	pub(lish-ed)		defici(ent-cy-ly)
	pub(li)sher		descri(ption)
	pub(lica)tion		diffic(ulty)
	prac(tice)		disch(arge-d)
	prac(tise-d)		disting(uish-ed)
	prac(tic)able		adver(tise-d-ment)
	prejud(ice-d-ial-ly)		

Exercise 124

Read, copy and transcribe

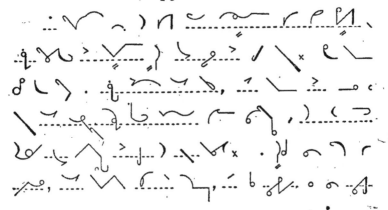

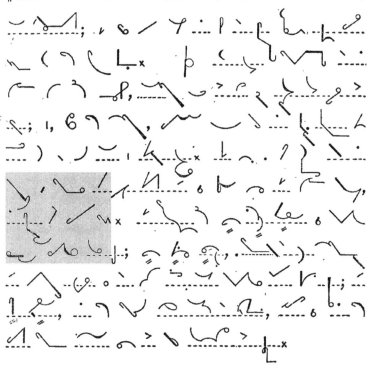

Exercise 125
Write in Shorthand

In-the *preliminary* announcement *published* on-Thursday
the *public* were made aware of-the *deficiency* in-the income
of-the *Performers* Society which *performs* a good work in a
most | *practicable* manner.   The offices of-the-society are
situated in a building which-is a fine example of-the
perpendicular architecture, but is in a state of decay.
Lately there- | has-been a discussion among-the-members
on-the powers of-the committee, and many divergent
views were expressed by-the-chairman and other members.
As a tribunal the committee | do-not always show a
dignified attitude.

Among other observations, some of-which were
extremely strong in tone, the chairman, a person of-
prejudiced views, said there-were many *difficulties* | in-the
way, but it-was-not at-all im*probable* that our new
patents would revive our trade in-the South-American
Republics, as-they-were *peculiarly* applicable to-the wants
of-its people.   (154 words)

Exercise 126

Read, copy and transcribe

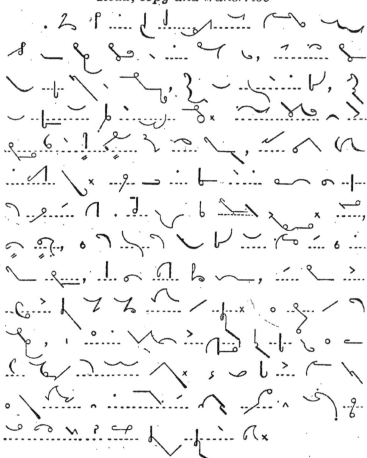

Exercise 127

Write in Shorthand

The chairman, in-the-course-of his speech, said that to-seek-the preservation of-the concern when-the profits were so un*substantial* and so dis*proportionate* to-the amount invested, | and when-the price of-the stock was so depreciated, was absurd, and-it was inadvisable to-carry on-the company.

The *advertisements* in-the paper are out-of all- | *propor-tion* to-the news, which-is very *deficient,* and-we marvel at-the prosperity of-the *publication* and-the confidence of-the *publishers.* It-has often *subscribed substantial* amounts to | *public* funds, opened its columns for national *subscriptions,* and given *distinguished* services to-the cause of charity.

The *performer* who *performed* at-the theatre is a Russian, and-his artistic | *performance* of-the play brought out all-the *peculiarities* of-the Slav race, although-there-was a dis*proportion* in-his acting which-would render a long engagement im*practicable.*   (148 words)

SPECIAL CONTRACTIONS : SECTION 2

	Jan(uary)			gov(ern-ed)
	cap(able)			gov(er)nment
	charac(ter)			fam(iliar-ity)
	charac(ter)is(t)ic			fam(ilia)rize
	commer(cial)			fam(iliar)iza-tion
	cross-ex-(amine-d-ation)			Feb(ruary)
	exch(ange-d)			finan(cial)
	exped(iency)			effici(ent-cy-ly)
	expend(iture)			suffici(ent-cy-ly)
	expens(ive)			manuf(acture)r
	esp(ecial-ly)			math(ematical-ly)
	esq(uire)			math(ematic)s
	estab(lish-ed-ment)			math(ema)ti-cian
	immed(iate)			max(imum) (see *minimum* in section 4.)
	impertur(bable)			
	mag(netic-ism)			mechan(ical-ly)
	manuf(acture-d)			metrop(olitan)
	exting(uish-ed)			mor(t)g(age-d)

Exercise 128

Read, copy and transcribe

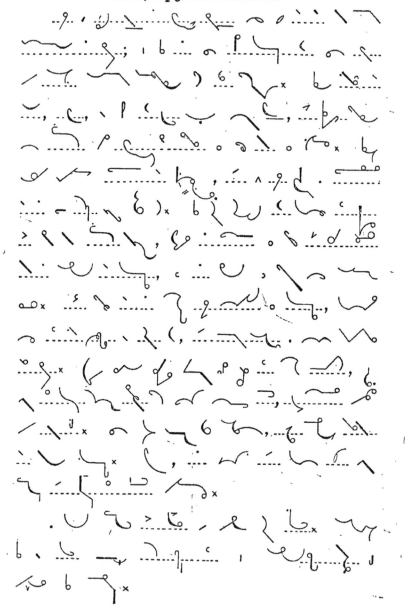

Exercise 129

Write in Shorthand

At-the meeting of-the-directors to-day it-was stated
that-the rates of-*exchange* in *January* and-*February* were
favourable to *manufacturers* in-this-country. Regarding-
the-matter | of *expediency*, to-discuss which the meeting
was primarily called, it-was thought that-the plan suggested might prove very *expensive* and cause endless trouble
in arranging-the necessary *mortgage*. | The chairman,
John Ogden, *Esq.*, a *commercial* magnate, is a very *capable*
mathematician, and he carries out all-his business with
mathematical exactitude. He-is hoping that-the *mechan-
ical efficiency* | of-the *establishment* may-be *sufficient* to-
check any unnecessary *expenditure* during-the coming
year. No-man is more *familiar* to-the-members of-the-
Exchange than he, and-his | speeches at social functions
are noted for-their humour, while-his placid manner is a
characteristic which compels the admiration of all. He-
is possessed of-great personal *magnetism*, and | it-is-due,
undoubtedly, to-his ability that-the company has an
almost unassailable position which-has surprised those-
who-are engaged in a similar *manufacture*. (176 words)

Exercise 130

Read, copy and transcribe

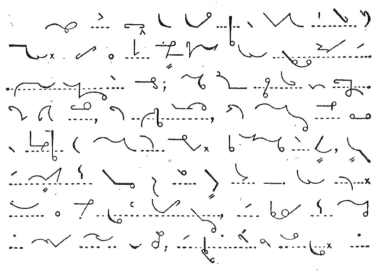

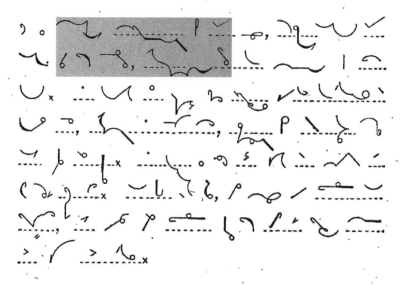

Exercise 131

Write in Shorthand

The new book of essays by a member of-the-*Government* contains some very worthy sayings : " A person of-*character* is in*capable* of a mean action, and-is able-to-| *govern* himself under all-circumstances. We-cannot-be wise-men unless we *familiarize* ourselves, and sympathize, with human-nature. Our *familiarization* with new scenes and new peoples shows us the | in*sufficiency* of-our educa-tion." In-the-*immediate* future we-expect to see-the author at-the head of-the cabinet.

In dealing-with-the charge against the prisoner the *metropolitan* | magistrate passed the *maximum* sentence after a close *cross-examination* of-the offender, and-after several-witnesses had-been *cross-examined*, and despite the fact that-the-prisoner's action had-| been *governed* by *financial* troubles over-which he had no control. The magistrate is a man of-wide tastes, and-is one of-the prime movers in-our Agricultural Show, | and he-is regarded as an authority on-most-matters relating to-the land. His model farm is a splendid example of scientific farming, and it-is a source of-| amazement to-the farmers in-the district, who-are mostly satisfied with seeking for-the best-results by empirical methods.   (200 words)

Special Contractions : Section 3

enthus(iastic-iasm)

incor(porated)

independ(ence-ent-ly)

indispens(able-ly)

individ(ual-ly)

inf(orm-ed)

inf(or)mer

interest

invest(ment) .

negl(ect-ed)

negl(ig)ence

{ nev(er)
{ Nov(ember)

sensib(le-ility-ly)

elec(tric)

elec(tri)cal

elec(tri)city

recov(erable)

irrecov(erable)

ref(orm-ed)

ref(or)mer

reg(ular)

irreg(ular)

relinq(uish-ed)

rep(resent-ed)

rep(resenta)-tion

rep(resentat)-ive

respons(ible-ility)

irrespons(ible-ility)

organ(ize-d)

orga(ni)zer

organ(i)zation

certif(icate)

uni(form-ity-ly)

{ unan(imity)
{ unan(imous-ly)

yest(erday)

Exercise 132

Read, copy and transcribe

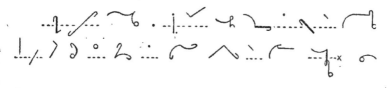

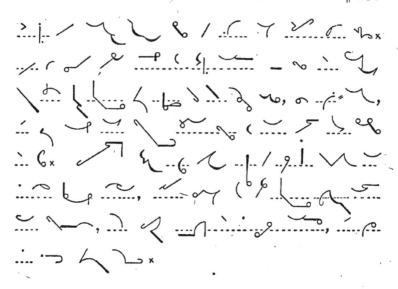

Exercise 133

Read, copy and transcribe

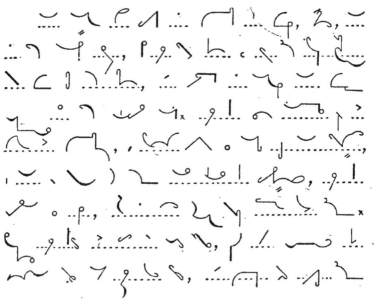

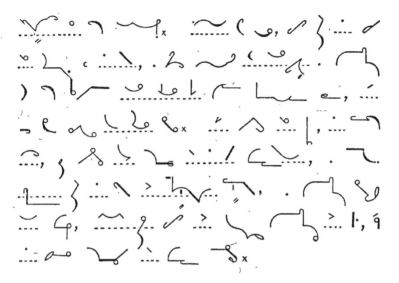

Exercise 134

Write in Shorthand

Great-*interest* is manifested in-the *electric* apparatus at-the local exhibition, the *capable organizer* of-which is very *enthusiastic* in following-the development of *electricity* and-all *electrical* appliances.

Our *representative* on-the council is *responsible* for-the *negligence* of-the *reform,* and our committee is of-the *unanimous* opinion that in-the future its support cannot-be given | to-one who-has shown so-much *neglect* of-his duties, and it purposes nominating another and a better candidate for-the *November* elections.

Yesterday the *investment* was sanctioned by-| those *interested* in-the improvement of-the-association, and it was hoped that-its previous position would soon be *recoverable.* When-the-association becomes *incorporated,* its *certificate* should-be recognized | by-all similar *organizations,* some of-which have shown considerable opposition towards-it, and displayed an inexcusable temper when-the committee refused to-*relinquish*-the policy formulated several weeks-ago. | (150 words)

Exercise 135
Read, copy and transcribe

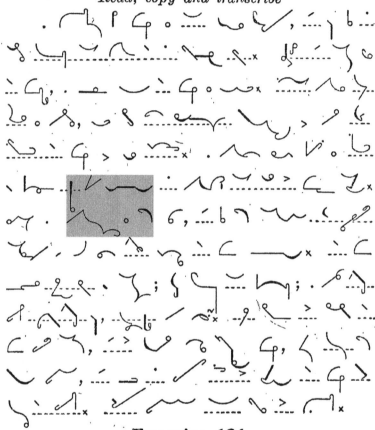

Exercise 136
Write in Shorthand

There-was a *unanimity* of opinion by-all-the *reformers* present that *organized* playgrounds were *indispensable* in-the education of children, and it-was resolved to-make a *representation* to-| the-council, and to ask it to introduce *uniformity* in-this-matter throughout-the county.　This resolution was singularly unfortunate, as-it-was-the cause of-friction between these *individuals* | and-the-council.

Regular subscribers to-the institution showed arrogance at-the *irregular* *practices*, and many *informed*-the Board that-they-would withdraw their support if-such

irresponsible actions were | allowed contrary to all-the
teachings of-the past. We-fear that no dis*interest*ed
person was-the *informer* in-this-matter, and-*probably* he
represented-the circumstances to be more | serious than
they really are. The resignation of-the secretary, however, will-be demanded, as-his attitude amounts to in-
subordination, and-this will cause-the regret of all, no
matter | what their *sensibility* may-be. The agenda of-the
next Board meeting will-be far from un*interest*ing, and
an apparently *irrecoverable* position may-be turned to-the
advantage of-the | institution. (181 words)

SPECIAL CONTRACTIONS : SECTION 4

	Parl(iament)-ary		int(elli)gent
	pros(p)ec(t)us		int(elli)gible
	tel(egraph)ic		En(gli)sh
	tel(egr)am		En(gli)shman
	satis(fact)ory		En(g)land
	adm(inistrat)or		leg(islat)ive
	adm(inistratr)ix		leg(isla)ture
	ques(tion)ab-(le-ly)		ar(bi)trate
	fals(ific)ation		ar(bi)trator
	amal(ga)mation		ar(bi)tration
	amal(ga)mate		ar(bi)trary
	mar(coni)gram		wheresoev(er)
	m(inim)um		whereinsoev(er)
	symp(athet)ic		whithersoev(er)
	inves(tig)ation		u(ni)verse
	insu(ran)ce		u(ni)versal
	know(l)edge		u(ni)versality
	acknow(l)edge		u(ni)versity
	in(con)siderate		howsoev(er)
	in(fluen)tial		whensoev(er)
	int(elli)gence		

Exercise 137

Read, copy and transcribe

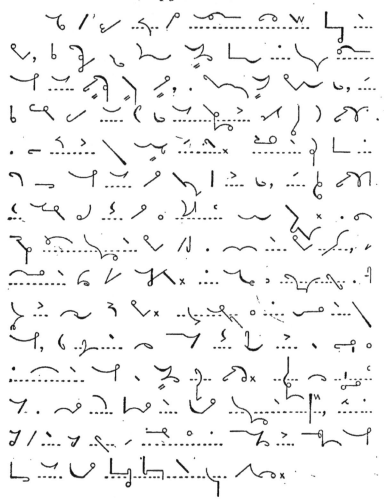

Exercise 138

Write in Shorthand

One who *arbitrates* is called an arbitrator, and-there-is
a growing tendency to-submit all disputes to *arbitration*
by a third-party. Such decision would frequently savo-

the disputants I from being *arbitrary* and harsh towards one another *whereinsoever* amends may-be-made. It-is thought by-some that a *universal* language would foster the spirit of *arbitration* throughout-the I *universe*, but as yet the attempts made to formulate such a method of intercommunication have-not-been very-*satisfactory*. There-can-be no-doubt that *telegraphic* communications, by-*telegram* and I *marconigram*, work for-the-cause of peace.

The *investigation* by-the *parliamentary* committee was *universally* acknowledged to be justified, and although-the *falsification* of-the reports was *established*, there-were-I many un*sympathetic* remarks, reflecting adversely on-the supposed failings of-members of-the *legislature*, by *influential* and un*influential* newspapers. All *Englishmen*, however, should-be proud of-the *legislative* bodies of I *England* and should-be *sympathetic* towards all endeavours to effect any *intelligent* progressive *reforms*. (164 words)

Exercise 139

Read, copy and transcribe

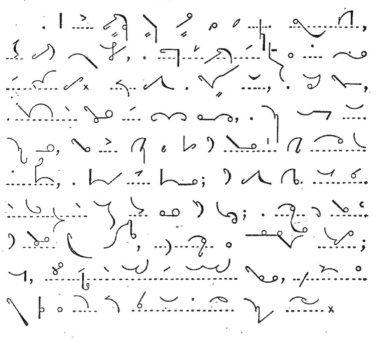

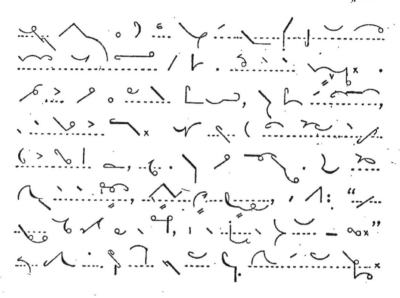

Exercise 140

Write in Shorthand

At a quarterly gathering of-our scientific society the *university* lecturer said an *intelligible* reason could-be given for-his theory of economics, but-the *universality* of-its acceptance by I economists was-not-to-be expected in-our present state-of-*knowledge*. On a future occasion he-is to-lecture on-the-subject of a *minimum* wage for workers. He-I is *acknowledg*ed to be a *capable* economist and a most excellent lecturer and writer on-the-subject for-which his name is famous.

The *prospectus* which-you forwarded *yesterday*, in I *acknowledg*ment of-mine of-last Monday, is un*questionably* very un*satisfactory howsoever* it-may-be considered. The *amalgamation* of two such prodigious concerns is very undesirable, and-the *intelligence* of-prospective I insurers should warn them of-the disadvantages of insuring under their tables. In-our company the *minimum* period for-such a policy of *insurance* is fifteen years, and it-is I *questionable* if-you-can secure better terms through any other *English* office. From-the-enclosed cutting you-will-find that-the *administrator* and *administratrix*, whom you-mention, were punished for I fraud in-connection with-the estate.

(186 words)

SPECIAL CONTRACTIONS : SECTION 5

Al(to)ge(ther)		unprincipled	
toge(ther)		n(o)t(withstand-ing)	
(circum)stan-tial		de(nomi)nation-(al)	
everything		in(can)descent	
thankful		in(can)descence	
something		enlarge	
remarkable		enlarger	
anything		in(con)ven(ient-ce)	
nothing		n(e)v(ertheless)	
whatev(er)		irrem(ov)able	
whenev(er)		rem(ov)able	
misf(ortune)			

Exercise 141

Read, copy and transcribe

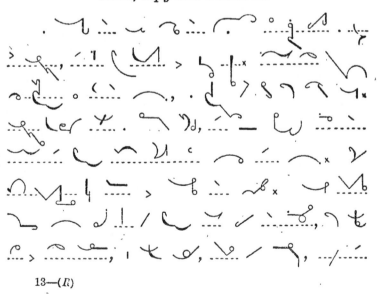

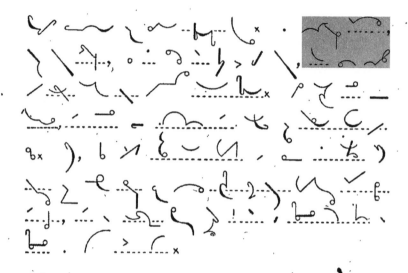

Exercise 142

Write in Shorthand

Dear-Sir,

My committee have-considered your communication of-the 12th-inst., drawing attention to-several matters relating to-the *denominational* schools in-your district.

The *enlarge*ment of-the Cross | Street Schools received special consideration, and my committee are of-the opinion that *something* should-be done *immediate*ly in-this direction. To *enlarge* them again as-they-were *enlarged* ten | years-ago seems-to-be necessary, and it-is hoped to commence building operations during-the coming summer ; and, to-save-time, my committee purpose giving the contract to-the | original builder of-the schools.

As-the whole of-the lighting of-the schools requires overhauling, my committee have arranged for a report on-the matter, and-as-the *incandescence* | of-the mantles in-the offices here is very-*satisfactory*, it-is *probable* that similar *incandescent* lights will-be fitted throughout.

Notwithstanding your remarks, my committee think-there-will-be | no unfairness to-the voluntary-schools of-the district owing to-the recent Circular coming into force in-the autumn, and are of-the opinion that *nothing* should-be done | to hinder its working.

Yours-very-truly,   (187 words)

Exercise 143

Read, copy and transcribe

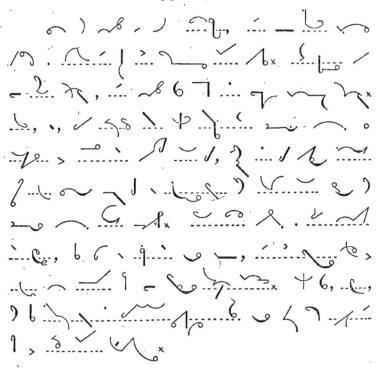

Exercise 144

Write in Shorthand

Dear-Sir,

I-thank-you for-your *circumstantial* account of-the centenary celebrations in-your town, the reporting and sending of-which show much consideration on-your part. *Whenever* I-| can help you in similar circumstances, I-shall-be only too-pleased to-do-so.

It-is *remarkable* that-such an insignificant matter as-the one you-mention should give | offence in newspaper circles.   One would-have-thought that-its very insignifi-cance would-have-been *sufficient* to ensure its acceptance. Certainly it-is difficult to understand how *anything* of-the| kind could-be described as *unprincipled* and unmannerly. It-is a *misfortune* that-such a quibble should-be raised

and-I-hope that *everything* will-be-done to-save any |
inconvenience to-those *interest*ed in-the-press. *Never-*
theless, I-do-not-think-the cause is *irremovable*, but rather
altogether removable, and-I-shall-be *thankful whatever* is
done to-bring-| the parties *together* again.

Yours-truly, (156 words)

Summary

1. Special Contractions are formed as follows—

  (*a*) By employing the first two or three strokes
     of the full outline.
  (*b*) By medial omission.
  (*c*) By using logograms.
  (*d*) By intersection.
2. As a general rule the same contracted form
     may represent either an adjective or an adverb,
     but where distinction is necessary the adverb
     should be represented by a joined or disjoined
     l, or by writing the full form for the adverb.
3. Dot *-ing* is generally used after contractions,
     but the stroke is used in a few cases.

CHAPTER XXXIV
ADVANCED PHRASEOGRAPHY

Principles of Phrasing. 207. Bearing in mind the most important rules of phraseography, that all phraseograms must be recognizable at sight, easily written, and not too long, the various abbreviating devices are made to do service for words, or the forms of words are changed, or words are omitted altogether, with the result that an unlimited number of facile and legible phraseograms may thus be formed. The principles of phrasing are considered under the following heads—

(1) Circles, Loops and Hooks, (2) Halving, (3) Doubling, (4) Omissions.

Circles. 208. (a) The small circle, besides being used for *as, has, is, his,* as in ↙ *it has been,*

↳ *it is not,* may be used to represent *us,* as in ↘ *from us,* ↙ *please let us know.*

(b) The initial large circle may be used to represent the following—

(1) *as we,*   as in (*as we think;*

(2) *as* and *w,* ,, ,, ↙ *as well as;*

(3) *as* and *s,* ,, ,, ↙ *as soon as.*

(c) The medial and final large circle may be used to represent the following—

(1) *is* and *s,*   as in ↓ *it is said;*

(2) *his* and *s,* ,, ,, ↙ *for his sake;*

189

(3)   s and s,   as in   ⟋   in this city;

(4)   s and has, ,, ,,   ⟋   this has been;

(5)   s and is,   ,, ,,   ⟋   this is.

Loops. 209. (a) The st loop is used for first, as in ⊢⁀ at first cost, ⟋⟅ Wednesday first; (b) the nst loop for next, as in ⟋⟅ Wednesday next.

Hooks. 210. (a) The r and l hooks are used in representing a few miscellaneous words, as in ⟍⟋ in our view, ⎰ it appears, ⟍⟍⟀ by all means, ⎰⟋ it is only necessary, ⟍⟍⟀ in the early part.

(b) The n hook may be used for the following—

(1) than, as in ⟋⟅ older than;

(2) own, ,, ,, ⟋⟀ our own;

(3) been, ,, ,, ⟋ I had been.

(c) The f or v hook may be used for the following—

(1) have, as in   ℓ   who have;

(2) of,   ,, ,, ⟋⟀ rate of interest;

(3) after, ,, ,, ⟍⟋⟀ Monday afternoon;

(4) even, ,, ,, ⟍⟋⟀ Monday evening;

(5) in such phrases as ⎰⟀ at all events, ⟍⟍⟀ into effect.

(d) The circle s and *shun* hook may be used for *association*, as in ⌒ₑ *medical association*, ⌇ₑ *political association*.

Halving. 211. The halving principle is used for indicating the following—

     (1) *it,*   as in   ∖   *if it ;*

     (2) *to,*   ,,   ,,   ∖   *able to ;*

     (3) *not,*   ,,   ,,   ⌐   *you will not ;*

     (4) *would,*   ,,   ,,   ⸜   *this would be ;*

     (5) *word,*   ,,   ,,   ⸜   *this word ;*

     (6) in such phrases as ⤳ *from time to time.*

Doubling. 212. Besides strokes being doubled for *there, their,* in a few cases they may be doubled for *other* and *dear,* as in ⌒ *some other,* ⌒ *my dear sir.*

Omissions. 213. These are arranged under (a) Consonants, (b) Syllables, (c) Logograms.

     (a) Consonants may be omitted as indicated in the following phrases—

⌐ *mos(t) probably,*   ⌐ *in (f)act,*

⸜ *in this (m)anner,*   ⌒ *animal (l)ife,*

∖ *in (r)eply.*

     (b) The syllable *con* may be omitted, as in ⌐ *I will (con)sider,* ⋀ *we have (con)cluded.*

(c) The signs omitted are chiefly logograms:

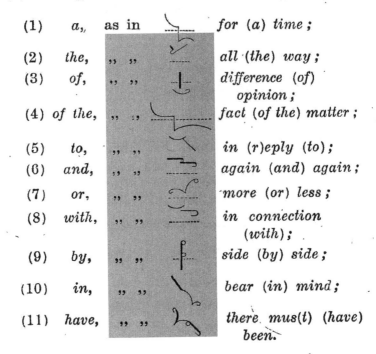

(1)   a,,   as in   *for (a) time;*

(2)   *the,*   ,, ,,   *all (the) way;*

(3)   *of,*   ,, ,,   *difference (of) opinion;*

(4) *of the,*   ,, ,,   *fact (of the) matter;*

(5)   *to,*   ,, ,,   *in (r)eply (to);*

(6)   *and,*   ,, ,,   *again (and) again;*

(7)   *or,*   ,, ,,   *more (or) less;*

(8)   *with,*   ,, ,,   *in connection (with);*

(9)   *by,*   ,, ,,   *side (by) side;*

(10)   *in,*   ,, ,,   *bear (in) mind;*

(11)   *have,*   ,, ,,   *there mus(t) (have) been.*

The student should seek to understand thoroughly the principles on which the phraseograms in the following lists are formed without seeking necessarily to commit the lists to memory. The lists are by no means complete. As stated above, the examples given merely show the general lines on which the phrases are formed, and the student in the course of his practice will find many opportunities of phrasing if he will keep in mind the general principles as illustrated above, and in the pages which follow. The exercises which follow each list should be written from dictation until they can be taken down with ease and rapidity.

ADVANCED PHRASEOGRAPHY : SECTION 1

agree with the

all circumstances

and in all probability

as fast as

as it were

as much as were

as the matter

brought forward

by and by

by the by

by some means

dealing with the

discuss the matter

every circumstance

I am certain that you are

I am inclined to think

I am persuaded

I am very glad

I think it is necessary

I think that you are

in his own opinion

in the meantime

in this country

in this matter

in this respect

notwithstanding such

notwithstanding that

on either hand

on either side

on the other hand

on the other side

on these occasions

on this occasion

on this matter

peculiar circumstances

per annum

per cent

percentage

quite agree

quite agreeable

so that we may

take the liberty

there were

those which we are now

those who are

those who were

through the world

to bring the matter

under all circumstances

very satisfactorily

you will agree

you will probably

Exercise 145
Read, copy and transcribe

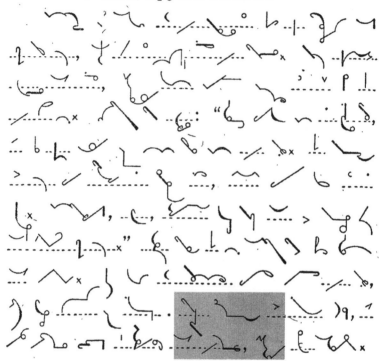

Exercise 146
Write in Shorthand

Dear-Sir,

I-am-very-glad to notice-that by-some-means you-are
hoping to-have-the new proposal brought-forward at-
the-next meeting of-the-directors, and-| I-am-persuaded
that in-the-meantime you-should-not discuss-the-matter
with anyone, because-it-is-necessary to be very cautious
under-all-circumstances as on-this-occasion. | You-will-
probably do what-can-be-done to-make-the case complete,
so-that-we-may-have every-circumstance detailed that-is
in-our-favour. I-think-that-you-| are-aware of-the import-
ance of-having ready a definite scheme if-we-would-be
successful, but as-the-matter is of-such vital importance
to-us, I-take-the-| liberty of-emphasizing-the point.
Awaiting your-reply, we-are, | Yours-truly, (132 words)

Exercise 147

Read, copy and transcribe

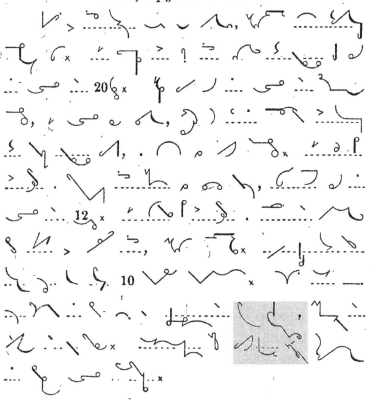

Exercise 148

Write in Shorthand

Dear-Sir,

I-am-certain-that-you-are-not fully conversant with-the-matter, or you-would-not urge those-who-were present on-these-occasions to-bring-the question | to-the notice of-the meeting. On-either-side there-are those-who-are always ready to hurry business as-fast-as they can, not-withstanding-that there-is-no-advantage | gained by un-necessary haste. By-and-by, I-am-inclined-to-think-that you-will-agree-with me on-this-matter, and-then you-will regret that-you unduly hastened-| the passing of-the rules with-which-we-are-now | dealing. Yours-truly, (103 words)

ADVANCED PHRASEOGRAPHY : SECTION 2
(*Circles, Loops and Hooks*)

from us		it is only necessary
please inform us		it can only be
to us		it may only be
as we have		they will only be
as we can		longer than
as we cannot		more than
as we do		any longer
as we think		no longer than
as we shall		rather than
as we-may		smaller than
as well as usual		at all your own
as well as can be		at all our own
as soon as we can		have been expected
as soon as they		have been informed
it is said		have been returned
for his sake		who have not
in this century		out-of doors
in this city		rate of interest
in this subject		state of affairs
of this statement		Thursday afternoon
this has been		Thursday evening
at first cost		at all events
Wednesday next		into effect
in our view		incorporated
in our statement		association
it appears		medical assocn.
it appears that		political assocn.
by all means		traders' assocn.

Exercise 149
Read, copy and transcribe

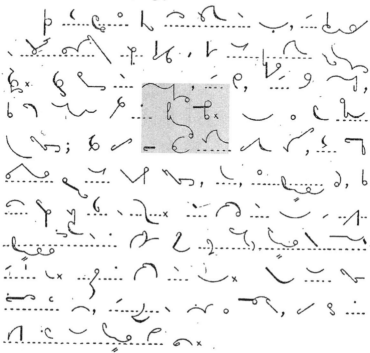

Exercise 150
Write in Shorthand

We-have-been-informed of-the-proposed meeting of-your county-association on-Wednesday-next, and to-us it-appears-that as-soon-as-the-members realize the state-of-| affairs they-will-be only too-glad to postpone a definite decision. We-are of-the opinion that-there-are many who-have-not agreed-with-the attitude of-the | executive, and who do-not-wish the proposals to be carried into-effect. At-all-events, at-all-our-own recent county gatherings, which-have-been rather smaller-than usual, | there-has-been much objection to-several proposals on-this-subject, and as-soon-as-we-can, we-are having a postal vote as-we-cannot decide certain matters without | knowing-the opinion of-members who-have-not-been in | attendance to-express any views on-the-questions.

(138 words)

Exercise 151

Read, copy and transcribe

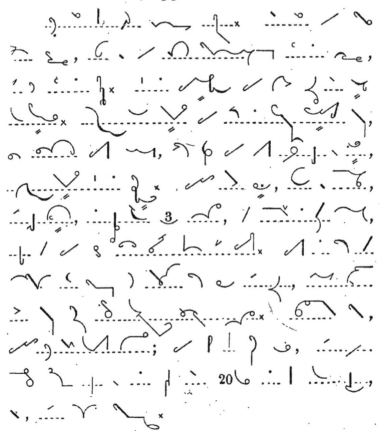

Exercise 152

Write in Shorthand

It-will-take longer-than we-expected to-finish the premises for-the political-association, but-we-shall-be-able-to get all-the out-of-doors work finished before-| the winter sets in ; and-then it-can-only-be a matter of weeks for-the completion of-the interior. Any-way, we-shall-be no-longer-than we-can | help. When finished, the building will-be one of-the | handsomest in-this-city.

(74 words)

Exercise 153
Read, copy and transcribe

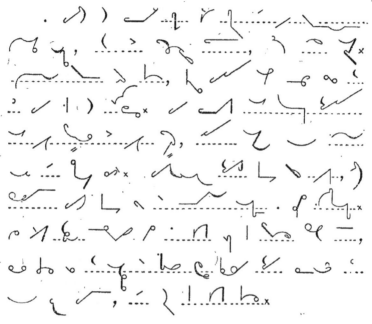

Exercise 154
Write in Shorthand

In-our-statement at-the Traders'-Association on-Thursday-evening it-will-only-be necessary to-mention briefly the high-rate-of-interest to be charged for-the loan on-| the new buildings, as-we-shall-have a full discussion of-the whole matter at-the-next meeting.   All-the voting cards have-been-returned and-in nearly all-cases | the vote is in-favour of-the-present president continuing in office.

We-shall-be-able-to purchase the materials at-first-cost, and as-we-do a very large | turnover our profits should exceed, rather-than fall below, those of-last-year. As-well-as-can-be estimated beforehand, we-shall-have to increase our stocks at-all-our-| own depôts, and as-we-may also require a new depôt at Acton, we-shall-be-obliged to increase-the initial order.   In-view-of-this we-shall-expect prices | to be much lower-than-the old rates.

(158 words)

ADVANCED PHRASEOGRAPHY : SECTION 3

(*Halving Principles*)

as if it were		I trust not
by which it was		I was not
if it is not		you cannot
if it be not		you may not
if it were		you must not
in which it is		you should not be
in which it has appeared		you were not
of which it has been		you are not
of which it must be		I would
able to make		if it would be
able to think		they would
I am able to think		they would be
I am unable to think		they would not be
we are able to make		we would
you will be able to		few words
I cannot be		in our words
I cannot say		many words
I cannot see		at any rate
I hope you will not		at all times
I may not be		at some time
I shall not be		at the same time
		for some time
		from time to time
		some time ago

Exercise 155

Read, copy and transcribe

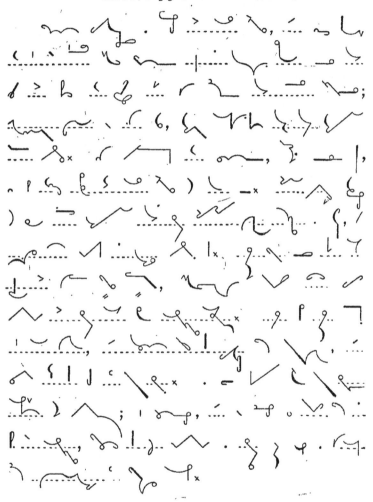

Exercise 156

Write in Shorthand

Dear Mr. Scott,

For-some-time past I-have-been unable to-write to-you as I-have desired and-as I-promised you when you-were here. I-hope-I you-will-not-be annoyed at-my apparent neglect. You-should-not-be, and-I-am-sure you-will-not-be when you-are-aware of-the-reason for-my | silence. I-have-no-doubt you-will-remember that I-was-not well previous to-your visit, but I-am-sorry to-tell-you I-have-been under-the care | of Dr. Brown ever-since-the day you left. Indeed, you-were-not gone an hour when I-had to-send for-the physician. I-do-not-know what-was-the | cause of-my illness; I-cannot-say that I-am-aware of anything to-which-it-may-be due. I-know of nothing to-which-it-can-be traced. At-| all-events, it-has-been very severe, and, for-some-time, my recovery was con-sidered hopeless. Of-course, I-am-not yet out-of-the wood, and-I-must-not | boast, but I-think I-am fairly on-the road to complete recovery. You-will-be-sorry to-learn that I-am-not yet strong enough to-leave my room, | but-you-must-not suppose that I-am in danger. I-trust I-shall-be-able-to-make an effort to visit you some-time during-the coming month. At-| any-rate, I-am hoping so. I-must leave off for-the-present, but will write again very-soon.

Very-truly-yours,
Thomas Makin.   (264 words)

Exercise 157

Read, copy and transcribe.

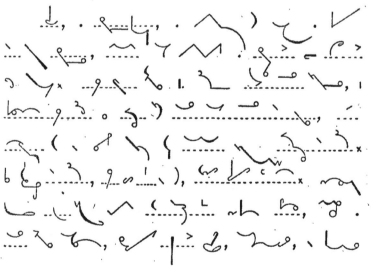

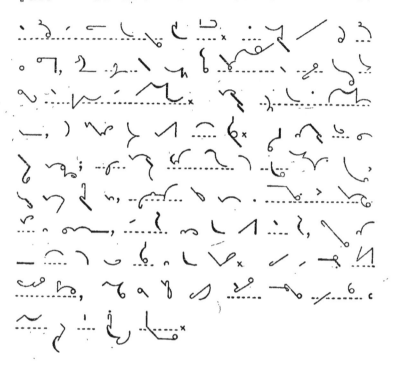

Exercise 158

Write in Shorthand

Dear Mr. Scott,

Since I wrote-you last I-have-heard that-you-were injured slightly in a railway accident. Is-this true? I-trust-not. If-it-is, you-| are-not likely to be improved by-my-letter. If-it-is-not you-will pardon my mentioning the report. In-any-case, you-might send me word, and-if-| you-can spare-the time, perhaps you-will come over on-Monday. If-you-cannot arrange this, please inform me from-time-to-time how you-are getting on with-| the new business, to-which-it-appears you-are devoting yourself. If-it-be as successful as you-were inclined-to-think you-will-be very fortunate, and-if-it-| be-not quite so profitable as you hoped, it-will still have proved an interesting experiment. At-all-events, it-was well worth a trial. At-the-same-time, you-| should-not work too hard. If-you do you-must-not-be surprised to-find your health giving way. I-have-no-doubt of-the ultimate success of-your patent, and-if-it-were-necessary, I could arrange to invest a consider-able amount in-the business. I-cannot-do anything in-the-matter of-the shares you spoke about until I-have-seen-you again. I-cannot-see that-there-is any hurry about-the affair. If-it-does happen that-the shares are all taken-up before I-make application I-shall-not mind very-much. I-am-trusting, however, that-you-will-be-able-to pay me a visit on-Monday and explain matters. I-have staying with me an old friend who-has-been out to South-America for three-years on business matters, and-I-am-sure you-will-be delighted with-his conversations on-the customs and manners of-the natives.

Yours-truly,
Thomas Makin.   (310 words)

ADVANCED PHRASEOGRAPHY : SECTION 4

(Doubling Principle)

above their	I know there will be
over their (or there)	I see there is
before there	I think there will be
before there is	I wish there were
from their	if there
has to be there	if there is
has been there	if there is to be
how can there be	if it be there
I am sure there is	in their case
I believe there will be	in their opinion
I have their	in their statement
I have been there	in which there is
I know there is	increasing their value
I know there is not	making their way

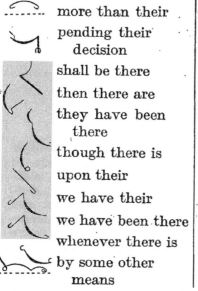

more than their

pending their decision

shall be there

then there are

they have been there

though there is

upon their

we have their

we have been there

whenever there is

by some other means

some other

some other way

some other respects

or some other

in other words

in order

in order that

in order to

my dear sir

my dear madam

my dear friend

my dear fellow citizens

Exercise 159

Read, copy and transcribe

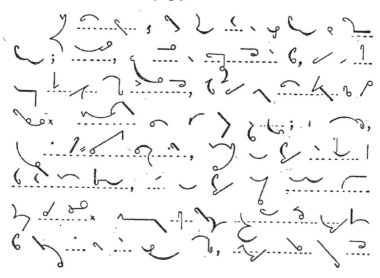

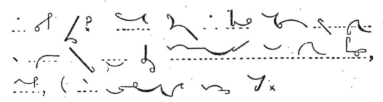

Exercise 160

Write in Shorthand

I-know-there-has-been a great-deal said, as-well-as written, about-the interest attaching to-the study of phrase and-fable, but I-know-there-has-not- | been sufficient said, in-view of-the importance of-the-matter, and-I-know-there-will-be a great-deal-more both said and written before-the subject is exhausted. | Whenever-there-is a subject of interest to-the general reader, and a desire expressed for information upon-it, there-will-be-found someone ready and willing to obtain-the | necessary knowledge and impart it to-others. As-we-have-seen, too, the work is from-time-to-time generally executed as-well-as-it-can-be, and-the-results | made known in-the very shortest time possible. This-is a great convenience to-most of-us, as-we-have-not-time to devote to-research in-these-subjects.   (149 words)

Exercise 161

Read, copy and transcribe

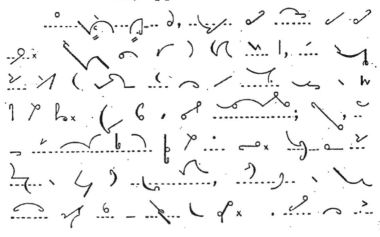

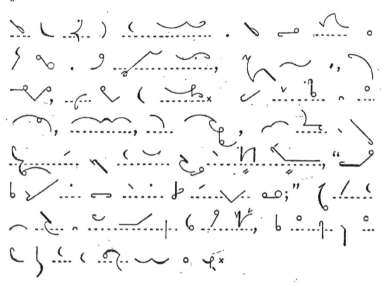

Exercise 162

Write in Shorthand

I-think-there-is room, indeed, I-am-sure-there-is room for-something-more on-the-topic I-have-mentioned before it-can-be-said that-the public is | tired of-it. There-are-some-people, however, who know very-little of-the origin and meaning of-many peculiar expressions of-frequent occurrence. For-their-sake, for-their-satisfaction | and-pleasure, as-well-as for-the educational advantage it-would-be to-them, I-wish-there-were some-means of-bringing before-their notice some of-the books already | published on-this-subject.   (94 words)

Exercise 163

Read, copy and transcribe

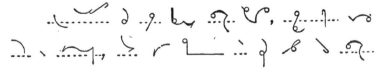

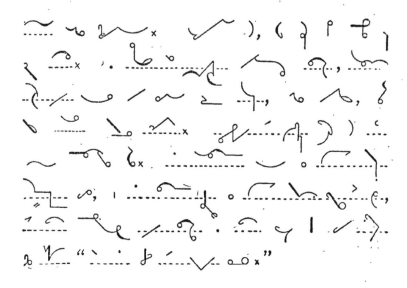

Exercise 164

Write in Shorthand

I-know-there-is a variety of opinion, however, on almost all-questions, and-if-there-be any of-my-readers who doubt-the benefit to be derived from such | a study as I-have referred to, and-if-they assert that, in-their-opinion, it-would-be a waste of-time as-well-as money to-procure such books, | I-ask-them, for-their-own sake and-for-that of-other-people in-their-position, who-may look at-the matter from-their own view, to-weigh-the following- | points as carefully and as-soon-as-they can : How often do we come across such phrases as "toad-eater," " salted accounts," etc., and-though-their meaning, from-their position | in-the-sentence, may-be pretty clear, should-we-not-have some difficulty in saying how they came to-have-their present signification ? Have-we-not all occasionally read some | phrase, or heard some allusion which-we-did-not-understand, and-have-we-not sometimes lost the beauty of a passage through our want of know-ledge ? I-think-there-will- | be few who-will dissent from this.   (187 words)

ADVANCED PHRASEOGRAPHY : SECTION 5

(Omissions: Consonants and Syllables)

I have (r)eceived

in other (r)espects

in (r)eply

we have (r)eceived

almos(t) certain

just now

jus(t) received

las(t) week

las(t) month

last year

mos(t) probably

mus(t) be

nex(t) week

there mus(t) be

you mus(t) be

you mus(t) not be

very please(d) indeed

in (f)act

in point (of f)act

telegra(ph) office

wor(th) while

in the (m)anner

and in like (m)anner

and in the same (m)anner

and in the same (m)anner as

in this (m)anner

nex(t mon)th

this (mon)th

as far as poss(ible)

as much as poss(ible)

as soon as poss(ible)

as well as poss(ible)

as if it were poss(ible)

jus(t) poss(ible)

betwee(n) them

foundatio(n) stone

o(n)e another

towards o(n)e another

industrial (l)ife

I (h)ope

I (h)ope you are satisfied

and the (con)trary

cannot be (con)- sidered

for (con)sideration

fully (con)sidered

further (con)- sidered

further (con)- sideration

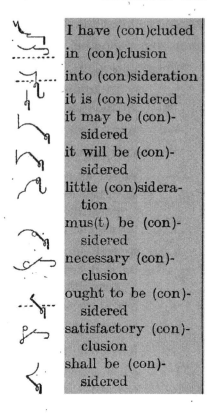

I have (con)cluded

in (con)clusion

into (con)sideration

it is (con)sidered

it may be (con)-
  sidered

it will be (con)-
  sidered

little (con)sidera-
  tion

mus(t) be (con)-
  sidered

necessary (con)-
  clusion

ought to be (con)-
  sidered

satisfactory (con)-
  clusion

shall be (con)-
  sidered

shall be (taken into
  con)sideration

should be (con)-
  sidered

some (con)sidera-
  tion

take (or taken) (into
  con)sideration

that (con)clusion

unsatisfactory
  (con)clusion

we have (con)-
  cluded

were (con)sidered

which will be
  (con)sidered

which will be
  (taken into
  con)sideration

Exercise 165

Read, copy and transcribe

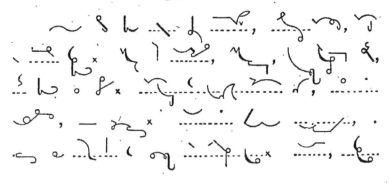

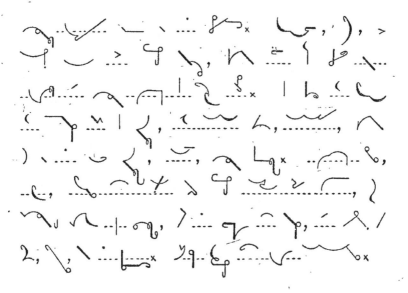

Exercise 166

Write in Shorthand

Dear Mr. Brown,

I-have-received your communication of-the 12th-inst., and-I-am-very-pleased-indeed to inform-you that-you-are almost-certain to-hear from-me | in-the affirmative next-week. Most-probably you-will-be asked to-come here the last-week in-the-last-month of-the-year, but-you-must-not-be surprised | if-you-are-requested to-give your lecture at an earlier date. ‹ Your lecture in-the autumn of-last-year was a great success; in-fact, un-paralleled in-the history | of-our literary organization. This-month and next-month we-are to-have a series of lectures on-the industrial-life of-our cities in-the nine-teenth century, and it- | is-just-possible that-we-may-have a famous economist as chairman at-the opening gathering. We-have-concluded that-these problems ought-to-be-con-sidered without-delay, especially as | economic questions are very-pressing just-now.

Yours-very-truly, (160 words)

Exercise 167

Read, copy and transcribe

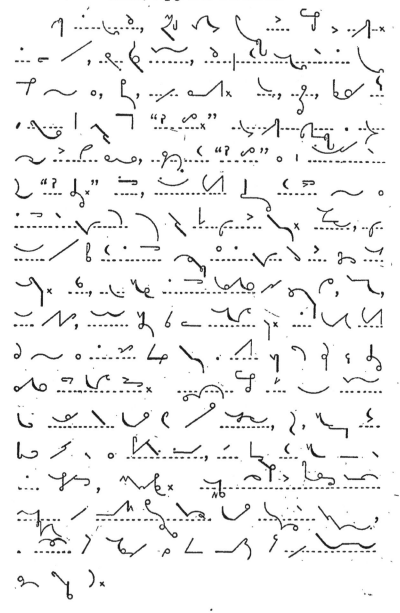

Exercise 168

Write in Shorthand

My-dear-Sir,

I-hope-you-will-think-it worth-while to-consider, as-far-as-possible, the alteration of-the date of-the laying of-the foundation-stone, and- | I-am-sure a little-consideration will lead you to a decision that will materially enhance the chances of a successful gathering. Is-it worth-while ignoring-the wishes of | a small but influential section of-your supporters in-this-manner when a slight alteration would-be of advantage ? In-other-respects I-think no-fault can-be-found with- | the arrangements.

Very sincerely yours,   (95 words)

Exercise 169

Write in Shorthand

Dear-Sirs,

We-have-received your-letter of-the 9th-inst., respecting consignments, and your-requests shall-be-considered in-the-same-manner-as your previous communications on-such-matters. | Our Mr. Burton is away at-present in-the-north of-Scotland. We-expect him back to-morrow, however, when-the whole-question shall-be-taken-into-consideration, and an | early-reply forwarded to-you. Doubtless a satisfactory-conclusion can-be arrived at which-will-be-considered agreeable to all concerned.

Yours-truly,   (83 words)

Exercise 170

Write in Shorthand

In concluding my report, I-would point-out that-there-are many-circumstances which-will-be-taken-into-consideration on a future occasion, but of-which it-is-considered unwise | to-speak now. One necessary-conclusion, however, is-that only in-the-manner I-have indicated is-it possible to arrive at anything like a true estimate of-the-motives | of-these men towards-one-another, and to judge impartially of-the letters which passed between-them. The incident at-the telegraph-office is-the-most-important.

(87 words)

ADVANCED PHRASEOGRAPHY: SECTION 6

(Omissions : Logograms)

as (a) rule

at (a) loss

in (a) few days

in (a) great (m)easure

in such (a) (m)anner as

for (a) moment

to (a) great extent

about (the) matter

all over (the) world

all (the) circum-stances

at (the) present day

at (the) present time

by (the) way

for (the) first time

I will (con)sider (the) matter

in (the) first instance

in (the) first place

in (the) sec(ond) place

in (the) th(ird) place

in (the) las(t) place

in (the) nex(t) place

into (the) matter

notwithstanding (the) (f)act

on (the) (con)trary

on (the) o(n)e hand

on (the) subject

under (the) circum-stances

what is (the) matter

as (a) matter (of) course

as (a) matter (of) (f)act

expression (of) opinion

in (con)sequence (of)

in (r)espect of

necessary (con)-sequence (of)

on (the) part (of)

out (of) place

short space (of) time

do you mean (to) say

expect (to) receive

face (to) face

from first (to) last

having (r)egard (to)

in (r)ef(eren)ce (to)

in (r)ef(eren)ce (to) which

in (r)elation (to)

in (r)eply (to)

in (r)espect (to)

it appears (to) me

it appears (to) have been

it seems (to) me

ought (to) have been

ought (to) have known

regret (to) say

regret (to) state

we shall be glad (to) hear

we shall be glad (to) know

wi(th) (r)ef(eren)ce (to)

wi(th) (r)ef(eren)ce (to) which

wi(th) (r)egard (to)

wi(th) (r)elation (to)

wi(th) (r)espect (to)

Exercise 171

Read, copy and transcribe

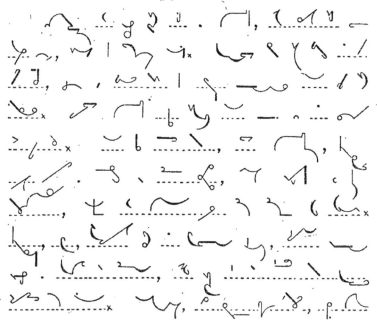

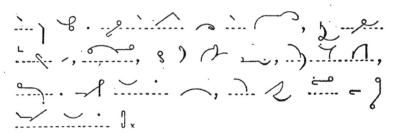

Exercise 172

Write in Shorthand

In-consequence of-the short-space-of-time at our-own disposal, and-having-regard-to all-the-circumstances under-which-the order was-given, we-are at-a-loss | to under-stand-the reason for-the delay in-the delivery of-the machine which ought-to-have-been here a week ago. We-shall-expect-to-receive it in-a- | few-days without fail. We-are face-to-face with a difficulty which-appears-to-have - been in -a - great - measure and to - a - great - extent brought about by-those- | who ought-to-have-known better, and-we-shall-be-glad if-you-will look into-the-matter for-us, notwithstanding-the-fact that-you-are so busy yourself. The | enclosed-statement gives you our position in-reference-to-the difficulty, and-we-shall-be-glad-to-have your expression-of-opinion on-the-matter at an early date.   (149 words)

Exercise 173

Read, copy and transcribe

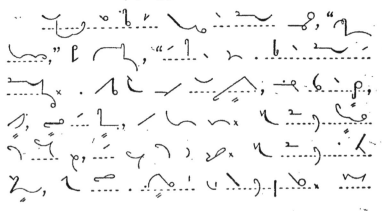

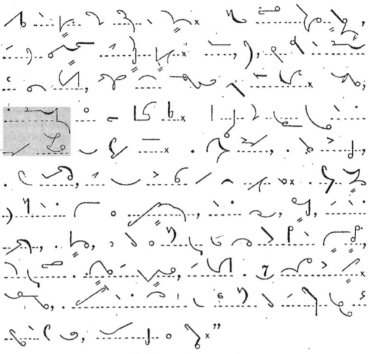

Exercise 174

Write in Shorthand

Dear-Sirs,

In-reply-to-yours of-the 11th-inst., we-regret-to-state that under-the-circumstances we-cannot-accept-the mere apology on-the-part-of your-client. | This conduct of-your-client has-been a source of annoyance for a considerable time, and-in-spite-of our requests that-such conduct should cease, and notwithstanding-the-fact | that legal proceedings have-been threatened, the statements of-which-we complain have continued. From-first-to-last we-have-been face-to-face with inconvenience in-consequence-of your-| client's attitude. Under-the-circumstances, and having-regard-to what-has happened an apology is out-of-the-question. On-the-contrary, we-shall-be compelled to-seek redress in-| the law-courts in-respect-of your-client's statements, and shall instruct our solicitors to-take action forthwith, unless your-client is prepared to pay-the amount of damages claimed. |

Yours-truly, (152 words)

Exercise 175

Write in Shorthand

The lecturer said : It-appears-to-me that at-the-present-time many of-the changes taking-place all-over-the-world are-the outcome of inviolable laws working for- | the-progress of-mankind. As-a-rule, man is apt to overlook-the silent working of-the laws of-the universe in-reference-to-which he-appears, as-a-matter- | of-fact, very-little concerned, or his interest lasts but for-a-moment when some striking incident compels his attention. Generally speaking, he takes things as-a-matter-of-course, | and, as a necessary-consequence-of this attitude, at-the-present-day the beauties of nature are a closed-book to a vast majority of-the inhabitants of-the globe. |

I-will-consider-the-matter and deal-with-the subject as briefly as-possible. In-the-first-place, it-seems-to-me that in-relation-to-the authorship there-is- | no-ground for supposing it to be doubtful. In-the-second-place, the statements in-the book are supported by contemporary accounts. In - the - third - place, all - the other known | works of-the author are of unimpeachable accuracy. Therefore, from-first-to-last, I-think-the criticisms are entirely out-of-place, and-I-cannot-understand what-is-the-matter | with-the reviewer that-he-should make such a violent attack, on-the-one-hand, upon-the probity of-our author, and-on-the-other, upon-the accuracy. of-his | statements.   (241 words)

Exercise 176

Read, copy and transcribe

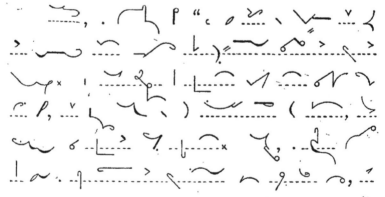

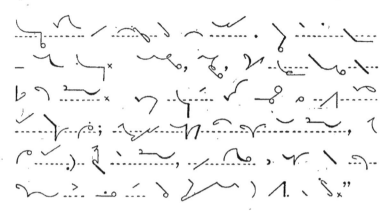

Exercise 177
Write in Shorthand

For-the-first-time in-the history of-the company, said-
the speaker, we-have to-report an adverse balance.
In-the-first-instance, we-have-had a serious strike | at-the
works, but-you-will-be-glad-to-know-that all disputes
have-been amicably settled.   In-the-next-place, we-have
had some very heavy law expenses with- | reference-to our
existing patents, and-with-reference-to-which a statement
appears in-the report. In-the-last-place, our annual
turnover has-not-been up to expectations, though, | by-
the-way, it slightly exceeds-the figures of-last-year.
You-will-be-glad-to-hear that our new manager has
introduced several excellent reforms which-will bear fruit |
in-the-near-future.

It-would-be out-of-place for-me in-the short-space-of-
time at my disposal to-try to-go fully into-the details of- |
the-accounts.   Moreover, we-expect-to-receive, very-
shortly, a further report from-the auditors.   Having-
regard-to-the present state-of-affairs, and-in-consequence-
of certain criticisms, we- | think-it best, under-the-circum-
stances, to-have an independent investigation, and-the
auditors have-been asked to-give a frank expression-of-
opinion in-reference-to-the affairs of- | the Company.   The
position is a difficult one.   On-the-one-hand we-are-told-
that as-a-matter-of-course the business ought-to be
prosperous, yet as-a- | matter-of-fact, the contrary is-the
case.   What-is-the-matter we-hope to-hear from-the auditors, who-are looking into-the-matter, and who-are
expected to- | report in-a-few-days.   (275 words)

ADVANCED PHRASEOGRAPHY : SECTION 7

(*Omissions : Logograms*)

	again (and) again
	dee(per) (and) deeper
	high(er) (and) higher
	lower (and) lower
	fast(er) (and) faster
	less (and) less
	more (and) more
	Mr. (and) Mrs.
	near(er) (and) nearer
	north (and) south
	east and west
	over (and) over again
	over (and) above
	here (and) there
	qui(cker) (and) quicker
	rates (and) taxes
	time (and) space
	ways (and) means
	side (by) side
	bear (in) mind
	borne (in) mind
	all parts (of the) world
	fact (of the) matter
	facts (of the) case

	for (the) purpose (of)
	history (of the) world
	out (of the) question
	peculiar circumstances (of the) case
	more (or) less
	one (or) two
	right (or) wrong
	six or seven
	sooner (or) later
	three or four
	two (or) three
	up (to the) present
	up (to the) present time
	in accordance (with)
	in accordance (with) the
	in accordance (with) the matter
	in connection (with)
	in connection (with) the
	in connection (with) their

Exercise 178

Read, copy and transcribe

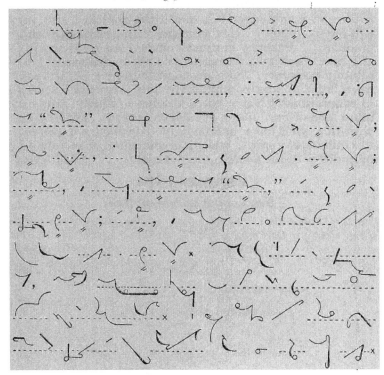

Exercise 179

Write in Shorthand

Ships of immense proportions are nowadays found in-all-parts-of-the-world, and docks have-to-be-made deeper-and-deeper in-order-to accommodate the huge vessels which- | are-constructed to-carry more-and-more and to-travel faster-and-faster as time advances. Distance between-us and-foreign parts is becoming less-and-less, and north-and- | south, and east-and-west are being brought nearer-and-nearer, so-that-the desire long-since expressed has almost-been accomplished, and time-and-space have-been practically annihilated | by-the progress of science and-the ingenuity of-man.   (100 words)

Exercise 180

Write in Shorthand

Owing to-the peculiar-circumstances-of-the-case such a course as you suggest is out-of-the-question, and you-will-have to-follow the procedure in-accordance-with I precedent. Further, you-must endeavour to secure Mr.-and-Mrs. Brown as witnesses, as their evidence is absolutely-necessary. The fact-of-the-matter is that-you have failed to I bear-in-mind the really essential features in-connection-with-the case and-have chiefly borne-in-mind one-or-two quite subsidiary points. Side-by-side with-this, you I have unfortunately displayed a more-or-less vindictive spirit, which, in-our-opinion, can-only-be prejudicial to-the success of-your claim.   (113 words)

Exercise 181

Read, copy and transcribe

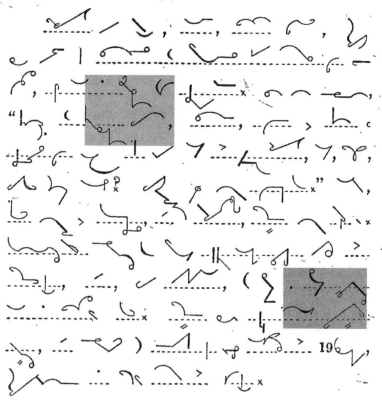

Exercise 182

Write in Shorthand

Over-and-over-again we-have-complained of-the rates-and-taxes in-connection-with our concern, and sooner-or-later we-shall-have to-discuss ways-and-means of | a successful agitation for-their reduction. Up-to-the-present-time we-have-been very heavily handicapped in-this-respect, and judging from-the present outlook our resources will-be-| called-upon more-and-more in-the-immediate future, unless-we-are-enabled to obtain-the relief we-think-we-are entitled to. Again-and-again, during-the-last six- | or-seven years there-have-been outcries against the upward tendency of-these local levies, and-in-connection-with-their collection many have urged that-the facts-of-the-case | required-the immediate attention of-the authorities. The history-of-the-world shows that-this-matter of-rates-and-taxes has always-been a sore point with people of-every- | clime and nation, and-whether right-or-wrong, it-is a fact that a great-many have suffered imprisonment rather-than pay what they-have deemed unjust impositions.   (178 words)

Exercise 183

Read, copy and transcribe

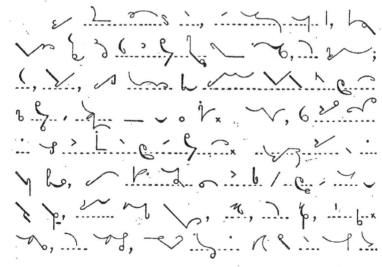

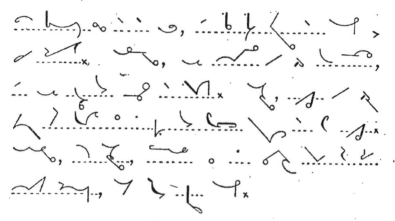

Summary

1. Abbreviations are utilized in advanced phraseography, as follows—

 (a) The small circle for *as, is, us.*

 (b) The large circle initially for *as we, as* and *w, as* and *s;* medially for *is* and *s, his* and *s, s* and *s;* finally for *s* and *has, s* and *is.*

 (c) The loop *st* for *first*, the loop *nst* for *next.*

 (d) The *r* and *l* hooks for a few miscellaneous words.

 (e) The *n* hook for *than, been* and *own.*

 (f) The *f* or *v* hook for *have, of, after, even*, and in a few common phrases.

 (g) The circle *s* and *shun* hook for *association.*

 (h) The halving principle for *it, to, not, would, word*, and in a few common phrases.

 (i) The doubling principle for *there, their, other, dear.*

2. The following may be omitted—

 (a) Consonants not essential to phraseograms.

 (b) The syllable *con-*, and a few other common syllables.

 (c) Any logogram or logograms providing the phraseogram is legible.

CHAPTER XXXV

INTERSECTIONS

The Use of Intersections. 214. The method of intersecting, or writing one stroke through another, is utilized for the brief, distinctive, and rapid indication of official titles, of persons or associations of various kinds, and of frequently-occurring colloquial phrases, etc. Where intersection is impracticable, the method of writing one stroke in close proximity to another is adopted instead; thus, ＿＿ *political party,* ＿＿ *party question,* ＿＿ *Labour Party,* ＿＿ *Party Bill.* When the word to be indicated by an alphabetic stroke is to be read first, the stroke is struck first, and the rest of the outline is cut through, or written in close proximity to it. The examples which follow illustrate the manner in which similar phrases may be dealt with.

P is employed to represent **party,** as in

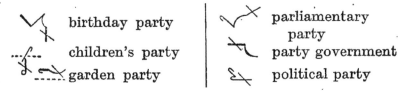

	birthday party		parliamentary party
	children's party		party government
	garden party		political party

Pr is employed to represent **professor,** as in

	Professor Jackson		Professor of Chemistry
	Professor Morgan		Professor of Commerce
	Professor Peake		Professor of Music

B is employed to represent the following—

(a) **bank,** as in

⟍	bank bills	⟍	City Bank
⟍	Bank of England	⟍	Mercantile Bank
⟍	bank pass book	⟍	Penny Bank
⤬	bank rate	⟍	savings bank

(b) **-bankment,** as in

⟍	sea embankment	⟍	Thames Embankment

(c) **bill,** as in

⟍	Finance Bill	⟍	Education Bill

T is employed to represent **attention,** as in

⟍	best attention	⟍	my attention has been called
⟍	careful attention	⟍	necessary attention
⟍	early attention	⟍	special attention
⟍	early attention to the matter	⟍	your attention

D is employed to represent **department,** as in

⟍	Department of Agriculture	⟍	Government department
⟍	electrical dept.	⟍	life department
⟍	engineering dept.	⟍	shipping dept.
⟍	foreign dept.	⟍	silk department

CH is employed to represent **Chancery,** as in

⟍	Chancery appeal	⟍	Chancery Judge
⟍	Chancery proceedings	⟍	into Chancery

J is employed to represent **Journal**, as,

Journal of Commerce		School Journal	
Journal of Education		Textile Journal	
Pitman's Journal		Weekly Journal	

K is employed to represent the following—

   (*a*) **Company**, as in

Barber & Co.		Gas Co., Ltd.	
Carriage Co.		Malleable Iron Co., Ltd.	
Delivery Co.		Weaving Co., Ltd.	

   (*b*) **Council**, as in

Borough Council		Parish Council	
Cabinet Council		Party Councils	
Councils of the Party		Privy Council	
County Council		Town Council	

   (*c*) **Capital**, as in

authorized capital		capital punishment	
capital charge		capital receipts	
capital expenditure		share capital	

   (*d*) **Captain**, as in

Captain Cook		captain of the ship	
Captain Dixon		captain of the team	
captain in the Army		ship's captain	

Kr is employed to represent the following—

(a) **Colonel**, as in

[shorthand] Colonel Anderson | [shorthand] Colonel Jackson

(b) **Corporation**, as in

[shorthand] investment corporation | [shorthand] Corporation of Leeds

G is employed to represent **government**, as in

[shorthand] English Government | [shorthand] government official

[shorthand] French Government | [shorthand] municipal government

F is employed to represent **form**, as in

[shorthand] entry form | [shorthand] form of Government

[shorthand] form of acknowledgment | [shorthand] form of the report

[shorthand] form of agreement | [shorthand] medical form

[shorthand] form of bequest | [shorthand] necessary form

V is employed to represent **valuation**, as in

[shorthand] low valuation | [shorthand] valuation of the site

[shorthand] valuation of the property | [shorthand] site valuation

TH is employed to represent the following—

(a) **Authority**, as in

[shorthand] authority of the manager | [shorthand] military authorities

[shorthand] authority of the représentative | [shorthand] sanitary authority

[shorthand] legal authority | [shorthand] well-known authority

[shorthand] local authority | [shorthand] written authority

(*b*) **Month,** as in

...✶... for a month

✶ in a month's time

✶ many months ago

✶ some months ago

S is employed to represent **society,** as in

...✶... dramatic society

✶ Hearts of Oak Society

✶ medical society

✶ Society of Compositors

✶ Society of Musicians

✶ Temperance Society

M is employed to represent the following—

(*a*) **Mark,** as in

...✶... auditor's mark

...✶... high-water mark

✶ low-water mark

✶ mark of respect

...✶... official mark

...✶... private mark

✶ save the mark !

✶ to mark time

(*b*) **Major,** as in

...✶... Major Anson

✶ Major General

✶ Major Jones

...✶... Serjeant Major Jones

N is employed to represent **national,** as in

...✶... national affair

✶ national bank

✶ national defence

✶ national desire

...✶... national disaster

...✶... national dividend

✶ national finance

✶ national reserve

✶ national revenue

✶ national society

L is employed to represent the following—

(a) **liberal,** as in

⌐\	Liberal Club	..⌐..	liberal discount
⌐⌐	Liberal· Govt.	..⌐⌐..	liberal manner
✕	Liberal Party	✕⌐	liberal payment
.✕⌒..	Liberal policy	..⌐..	liberal view

(b) **limited,** as in

⟍⟋	Pears' Limited	....⟋✕⟍....Lupin Limited

R (down) is employed to represent **arrange-d-ment** in colloquial phrases like the following—

⟍⟋	better arrangement	⎰	it was arranged
⟋⟍	I shall arrange		please make arrangements
..⎳⟍..	if you can arrange	⟋✕⟍	we will arrange the matter

R (up) is employed to represent **railway,** as in

....✕..	Cambrian Railway	✕⟍	railway officials
..⎰⟍..	difficulties of the railway	⟋⟍	railway rates
⟍✕	Metropolitan Ry.	..⌐..	railway ticket
⟋⟍	railway company	.⌐..	railway time
✕⎰b..	railway facilities	..⌐...	railway time table

Sr (up) is employed to represent **conservative,** as in

⟋⟍	Conservative Club	✕	Conservative Party
⟋⟍	Conservative Government	✕⌒	Conservative policy

Exercise 184

Read, copy and transcribe

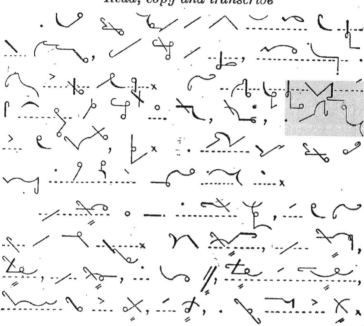

Exercise 185

Write in Shorthand

Messrs. Barber-and-Co., the New Carriage-Company, and-the Dorset-Supply-Company, are to be converted into limited-companies. The annual reports of-the Malleable-Iron-Co.,-Ltd., Smith,-I Brown-and Co.,-Ltd., and-the Weaving-Co.,-Ltd., all bear testimony to-the prosperity of-trade during-the past year. A Government-official, a well-known railway-official, and I a clerk in-another Government-department have all advised me to-take shares in Lee's-Brewery-Company, but, as a member of a temperance-society, I-do-not like-the I idea. The local-authorities have invited the committee of-the Agricultural-Society to arrange a show here, and-the local Society-of-Musicians has undertaken-the charge of-the musical-I arrangements. It-is hoped the committee will-arrange-the-matter. Please-make-arrangements to-come over on-the first-day if-possible. (142 words)

Exercise 186

Read, copy and transcribe

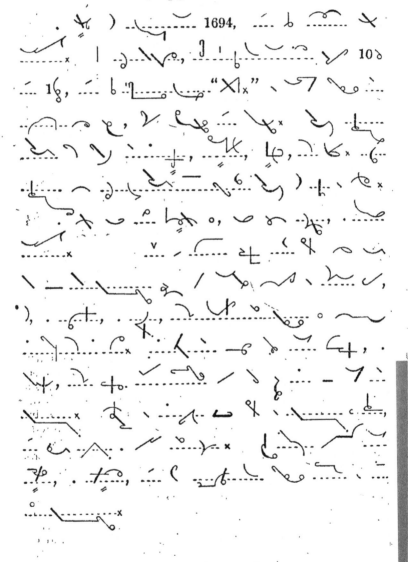

Exercise 187

Write in Shorthand

We give a liberal-discount on all cash-orders. The committee treated him in a liberal-manner and allowed him a most liberal-payment for-his services at-the Liberal-| Club. On-the-authority-of-the-representative ___ we-are-bound-to-say that-the valuation-of-the-site is a very unsatisfactory-one in-view of-the yearly-valuation which-| has-been made for-the last twelve years.

Our national-society is very-much interested in national-affairs, and it-is desirous of securing the strengthening of-our national-defence.| The other evening Major-Jones opened a debate on capital-punishment, and-after an interesting discussion in-which Captain-Dixon, Colonel-Beach and Professor-Peake took-part, we-regret-to-| say that a majority voted for-its retention.   (128 words)

Summary

An intersection is formed by allocating a definite word or words to an alphabetic stroke when intersecting, or written in close proximity to, another stroke, as follows :—

P	=	*party*	G	= *government*
Pr	=	*professor*	F	= *form*
		bank	V	= *valuation*
B	=	*bankment*	TH	= *authority*
		bill		*month*
T	=	*attention*	S	= *society*
D	=	*department*	M	= *mark*
Ch	=	*Chancery*		*major*
J	=	*journal*	N	= *national*
		company	L	= *liberal*
		council		*limited*
K	=	*capital*	R (down) =	*arrange-d-*
		captain		*ment*
Kr	=	*colonel*	R (up)	= *railway*
		corporation	Sr (up)	= *conservative*

16—(R)

CHAPTER XXXVI

BUSINESS PHRASES

Phraseography in Business. 215. When the requirements of particular businesses have to be met, the principles of phrasing and intersecting may be given a special application according to the purpose for which they are required. Thus, while in a general sense ＼ p intersected indicates the word *party*, it may be used to represent the word *policy* in an insurance office, and the word *pump* in an engineer's office. This allocation of a special meaning to an alphabetic stroke and a further application of the rules of phrasing are set out in the following lists. The following examples are intended to be suggestive of similar phrases to be met with in various branches of business.

GENERAL BUSINESS

account sales
additional cost
additional expense
at your earliest convenience
best of my ability
best of our ability
best of their ability
best of your ability
bill of exchange
bill of lading
board of directors
by passenger train

by return of post
declare a dividend
directors' report
discount for cash
early convenience
enclose-d herewith
faithfully yours
from the last report
goods not to hand
I am directed to inform you
I am directed to state

I am in receipt of your esteemed favour

I am in receipt of your favour

I am in receipt of your letter

I am instructed

I am instructed to inform you

I am instructed to state

I am requested to inform you

I beg to acknowledge receipt of your favour

I beg to acknowledge receipt of your letter

I beg to call attention

I beg to enclose herewith

I enclose herewith

I have to acknowledge receipt of your letter

I have to call attention

I regard

I regret

in reply to your esteemed favour

in reply to your favour

in reply to your letter

in your reply to my letter

not yet to hand

ordinary rates

postal order

referring to our invoice

referring to our letter

referring to your favour

referring to your letter

referring to yours

registered letter

respectfully yours

under bill of sale

we beg to quote

we respectfully request

your esteemed favour

your favour

your obedient servant

yours faithfully

yours obediently

yours respectfully

yours sincerely

Exercise 188

Write in Shorthand

Dear-Sir,

In-reply-to-your-favour of-the 16th-inst, we-regret that-we-cannot undertake-the responsibility of adopting your suggestions with-regard-to-the machine. We-are | willing to-execute the repairs to-the best-of-our-ability, and-on-the lowest-terms possible, but as we stated in-our last-letter, the methods you-propose would-| be attended with great risk to-the rider. If-you decide to-leave-the-matter to-us you-might inform-us by-return-of-post, and-we-will put-the | work in-hand at-once, so-as-to-be-able-to dispatch-the machine by-goods-train on-Saturday. We-need hardly-say that-we pay-the best-price for | all-the-materials we use, and-we guarantee them to be of-the best-quality obtainable. Referring-to-your-letter of-the 9th-inst., we-have-done our best to | induce-the carriers to-quote special-rates for-the-goods consigned to-you, but-they decline to-make any reduction on-the ordinary-rates unless-the traffic is considerably increased. | With-reference-to-our statement-of-account for last quarter, we-beg-to-call-attention to-the fact that-the balance due has-not-yet-been received, and-| we-will-thank-you for a cheque or a postal-order for-the-amount at-your-earliest-convenience. We-shall-give early-consideration to-your inquiries for-the special tandem, and-will-| forward-the specification desired as-soon-as-convenient.

Yours-faithfully,   (250 words)

Exercise 189

Write in Shorthand

Dear-Sir,

I-am-in-receipt-of-your-letter of-the 24th, and I-regret-to-state that I-am-unable to-give you-the information you-require. I-| can-assure-you I should-be-pleased to-do-so if-it-were-possible. I-am-surprised to-hear from-you that-the funds of-your society are in-such | a bad-way. I-regard-the objects of-the-society as most praiseworthy, and I-cannot-understand how it-is that public support should-be withheld. I-enclose-cheque for | ten-pounds as a subscription, and shall-be-glad to-give-the same-amount next year. I-am-much-obliged-to-you for-the copy of-the report.

Yours-faithfully, | (120 words)

Exercise 190

Write in Shorthand

Dear-Sir,

I-brought your-letter before-the Board-of-Directors at-their-meeting yesterday, but after some discussion they-were-obliged to postpone further-consideration of-the-matter until | the next Directors'-meeting, which-will-be held on-the last Tuesday-afternoon of-this-month. I-think-the Directors would-be-glad if-you would kindly set-forth your- | proposals more fully than is done in-your-letter. The first-cost of-the-material is very-low, but-the question of-the additional-cost of-preparing it for-sale, | and-the additional-expense which-will-probably be incurred in advertising it is sure to be taken-into-consideration by-the-Directors, and-if they-had your estimate of what- | the total expenditure is likely to amount to, it-would-no-doubt help them in coming to a decision. If-you-will make-an-appointment for-some day next-week | I-shall-be-glad to see-you, and it-is-just-possible that I-may-be-able to-give-you some further-particulars. Meanwhile, I-have-the-pleasure to enclose | copy of-the-Directors'-Report published last-month.

Yours-faithfully,   (190 words)

Exercise 191

Write in Shorthand

Dear-Sirs,

In-reply-to-your-letter of-yesterday, we-beg-to-state that-the bill-of-lading and-the bill-of-exchange were forwarded to-you by-first-post | on Tuesday-morning last, in registered-letter, addressed as-usual, and-we-are-surprised that-they-have-not reached you. We-will make inquiries here, and-in-the-meantime, if-| you-receive-the letter kindly inform-us by wire at-once. Referring-to-our-letter of-the 27th ult., and your-reply to-same, we-have written-the works | pressing-them to-give early-attention-to-the-matter and to-make-the necessary-arrangements for forwarding-the goods to-the finishers as-soon-as-ready. We-have-instructed the | latter to-give-the-material the best-finish, and-we-have-no-doubt they-will-do-so. We-have-also mentioned your complaint as-to-the finish of-the last | consignment, and-we-are-assured that special-care will-be taken to-prevent a repetition of-the-mistake in-the future.   Yours-faithfully,   (173 words)

CHAPTER XXXVII

POLITICAL PHRASES

Phraseography in Political Matter. 216. The following phrases are illustrative of the kind commonly met in taking notes of political speeches, etc. The shorthand writer should keep himself informed in regard to the political questions of the day, and familiarize himself with the phrases which almost invariably accompany the introduction of any special legislation. The list of phraseograms here given will serve as models for similar phrases.

POLITICAL

Act of Parliament

at the first reading

at the second reading

at the third reading

British Constitution

British Empire

Cabinet meeting

Chairman of Committee

Chancellor of the Exchequer

colonial preference

Commissioner of Works

Conservative Party

freedom of the people

freedom of the press

freedom of trade

Home Rule Party

hon. and learned member

hon. gentleman

hon. member

hon. member for Preston

House of Commons

House of Lords

Houses of Parliament

238

Imperial Parliament	Parliamentary Committee
in committee of supply	party leaders
in the House of Commons	plenipotentiary
in the House of Lords	Postmaster-General
Labour Party	Prime Minister
Leader of the House	President of the Board of Agriculture
Leader of the Opposition	President of the Board of Trade
Leader of the Party	President of the Local Government Board
Liberal Party	proportional representation
Liberal Unionist	ratepayers
Liberal Unionist Party	right honourable
Local Government Board	right hon. gentleman
Lord of the Admiralty	Secretary of State
Lord of the Treasury	Secretary of State for the Colonies
member of Parliament	Secretary of State for the Home Department
my hon. and gallant friend	Secretary of State for War
my hon. friend	Secretary for War
National Insurance Act	Tariff Reform
nationalization of railways	United Kingdom
naval estimates	United States

Exercise 192

Write in Shorthand

The right-hon.-gentleman, the member-for-Preston, speaking in-the-House-of-Commons, on Tuesday-evening, on-the-proposal to increase-the numerical strength of-the Army-and-Navy, | referred to-the extraordinary growth of-the British-Empire during-the-last fifty years. He asserted with-much vigour that freedom-of-trade, freedom-of-the-people, and freedom-of- | the-Press, were-the rule in every-part of-His-Majesty's dominions, and he declared that every free-trader was bound to-give-the measure his support. His Majesty's-Government | had given most careful-consideration to-this-matter, and Ministers in both Houses-of-Parliament were quite unanimous in-the-conviction that-such a measure was-necessary for-the safe-guarding | of-the vast interests committed to-their care. His right-honourable-friend, the Secretary-for-War, had shown exactly how-the proposed increase would-be distributed, and-the Chancellor-of- | the-Exchequer, the First-Lord-of-the-Treasury, and-the First-Lord-of-the-Admiralty had each advanced weighty reasons for-the adoption of-the-proposal. It-was-not a | party-question, and he trusted that-the right-honourable-gentleman, the leader-of-the-Opposition, would-not attempt to-make party-capital out-of-it. It-was true, as-the | President-of-the-Board-of-Trade and-the Secretary-of-State-for-the-Home-Department had both candidly admitted, there-were several minor details of-the-measure open to amendment, | but-they-would, no-doubt, be amended in-committee, when-the Chairman-of-Committee would-give honourable-members, and especially the honourable-and-learned-member for Bath an opportunity of | debating these-points. The Leader-of-the-Opposition took exception to-the-manner in-which-the proposal had-been brought before-the House, and declared that sound reasons had-not- | been advanced for-its adoption. As Leader-of-the-Party in Opposition he claimed that fuller discussion should-be given to-the-measure before-the Government pressed it forward to | a division. The Secretary-of-State-for-War replied for-the-Government, and-the-motion was carried by a very large majority.   (352 words)

Exercise 193

Write in Shorthand

Topics of-considerable interest were discussed at-the district conference of-the Labour-Party. There-was much praise for-the National-Insurance-Act. The question of-the nationalization-of-railways | in-the United-Kingdom raised a lengthy and-interesting discussion. With-regard-to proportional-representation it-was asserted that-it-was opposed by party-organizers because it-would open-the | way to-government by groups which-would-be contrary to-the traditions of-the-British-Constitution. Much objection was-taken to-the increase in-the naval-estimates for-the-| current year, and-some speakers averred that our plenipotentiaries abroad might do more to-check-the desire for increased armaments. The condition of-the working-classes in-the United-States | and-Germany was-given as an argument against tariff-reform, while it-was argued that-the whole question of colonial-preference could-only-be satisfactorily settled by an Imperial-Parliament. |　　　　　　(150 words)

Exercise 194

Write in Shorthand

The Treasury had consented to enlarge-the land-department. There-would-be one additional Sub-Commissioner and-four Assistant Sub-Commissioners. The Treasury had also sanctioned an additional clerical staff to-the | number of eleven persons. A matter of-great importance and difficulty at-the beginning of-this work had-been-the obtaining of-suitable land. A great-deal of-land was | expressly excluded by-the Act. In-some-places there-was-not enough suitable land for all-the applicants, and-there-were cases in-which-the only remedy for congestion was- | the migration of-some of-the appli-cants to other-parts of-Scotland. There-were various causes which-made rapid progress impossible in-the-first year, but-these-would diminish as | time went on. He hoped the Board would-be-able-to bring into use for small-holders land which now was either not cultivated or not being used to-the | best-advantage. During-the past century a large area of arable cultivation had passed into permanent pasture, and he hoped it-would-be possible

to-place many small landholders on | land of-that kind—
a process which-would increase-the number of-men maintained on-the soil.   As-to deer forests, there-were
two-cases in-which owners had offered | to negotiate for
a settlement, and-there-were several other cases in-which
negotiations were going on. . The question of compensa-
tion might make-the taking of a small piece of- | land
in-the-middle of a deer forest an extremely costly business.
The first report showed that by-the end of-the-year,
subject to-the decision of-the land | Court, arrangements
had-been made to-provide for 500 applicants, and-since-
then a great-deal of work had-been-done.   Many hun-
dreds of-cases were in various stages | of development.
The Board were anxious, not-only to-find land for small
holdings, but also to assist their successful cultivation by
giving the holders opportunities of-practical instruction
and | demonstration, of-learning the best-methods of-
cultivation, of keeping up-the quality of-their stock, and-
by encouraging poultry and everything which-would-
make-the small holdings profitable.   Co-operation |
amongst small-holders was-making satisfactory progress,
and-the-Board were at-present in communication with-the
Scottish-banks for-the-purpose-of seeing whether-they
could offer better credit | facilities.   (391 words)

CHAPTER XXXVIII
BANKING AND STOCKBROKING PHRASES

Phraseography in Banking and Stockbroking. 217.
The shorthand writer engaged in banking or stock-broking will meet with many terms peculiar to these branches of business, and he should equip himself with suitable and easily written phraseograms for their rapid representation. It will not be sufficient, however, for him to know the shorthand outlines for these phrases. He should make himself master of the meanings of the terms and their correct use. A study of the following lists will enable him to frame similar contractions for any phrase not included in the lists.

BANKING

accepted for the honour of

accepted payable in London

ad valorem stamp

advance against a life policy

arbitration of exchange

bank note

bank post bill

cable remittance

cancel the cheque

circular note

clearing house

country cheque

course of exchange

date of the maturity of the bill

deed of transfer

draft on demand

English Government Securities

form of indemnity

in case of need

Joint Stock Bank

last indorser

London clearing bankers

long exchange

memorandum of deposit

metropolitan cheque

negotiable instrument

negotiable security

nominal consideration

not negotiable cheque

orders to retire acceptances

paying-in slip

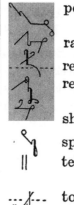

per procuration acceptance

rate of exchange

refer to drawer

restrictive indorsement

short exchange

specially indorsed

telegraphic transfer

town cheque

without recourse

written authority of the drawer

Exercise 195

Write in Shorthand

My-brother and-I are in Joint-Stock-Banks in-London. He-is in-the foreign-department and consequently he-is specially acquainted with-such expressions as arbitration-of-exchange, | course-of-exchange, rate-of-exchange, long-exchange, short-exchange, cable-remittance and tele-graphic-transfers, and a draft-on-demand. The phraseo-logy used in-connection-with bills is very interesting | to-him, and-in dealing-with a bill he-has, of-course, to note the date-of-the-maturity-of-the-bill, whether it-is specially-indorsed, or has a | restrictive-indorsement, or has on it the words without-recourse, or in-case-of-need Bills are sometimes accepted-for-the-honour-of any party thereon, or accepted-payable-in- | London, or they-have a per-procuration-acceptance. A bank may-receive orders-to-retire-acceptance. I-am specially concerned with cheques which-may-be town-cheques, metropolitan-cheques, or | country-cheques, paying-in-slips, various bank-notes and circular-notes. Our-bank occasionally consents to-grant an advance-against-a-life-policy and accepts deeds accompanied by a memorandum- | of-deposit.

(182 words)

Exercise 196

Write in Shorthand

I-understand-the significance of a nominal-considera-tion; which-is given for-the-purpose-of avoiding paying ad-valorem-stamp duty, a deed-of-transfer, a negotiable-instrument, and a | negotiable-security, among-which last English-Government-Securities take a premier place. A form-of-indemnity is used in-connection-with-the loss of documents, and-in other matters. Sometimes | I-have to-write on a cheque " refer-to-drawer," and occasionally a cheque is-not honoured without-the written-authority-of-the-drawer, or-the advice to " cancel-the-| cheque " is received. I-have to pay particular attention to a " not-negotiable "-cheque. Without-the Clearing-House the London-clearing-bankers would-be unable to-cope with-the huge | number of cheques which pass daily through-their banks, the daily average being about £50,000,000. The amount of-labour, both physical and mental, repre-sented by-this vast sum, | is indeed wonderful. There-are four clearings each day : Metropolitan, Town (morning), Country, Town (afternoon), at-each of-which-the respective-cheques are cleared. The busiest days are-the fourth | of-the-month when so-many bills are payable, and-the Stock-Exchange settlement days. (195 words)

STOCKBROKING

	bearer shares			cum dividend
	blank transfer			cumulative prefer-ence shares
	buying for control			day to day money
	capital liabilities			demoralized markets
	carry-over facilities			directors' qualification
	concentrating plant			dwts. per ton
	consolidated annuities			ex-dividend
	convertible gold bonds			first mortgage debentures

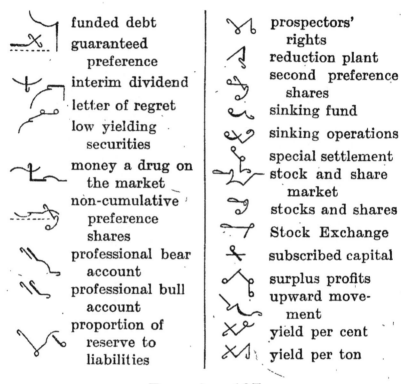

funded debt	prospectors' rights
guaranteed preference	reduction plant
interim dividend	second preference shares
letter of regret	sinking fund
low yielding securities	sinking operations
money a drug on the market	special settlement
non-cumulative preference shares	stock and share market
professional bear account	stocks and shares
professional bull account	Stock Exchange
proportion of reserve to liabilities	subscribed capital
	surplus profits
	upward movement
	yield per cent
	yield per ton

Exercise 197

Write in Shorthand

The young investor is apt to be nonplussed by-the business vocabulary of-the stockbroker. If-he reads the financial articles on-the stock-and-share-markets he-will come | across such expressions as buying-for-control, carry-over-facilities, day-to-day-money, money-a-drug-on-the-market, demoralized-markets, professional-bear-account, professional-bull-account and upward- | movement. In-the-mining market section he-will read of-prospectors'-rights, concentrating-plant, reduction-plant, sinking-operations, and-the report of a year's working will mention dwts.-per-ton, | yield-per-ton, and yield-per-cent. He probably knows little of-directors'-qualifications, and-is liable to be misled into buying low-yielding-securities. Among-the various investments there- | are consolidated-annuities or consols, a funded-debt of-the-government, cumulative-preference-shares, non-cumulative-preference-shares, first-mortgage-debentures, second-preference-shares, and so on. He-may come | across blank-transfers and bearer-shares, and-have to study the subscribed-capital, the capital-liabilities, the proportion-of-reserve-to-liabilities and-the surplus-profits of going concerns.   (179 words)

Exercise 198

Write in Shorthand

He-will-have to pay special-attention to-the sinking-fund, an amount which-is annually set aside out-of revenue and-invested with-the interest accruing to-provide, at | a future date, for-the redemption of a loan or a series of debentures, or for recouping the gradual shrinkage in value by exhausting the known profit-bearing resources of | a mine or similar undertaking. When taking-up stocks-and-shares he-will, of-course, be influenced by interim-dividends, and-whether-the stocks-and-shares are cum-dividend or ex- | dividend, and-in-some-cases after much trouble and-some worry he-may-receive a letter-of-regret. In-the-case-cf companies being floated he-must notice if-the | Stock-Exchange is giving a special-settlement. Certainly the investment of-money so-as-to produce a satisfactory return is-no easy-matter, and-whether convertible-gold-bonds or guaranteed- | preference shares are held, it-is-necessary to-exercise the greatest caution. Even-the most astute investor may-be deceived at-times by prospectuses, and balance-sheets may fail to- | reveal the true state-of-affairs of a company.   (189 words)

CHAPTER XXXIX

INSURANCE AND SHIPPING PHRASES

Phraseography in Insurance and Shipping. 218.
The following lists of phrases in common use in
insurance and shipping are only a small selection of
the total number of such-like phrases to be met with
daily in either of these important branches of business. The shorthand-writer entering upon work in
either an insurance or a shipping office should immediately set about familiarizing himself with the
terms he will be called upon to write in shorthand
and with their meanings. His value to his employers
and his chances of promotion will depend largely
upon his intelligent understanding of the terms
employed and his unceasing efforts to extend his
knowledge of the business.

INSURANCE

Accident Insur-
ance Co.

approximate rate
of premium

automatic
sprinklers

bonus year of the
company

casual employ-
ment

claim for com-
pensation

combined accident
and disease
policy

damage by fire

damage to
premises

damage to tyres

date and term
of insurance

dislocation of the
wrist

fire insurance

immediate benefit

in full discharge of
all claims

incombustible
materials

Insurance Co.

interim bonus

248

life insurance

life policy

loan on the policy

medical examination

morale of the risk

motor-car

negligence of the chief engineer

ordinary accident policy

Personal Accident Insurance

personal injury

policy is declared void

policies are declared void

proposal form received

quinquennial valuation

registered number of the car

renewal of the policy

responsibility of the company

situation of the crane

situation of the lift

Third Party Indemnity Insurance

Workmen's Compensation Act

Exercise 199

Write in Shorthand

The operations of insurance-companies now cover a very extended field and are continually growing consequent upon legislative enactments and improved methods of-locomotion. There-is-the Workmen's-Compensation-Act | which deals with accidents arising out-of and-in-the-course-of employment, and-claims-for-compensation are made for minor-accidents such-as-the dislocation-of-the-wrist and | unhappily also for fatal accidents. Often this compensation is paid in a lump-sum in-full-discharge-of-all-claims. Evidence of a definite contract or arrangement must-be shown | in-the-case-of casual-employment before compensation can-be claimed. Third-Party-Indemnity-Insurance is concerned with-the liability of persons to-third-parties in-respect-of personal-injury | and damage-to-property.   (124 words)

Exercise 200
Write in Shorthand

The rate-of-premium depends on-the *morale*-of-the-risk. In-the-matter of-motor-car insurance there-are-considerations of damage-by-fire and damage-to-tyres, and- | in-all-cases the registered-number-of-the-car must-be given. Then there-is indemnity for accidents in-connection-with lifts, cranes and hoists in-which-the situation-of- | the-cranes, and-the situation-of-the-lifts are of-much importance. Personal-Accident-Insurance may-be covered by an ordinary-accident-policy or a combined-accident-and-disease-policy. | Fire-insurance covers damages-to-premises by fire, and among other precautions automatic-sprinklers are insisted upon where there-are other-than incombustible-materials. Life-insurance is often associated with | a medical-examination and policies-are-declared-void and-the responsibility-of-the-company ceases if material facts are hidden by-the insured.   (143 words)

Exercise 201
Write in Shorthand

Most insurance-companies have what-is termed-the bonus-year-of-the-company, and-some declare an interim-bonus. A quinquennial-valuation is taken by life-offices when bonuses are | declared and-provisions made for shareholders'-dividends where-the office is a proprietary one. It-is-true that-the holders of-life-policies, payable with bonus pay a higher premium | than-the holders of life-insurance-policies payable without bonus, but it-is-not correct to assume that-the holders of bonus-policies merely receive back in-the form of | bonus the excess premiums paid to-the Life-Insurance-Company. If a life-office could predict exactly its future mortality experience, rates of interest realizable, and rates of-expense, it | could fix its premiums so-that it-would show neither profit nor loss. One-of-the-most attractive features of-life-insurance is-its simplicity. There-are-no legal costs | or charges to be faced, there-are-no trying and complicated investigations to be-made, requiring the skill and experience on-the-part-of-the principal personally or by deputy, | and-the business of obtaining a life-policy can-be completed in-the-course-of a very-few hours, without incurring a single farthing of unproductive expense.   (207 words)

SHIPPING

advances against shipment

advances on acceptances

bill of lading in set of four

Board of Trade regulations

cable exchange rate

captain's receipt for documents

case of total loss

cash against bill of lading

Chamber of Commerce

charter party

constructive total loss of cargo

consular invoice

cost, insurance and freight(*c.i.f.*)

documents of title

indorsed and confirmed

errors and omissions excepted (*e. & o. e.*)

foreign general average

free of general average

free on rail (*f.o.r.*)

free on board (*f.o.b.*)

London office of the bank

Marine Insurance Act

marine insurance policy

Merchant Shipping Act

nature and cause of damage

not responsible for the damage

Port of London Authority

remit draft on Paris

remit proceeds of bill

salvage charges

shipping documents enclosed

telegraphic codes

to be approved by the underwriters

value to be declared

voyage policy

weight subject to correction

York-Antwerp Rules

Exercise 202
Write in Shorthand

The Port-of-London-Authority extends its sway over-the greatest and richest highway of-commerce ever-known to history, and it-is continually improving the conditions of shipping on- | the Thames. In matters relating to shipping the Board-of-Trade-regulations have - to be carried-out, while-the various chambers-of-commerce seek to-improve and modify any enactments | affecting the interests of-their-members. The Merchant-Shipping-Act, the York-Antwerp-Rules, and-the Marine-Insurance-Act have an important-bearing on-the importation and exportation of-produce. |' When goods are exported various documents are used according-to-circumstances. Among-these documents may-be a bill-of-lading-in-set-of-four, an invoice, marked *e.- &-o.-* | *e.*, a consular-invoice, and a marine-insurance-policy, which-may-be a voyage-policy.   (135 words)

Exercise 203
Write in Shorthand

These documents, which-are frequently accompanied with a bill-of-exchange, form-the documents-of-title. If an advance-against-shipment is required, the documents-of-title, including-the Consular-invoice, | are forwarded to-the London-office-of-the-bank. The advice should-be marked " shipping-documents-enclosed." If a bill-of-exchange is sent through-the bank for-collection, any | special-instructions as to-the proceeds should-be given; for-instance, remit-proceeds-of-bill to-London; or, remit-draft-on-Paris. Sometimes a charter-party is employed, and for | all-these a captain's-receipt-for-documents is given. A shipper's prices may-be *f.-o.-b.*, *f.-o.-r.*, or *c.-i.-f.*, and insurance may-be free-of-general-average, or according-to foreign- | general-average. In-all-cases risks must-be approved-by-the-underwriters, or they-will-not-be responsible-for-the-damage which-may occur. In making a claim the nature- | and-cause-of-damage must-be given, and-there-may-be a case-of-total-loss or constructive-total-loss. If salvage is-necessary the ship, freight, and cargo must | each pay its-own share of-the salvage-charges. Consignees may-be written to by post with shipping-documents-enclosed.   (207 words)

Exercise 204

Write in Shorthand

Arrangements are often made for bankers to-make advances-against-shipments, or advances-on-acceptances. The banker forwards the documents to-his agent abroad who presents-the bill-of-exchange | for acceptance or payment upon-which-the agent will surrender the shipping-documents. The London-office-of-the-bank will-be advised and-the shipper will-be credited with-the | margin, or difference between-the advance made and-the amount-of-the-bill. Instructions are often given to remit-draft-on-Paris, to remit-proceeds-of-bill by telegraphic-transfer, | or to cable-exchange-rate, and telegraphic-codes are employed. These usually consist of key-words or figures, each word or group of figures representing a complete sentence.   (118 words)

CHAPTER XL

TECHNICAL AND RAILWAY PHRASES

Phraseography in Engineering and Railway Offices.
219. There is no more difficult form of note-taking than that to be met with in the offices of electrical and mechanical engineers or certain departments of railway work. Special care is, therefore, necessary on the part of the shorthand writer undertaking such work. It is not, of course, to be expected that he should have a great deal of technical knowledge ; but it is very desirable that he should endeavour to acquire at least a general knowledge of the difference in meaning of terms which are more or less similar in sound. He will find that the terms used are dictated at a fairly rapid rate, and that his outlines for them must be clearly and easily written. Very much more extensive lists of phrases are given in the publishers' series of Shorthand Writers' Phrase Books, to which the shorthand writer entering for the first time the office of an engineering concern or a railway is referred.

ELECTRICAL AND ENGINEERING

alternating current	discharge chamber
automatic apparatus	earth currents
Bessemer steel	eddy currents
block signal	electric current
civil engineer	electrical engineer
combustion chamber	energy current
current density	energy resistance
discharge resistance	exhaust valve
	free charge

254

heating apparatus

high resistance

high voltage

induction coil

lever and weight
  safety valve

low pressure
  cylinder

low voltage

mechanical stokers

monophase
  generator

no voltage attach-
  ment

pressure gauge

primary battery

primary coil

primary currents

railway engineer

residual charge

resistance board

resistance of
  copper circuits

rotary converter

rotary transformer

secondary coil

secondary current

sight feed
  lubricator

spring balance
  safety valve

vacuum brake

water cooling
  plant

Exercise 205

Write in Shorthand

The history of engineering is a very fascinating subject,
and-the remains of-remote antiquity, as exemplified
in-the pyramids of Egypt, and-of Stonehenge in-our-own
island, testify | to-the early skill of-men in matters relating
to engineering.   It-was about-the middle of-the 18th-
century that-the-profession of engineering originated,
and to-day it- | is-one of-the foremost in-the-world.
There-are many subdivisions such-as military, mining,
mechanical, civil, railway, sanitary and electrical, and-as
electricity is-now so generally applied | it-is-necessary
for-most engineers to be electricians a'so.   Electricians
must understand what-is-meant by earth-currents, eddy-
currents, electric-currents, alternating-currents, residual-
charge, resistance-board, rotary- | transformer, or rotary-
converter.   (124 words)

Exercise 206

Write in Shorthand

The railway-engineer is concerned, more-or-less, with block-signals, heating-apparatus, Bessemer-steel, and vacuum-brakes, while-the mechanical-engineer pays special-attention to automatic-apparatus, combustion-chambers, | exhaust-valves, low-pressure-cylinders and high-pressure-cylinders, mechanical-stokers, sight-feed-lubricators and water-cooling-plants. He-has to-consider-the advantages and disadvantages of-the lever-and- | weight-safety-valve and-the spring-balance-safety-valve, and also of-the surface-condenser, which-is a device employed for condensing exhaust-steam without mixing-it with cold-water. | The method is-now universally used in marine engines. (99 words)

Exercise 207

Write in Shorthand

Among other things, the electrical-engineer should-know-that power delivered from-the monophase-generator is pulsating, that from-the multiphase-generator is con-stant ; that current-density is-the amount | of current per unit of area of a cross-section of a conductor ; that an induction-coil is an apparatus used for obtaining a very-small-current at a very | high-voltage from a battery-current of low-voltage, and hence really a transformer especially adapted to work a continuous-current from a few cells ; that a primary-coil is-| that coil of an induc-tion-coil, transformer, etc., through which flows a primary-current, with-the original-current, whose fluctuations are to be utilized in-order-to induce another or | secondary-current in-the secondary-coil of-the apparatus ; and-that copper-loss is-the waste of-energy through-the resistance-of-copper-circuits in electric-plant, the energy being | dissipated in-the form of heat. The dynamo is a rever-sible machine, that-is-to-say, it-may-be used either as a dynamo or as a motor. In-the-| first-case, the machine is driven by a steam-engine or gas-engine or turbine, and gives out electrical-energy. In-the-second-case, electrical-energy is imparted to-the | machine. (211 words)

RAILWAY

break down plant
Caledonian Ry.
Charing Cross
    Station
chief mechanical
    engineer
dining car
district traffic
    manager
fast passenger
    train
general manager
goods traffic
    committee
Great Central
    Railway
Great Eastern
    Railway
Great Northern
    Railway
Great Western
    Railway
King's Cross
    Station
Lancashire and
    Yorkshire Ry.
locomotive and
    engineering
    committee
locomotive
    superintendent
L. & N.E. Ry. Co

L. & N.W. Ry. Co.
L. & S.W. Ry. Co.
London, Midland
    and Scottish Ry.
Midland Railway
North British
    Railway
Paddington
    Station
passenger brake
    van
passenger traffic
    committee
passengers'
    luggage
permanent way
    committee
railway directors
railway manager
railway receiving
    station
St. Pancras
    Station
second class com-
    partment
sleeping saloon
Southern Railway
superintendent of
    the line
telegraph super-
    intendent
traffic manager

Exercise 208

Write in Shorthand

It-was in-the first half of-the 19th-century that-the-majority of-the great railway undertakings in-this-country received parliamentary sanction. Commencing with-the-year 1834, | the following is-the-order in-which-the companies named received their Act : London-and-South-Western-Railway, Midland-Railway, Lancashire-and-Yorkshire-Railway, North-British-Railway, Caledonian-Railway, Great- | Central-Railway, London-and-North-Western-Railway, Great-Northern-Railway, Great-Eastern-Railway, Cambrian-Railway, and Great-Western-Railway. London is-the centre from which radiate all-the great English- | railways, and among-the well-known termini are King's-Cross-Station, Paddington-Station, Charing-Cross-Station, and St.-Pancras-Station. Many of-the railway-companies have-been amalgamated under new | names, as-follows:—the London-Midland-and-Scottish-Railway; the London-and-North-Eastern-Railway; the Southern-Railway, and-the Great-Western-Railway.   (143 words)

Exercise 209

Write in Shorthand

For-purposes-of administration the work of a railway is divided into many-departments under-the-control of-the general-manager, who ultimately settles all disputes. Then there-are-the | chief-mechanical-engineer, who-is-the head of-the locomotive-department which-has very complicated matters to negotiate, the traffic-manager, the locomotive-superintendent, the superintendent-of-the-line, the | telegraph-superintendent, and so on ; while various committees, such-as-the goods-traffic-committee, the locomotive-and-engineering-committee, the passenger-traffic-committee and-the permanent-way-committee decide important- | matters concerning-the working of-the line. The settlement-of-claims made by-clients of-the railways is a very difficult problem, and often leads to actions in-the-law- | courts.   (121 words)

Exercise 210

Write in Shorthand

To cope with-these and other-matters, such-as-the rating of-the railway by public bodies, a staff of fully-qualified solicitors is employed by-each-company. The very- | important and complicated work of-the equitable division of-receipts for-the carriage of passengers and goods, demurrage on wagons, etc., is performed at-the Railway - Clearing - House. Long - distance | passenger - trains may-have sleeping-saloons and dining-cars, and many companies have discontinued second-class-compartments on all-trains. Nearly all passenger-trains have a passenger-brake-van for | passengers'-luggage and merchandise and perishables for quick transit.   (99 words)

CHAPTER XLI

LEGAL PHRASES

Phraseography in Legal Work. 220. The law has, to a large extent, a vocabulary and terminology of its own, and the shorthand writer engaged upon legal work, whether in taking notes of correspondence and of documents, or as note-taker in courts, must have a fairly wide acquaintance with the peculiar style of language employed. The court reporter must also be familiar with quite a number of leading cases, because reference to these is of everyday occurrence, and ignorance of them would make his work difficult, if not, indeed, impossible. Neatness of outline formation in legal note-taking of any description is of the utmost importance, and absolute accuracy of transcription is essential. No pains, therefore, should be spared by the writer to make himself thoroughly efficient, both in general knowledge of the matter he will be sure to meet with in the course of his work, and in regard to the actual writing of his shorthand notes.

LEGAL

affidavit
Articles of Association
bankrupt
bankruptcy
breach of promise of marriage
Central Criminal Court
Chancery Division
circumstantial evidence

counsel for the defence
counsel for the defendant
counsel for the plaintiff
counsel for the prisoner
counsel for the prosecution
Court of Criminal Appeal

Court of Appeal

deed of settlement

deed of trust

deed of assignment

documentary
   evidence

EcclesiasticalCourt

employers' liability

equity of redemp-
   tion

examination in
   chief

executor

executrix

grand jury

Habeas Corpus

heirs, executors,
   administrators
   and assigns

heirs, executors.
   administrators
   or assigns

High Court of
   Justice

increment duty

judgment
   summons

jurisprudence

justice of the peace

King's Bench

King's Bench
   Division

King's Counsel

learned counsel

learned counsel for
   the defence

learned judge

legal estate

legal personal
   representative

Lord Chancellor

Lord Chief Justice

marriage settle-
   ment

may it please your
   honour

memorandum of
   association

my learned friend

official receiver

official writer

originating
   summons

power of attorney

Probate, Divorce,
   and Admiralty
   Division

real estate

recognisance

reversionary bonus

trust funds

verdict for the
   defendant

verdict for the
   plaintiff

warrant of
   attorney

will and testament

your worship

Exercise 211

Write in Shorthand

Re SMITH, a Bankrupt

T. B. GILL, Esq.

Dear-Sir,

The action brought by-the Official-Receiver to-test the validity of-the Bill-of-Sale given to-you by | Mr.-Smith, came on for trial to-day in-the King's-Bench-Division of-the High-Court-of-Justice, before Mr. Justice Bright. I-regret-to-say that-the learned-judge, | after hearing the arguments on both-sides, decided against you on-the ground that-the document is-not in-accordance-with-the form prescribed by-the Act-of-Parliament relating | to Bills-of-Sale. You-will-remember that I-have many-times pointed out to-you that-the Bills-of-Sale Act is so obscurely worded that great-numbers of | Bills-of-Sale prepared by-the-most eminent conveyancers have-been set aside on-the-same-ground. It-is open to-you to-carry-the matter to-the Court-of- | Appeal, but I-do-not advise that course.

Yours-truly,   (160 words)

Exercise 212

Write in Shorthand

Mr. Walter Morton's progress at-the Bar has-been unusually rapid. He-was called in 1887. Before he had-been two-years at-the Bar | he had-been counsel-for-the-plaintiff in an action for breach-of-promise-of-marriage, counsel-for-the-defendant in an action in-the Probate,-Divorce,-and-Admiralty-Division, | had appeared once in-the Ecclesiastical-Court, and-once before-the Lord-Chancellor in a Habeas-Corpus case. In every-instance he-was successful. If-he represented-the plaintiff the result was a verdict-for-the-plaintiff, and-if-he represented-the defendant the result was a verdict-for-the-defendant. He-is respected in-the High-Court-of-Justice | for-his thorough-knowledge of-the Common-Law, and-is always heard with marked attention in-the Divisional-Court. He argued with great ability a novel point raised on a | commercial-summons in-the King's-Bench last-week. He-has-been retained in an important action on a bill-of-lading, and also in-several assessment appeals

arising out-of- | the recent quinquennial-valuation. He-is
an authority on-the vexed question of employers'-liability
under-the   Workmen's-Compensation-Act,   and-is   as
successful with a Common-Jury as with- | the Judges.

(212 words)

Exercise 213

Write in Shorthand

Those-who heard his arguments the other-day as-to-the
difference between-the meaning of-the two phrases,
"heirs, - executors, - administrators, - *and* - assigns," and
"heirs,-executors,-administrators,-*or*-assigns," | will-not
soon forget his keenness. He-was equally brilliant lately
when-the notary-public was sued on a warrant-of-attorney.
As-he refuted the arguments of-the learned- | counsel-
for-the-defendant, "my-learned-friend" must-have felt
overwhelmed. In-consequence-of the death of-his-father,
under whose will-and-testament he inherits considerable
personal-estate   and | real-estate,   he-is-not   dependent
upon his profession. People are already speculating as-to
when-he-will-be-made a King's-Counsel. He-has-been
nominated as a Justice- | of-the-Peace for Surrey, his
father's county. He-is-the prospective candidate for a
very large constituency in-the-North of England and
he-is in great demand as | a political speaker. There-is-
no-doubt that at-the first opportunity he-will-be elected
to-represent-the constituency in-Parliament. His inti-
mate friends are hopeful that in-due | time he-will fill the
highest judicial position in-the land, and-they feel sure
he-would-be an ornament to-the office.   (203 words)

CHAPTER XLII

, THEOLOGICAL PHRASES

Sermon Reporting. 221. Very many students of shorthand make an opportunity of practising the art by taking notes of the sermons delivered in the various places of worship in their neighbourhood. There are peculiar difficulties in this kind of note-taking, because of the necessity for taking notes without a firm rest for the note-book. A piece of stiff cardboard, or of thin wood, attached to the back of the note-book will be found to answer the purpose of a knee-rest very well, and practice will make the note-taking under these conditions a fairly easy task. The writer must guard against allowing the neatness of his notes to be affected by the unusual conditions under which they are taken.

THEOLOGICAL

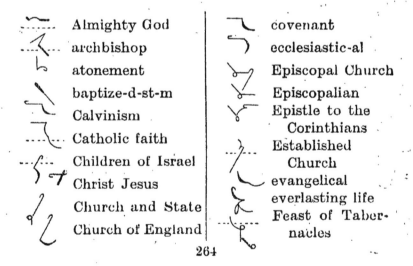

Almighty God		covenant	
archbishop		ecclesiastic-al	
atonement		Episcopal Church	
baptize-d-st-m		Episcopalian	
Calvinism		Epistle to the Corinthians	
Catholic faith		Established Church	
Children of Israel		evangelical	
Christ Jesus		everlasting life	
Church and State		Feast of Taber-nacles	
Church of England			

264

fellow-creature

fruits of the Spirit

glad tidings

goodness of God

gospel of peace

Greek Church

Heavenly Father

Holy Scripture

Holy Word

House of Israel

in Jesus Christ

in the presence of God

in the providence of God

in the sight of God

in the words of the text

Jewish dispensation

kingdom of Christ

kingdom of God

kingdom of heaven

knowledge of Christ

Lord and Saviour Jesus Christ

Lord Jesus

minister of the gospel

Methodism

my beloved brethren

my text

New Testament Scriptures

Nonconformist

Nonconformity

Old Testament

passage of Scripture

Presbyterian

resurrection of Christ

Revised Version

Right Reverend

Right Rev. Bishop

Roman Catholic

Roman Catholic Church

Sabbath day

Sermon on the Mount

tabernacle

transubstantiation

United Free Church of Scotland

Virgin Mary

Wesleyan Methodist

world without end

Exercise 214

Write in Shorthand

Humanity owes much to-the Church-of-Christ, in-which-the true children-of-God have-been animated by-the Holy-Spirit to Christian-faith and-practice, and to-the I advocacy of-the gospel-of-peace and-the promotion of a love of-our fellow-creatures in every child-of-God. Though-the relations of Church-and-State in various I lands have-not-been always what could-be desired, yet in-the-providence-of-God the fruits-of-the-Spirit have-been revealed, so-that in-the-Church the knowledge- I of-Christ has increased, and-in-the-world in-the-pro-vidence-of-God there-has-been an extension of-the king-dom-of-Christ. The blessing of-the divine Head-of- I the-Church, and-the outpouring of-the Holy-Spirit, have-been often asked on foreign-missions and home-missions, as-well-as on Sunday-school work, and other methods in- I which Christian activity has manifested itself to-bring into-the kingdom-of-God the ignorant and indifferent, by taking to-them a knowledge-of-Christ and-of-the Holy-Word, I by bringing to-them the glad-tidings of-the goodness-of-God and a knowledge of-the kingdom-of-heaven, and of-Him who-is at-the-right-hand-of- I God.

The minister-of-the-Gospel selected a passage in-the-word-of-God from-the Revised-Version, and-said that in-the-words-of-the-text, or in my- I text, taken from St.-Paul's-Epistle to-the Colossians, they-would-find authority for-his addressing-them not as my-beloved-brethren, my-brethren, or my-dear-friends, but as- I he proposed to-do in-the-sight-of-God, and feeling that-they-were in-the-presence-of-God, as faithful brethren in-Christ, accepting the Catholic-faith, looking to- I the-same Heavenly-Father, having-the-same trust in Almighty-God, and believing in an everlasting-God, world-without-end, the ruler over heaven-and-earth for-ever-and-ever. I

(330 words)

Exercise 215

Write in Shorthand

Christianity as represented in-the-Christian-Church is-the religion of-the European race, the principal bodies engaged in-its maintenance or dissemination being-the Roman-Catholic-Church, the Greek- I Church, the various national Established-Churches, the Free-Churches, and many other organizations which find their faith and-practice in-the New-Testament-Scriptures. There-are, at-the-same-time, | scattered among-the nations-of-the-earth, descendants of-the Children-of-Israel who obey the Mosaic-law, observe-the Sabbath-day, the Feast-of-Tabernacles, and-the Festival of- | the Passover, and-find spiritual guidance in-the Old-Testament.

Our-Lord-Jesus-Christ was-born under-the Jewish-dispensation, and-with-his parents visited Jerusalem in-his twelfth year. | Here he-was found by Joseph and-his mother, the Virgin-Mary, among-the great-ones of-the House-of-Israel. John the Baptist bore testimony that-the Lord-Jesus- | Christ was-the Lamb-of-God, and at-the first call of-the disciples, testimony was-borne that-the Lord-Jesus was-the Son-of-God. At-the second call, | the first four in-the Apostolic College were chosen. Among-the-words of-the Lord-and-Saviour recorded in-the Gospels, the Lord's-Prayer is-the-most widely known and | used ; and-of our-Saviour's teaching, the Sermon-on-the-Mount is perhaps | most generally quoted. The institution of-the Lord's-Supper is recorded by three of-the Evangelists, and- | the-last discourses of-the Lord-and-Saviour-Jesus-Christ by St.-John.   (253 words)

CHAPTER XLIII
SPECIAL LIST OF WORDS

222. (*a*) The fact that the English language contains very many words which have a similar consonantal structure was early recognized by the Inventor of Pitman's Shorthand, and provision was accordingly made in the system for the easy differentiation of these words by distinguishing outlines, so that the writer would have no difficulty either in the writing or in the transcription of these similarly constructed words. It is, indeed, mainly this inherent power of readily distinguishing similar words that makes Pitman's Shorthand at once legible and capable of being written with extreme rapidity.

(*b*) It will be found that the application of the ordinary rules of the system provides distinguishing outlines in the great majority of cases, but where this is not so, distinction is obtained by the insertion of a vowel or, in a few cases, by placing the outline out of position, or by writing a full outline instead of applying an abbreviating principle. In studying the following list of outlines, the student should seek to appreciate fully the reasons for the various forms and positions. Where a line contains more than one word, the first word is the root word, the others being derivatives. The list of words here given is not, of course, exhaustive. The student may easily compile further lists for himself and, proceeding upon the method here illustrated, he may at one and the same time test his vocabulary and enlarge it by starting with a few root words and from them building up lists of words formed from them by the addition of prefixes and suffixes.

Exercise 216

Read, copy and transcribe

1. Compatible
2. Pity
3. Petrify
4. Putrefy
5. Patron
6. Passion
7. Patient
8. Poor
9. Pure
10. Purpose
11. Perhaps
12. Propose
13. Prepare
14. Proper
15. Property
16. Propriety
17. Appropriate
18. Protect
19. Product
20. Compare

Exercise 217

Write in Shorthand

Is-it compatible with fairness to-call-the trader a useless member of society, one that stands between producers and takes toll of-the-goods that are exchanged ? That-is | a proper question, for-we-have-seen-that, although money intervenes in-order-to facilitate exchange, the appropriate fact is-that commodities are exchanged for commodities, the pure wheat of | Canada for-the railway-material of Warwickshire, the beef of-the Argentine for-the woollens made and-prepared in Bradford. The farmer of-the far-stretching fields beyond Winnipeg works, | perhaps, for-the-purpose-of feeding-the operatives in an engine-shop at Birmingham. Men tend cattle on-the great plains of-South-America so-that British workers may-be-| the better fed. And-the poorest worker here toils for-those separated from-him by wide areas of sea and land. It-is-not improper or inaccurate to say that- | we-are all exchanging services. We-may ask with perfect propriety, is a middleman, a trader, necessary ? We-are-prepared to say that-he-is ; it needs little thought or | comparison of argument to-bring home to-ourselves how indispensable the trader's work is. The proposition is almost self-evident. When, as happened occasionally during-the pitiable days of-the war, | the Government felt constrained to-take into its-own-hands the distribution of-some commodity—petrol, or meat, or accommodation on-board steamers—it-was obliged to appoint armies of | officials who did, after a certain amount of-preparation and-training, what traders had done cheaply and smoothly before. The work was, of-course, incompatible with their intentions in | early-life, but it-was important, and required patience to-carry it through. There-is-no essential difference between-the work of-the-trader and-the work of another man. | The trader is helping to-move products—and to-move things is-the only act that-man is capable of ; the trader helps-the commodity along its lengthy journey from-| its production to-its consump-tion. The trader seeks to-place commodities where-they shall-be of-most service for-men. That is-his purpose or business in life. He-must- | know where-the best and cheapest commodities are to be had ; he-must-know also where-these commodities will satisfy-the keenest demand.

(383 words)

Exercise 218

Read, copy and transcribe

1. Operate
2. Porter
3. Proffer
4. Prefer
5. Provide
6. Pervade
7. Persecute
8. Prosecute
9. Person
10. Parson
11. Pursue
12. Perish
13. Prominent
14. Permanent
15. Pre-eminent
16. Prince
17. Beauty
18. Bribe
19. Birth
20. Bury

Exercise 219

Write in Shorthand

We-are all sellers and buyers. Parson or layman, prince or peasant, we-are all either providers or consumers of things. We proffer services or offer goods to others and- | if-we-are keen we-prosecute a person who illegally tries to-prevent us from carrying-on our legitimate business. We live by exchanging, by bargaining; and- for our-own | sakes it behoves us to acquire some skill in-the operation or making of bargains. This-is true whether-we-are exporters or importers, manufacturers or merely dealers. In-any-event, we | sell our services and so buy money. This money we change into those-things we-desire most—and which-are provided by-others—into- the necessaries and comforts of-existence, | a beautiful house, an extensive library of-permanent value, or what- ever we-may prefer to add to-our reasonable enjoyment of-life. In agriculture itself, people are ceasing to- produce- | the things they consume : the farmer sells his milk-and-cream and buys butter, or contents himself with- the substitute that tropical Africa has lately added to-our tables ; he | sells his cattle and buys beef of-the butcher who carves an ox fed on-the pampas of-South-America ; he no-longer makes even his-own flour. The essential, | all-pervading fact of-our economic life is exchange. Apart from agriculture, we should-be unable to-produce sufficient to sustain-the simplest life, and-we should perish. By- means- | of exchange and-the co-operation it brings- about, we-are-enabled to-produce enough to satisfy a very complex life. We go to-the-market with our goods, perishable or | imperishable. Our goods may-not-be embodied in commodities that can-be weighed or meas- ured ; they-may-be, and usually are, merely proffered services. But-whether-we offer our services | for-the permanent or temporary accommodation of others—or whether-we-have visible and tangible commodities—pairs of boots, or pounds of bacon, or attractive ties, or suc- culent fruits—makes | no difference. It-is-our supply, and-this-is-the course to pursue if-we-would-be a seller of what we-have. In-our minds we attach a minimum | price to-it, what-the auctioneer calls a reserve price. Unless we get that-price we-shall withdraw from-the market, and-no briber can bribe us to-sell at | a figure below that-price.   (395 words)

Exercise 220

Read, copy and transcribe

1. Abundant
2. Abandon
3. Tuition
4. Temporal
5. Temper
6. Attend
7. Continue
8. Continent
9. Travel
10. Trivial
11. Iterate
12. Debt
13. Doubt
14. Audit
15. Edit
16. Detriment
17. Determine
18. Differ
19. Defer
20. Adverse

Exercise 221

Write in Shorthand

Unless a business man has an abundant knowledge of-the fundamental art of-calculating he-will-be hopelessly outclassed in-the keen competition of-modern-times, and might even have | to abandon a business-life. An apparently trivial amount, a tiny fraction may-make-the difference between profit-and-loss and turn a favourable amount into an adverse balance. In | no branch of commerce is-this more evident than in transactions with-the continent and other-parts-of-the-world. So-many factors have-to-be-taken-into-consideration that-the | middleman, by whose offices such transactions are settled, must calculate to a nicety. He-cannot afford to-make a rough estimate, or leave-the-matter to an inefficient man or | woman. Men or women inexperienced in figures would-be useless in-such offices. He carries on-his business of bill-broking—of buying from those-who-have credit abroad and selling | to-those-that seek credit— largely on borrowed money for-which he pays interest. He-cannot charge very high for-his services for two-reasons. Other brokers are available ; and- | there-are other-ways of settling debts than-the buying of a draft to-send abroad. The debtor may procure gold and him-self dispatch it, or he-may send a | security to-his foreign creditor—a railway-debenture, a municipal bond, a mortgage on-land, though he-would-not-be indifferent as-to-the choice. For in a sense we- | can, in-these-days, so closely identified is property with-the legal title to-it, export our fields and-factories, our railroads and canals, to pay for our imports. However, | a debtor resorts to-the export of-gold or securities only as a temporary measure, when-the bills-of-exchange are at-a-price he judges exorbitant. What-is this | exorbitant price which deter-mines his choice ? It-is a price beyond that-which he-would-be-required to pay for gold and-for-the-expenses of-sending it to-his | creditors, or for-the security that-would in-the foreign-country command enough credit to cancel the debt. When-we-are guided, as normally we-are, by economic considerations, we | elect the cheaper instrument for performing a necessary operation ; we-do-not give good-money when poorer will suffice. That-would-be detrimental to-our business, as-the audited accounts | would afterwards show.   (393 words)

Exercise 222

Read, copy and transcribe

1. Diverse
2. Decease
3. Disease
4. Dear
5. Agent
6. Act
7. Cause
8. Access
9. Excise
10. Exercise
11. Cultivate
12. Column
13. Culminate
14. Calumny
15. Create
16. Carry
17. Credence
18. Credit
19. Accord
20. Guide

Exercise 223

Write in Shorthand

The view taken of-the very diverse changes and chances of-life varies with different people, and-with-the same people at different times. Some there-are who-would perform- | the same journey, work at-the-same desk, have lunch at-the-same table day after day, year in and year out. They-are, apparently, merely mechanical agents, and-nothing | short of sickness, culminating in chronic disease, would alter their habits. They cultivate a disinclination to-exercise their undoubted right to change. They prefer routine to-risk, and are appalled | when-they consider-the uncertainties that dog their paths from one cause or another. They carry-on, accordingly, in-the-same-way, year after year, until their decease. Our modern | trade facilities have, indeed, removed from tolerably civilized societies many of-the risks of famine or scarcity or sudden death or ruin that-men ran in ruder times. We-have | a security of-person and-property such-as was-not enjoyed in-the best days of-the Roman peace ; and-the cheapness and ease of-transport enable-the surplus of- | one area to-supply-the deficiency of another. Modern conditions have created a different atmosphere, and-we-are, in a sense, very different creatures. We-are freed from-the drawback | of-which Mill speaks : "In poor and backward societies, as in-the-East, and-in Europe during-the Middle-Ages, extraordinary differences in-the-price of-the-same commodity might | exist in-places not very distant from each-other, because-the want of-roads and canals, the imperfection of-marine navigation, and-the insecurity of communications generally, prevented things from | being transported from-the places where-they-were cheap to-those where-they-were dear. The things most liable to fluctuations in-value, those directly influenced by-the seasons, were | seldom carried to any great-distances. Each locality depended, as-a-general-rule, on its-own produce and-that of-its immediate neighbourhood. In-most years, accordingly, there-was, in- | some part or-other of any large country, a real dearth. . . . . In modern-times there-is-only dearth where there formerly would-have-been famine, and sufficiency everywhere when anciently | there-would-have-been scarcity in-some-places and superfluity in others."   (372 words)

Exercise 224

Read, copy and transcribe

1. Good
2. Guard
3. Grade
4. Grant
5. Guarantee
6. Factor
7. Favour
8. Fall
9. Felon
10. Fortune
11. Four
12. Far
13. Further
14. Fresh
15. Form
16. Farm
17. Firm
18. Evident
19. Confide
20. Avoid

Exercise 225

Write in Shorthand

It-is evident that-we-shall hardly succeed in-our business-relations unless we-understand something of-the law that guards and guarantees our legal rights, and-in-the-last | resort enforces the performance of bargains. We-must in-our duties as ordinary-citizens have-some degree of knowledge in-the-laws in-order-that-we-may protect ourselves against | the felonious acts of felons or would-be felons. In matters of business we-need to-have a keener appreciation of-our rights-and-obligations, or we-shall-probably fall | into serious mistakes and, possibly, lose our whole fortune. Certainly we-are-not to-suppose that-men act honourably in business merely because they-are constrained by-the law. Merchants, | factors, agents and owners of factories perform their contracts without thinking about-the possibility of a law-suit, even as-they respect-the property of-their neighbours from-other motives | than a dread of punishment for thieving. Confidence in-the honesty of others there-must-be, or business would-be-impossible. Contracts were performed long-before there was a law | of contracts ; and number-less bargains are effected that-the law would-not-think of enforcing. Much of-our mercantile law is, in-fact, simply the custom of-merchants made authoritative | and applicable to all-grades of business. What men have-found convenient to-do, what-has conduced to-the smooth working of buying and selling, has-been adopted and made | effective, and few seek to-avoid their obligations. The merchants enjoyed special privileges and-were subject to special duties ; and-their usages were binding only upon them. These usages were | a body of customs by-which trade was facilitated and-they-were more firmly established as time passed. Recognized as binding by-the merchants this body of customs was gradually | incorpora-ted into-the law that-everyone, whether merchant or farmer, factor or agent, is constrained to observe. Such law is, as-was declared by a judge of a case in | 1875, " neither more-nor-less than-the usages of-merchants and-traders. They-have-been ratified by-the decision of-courts-of-law, which, upon such usage being | proved before them, have adopted them as settled law." In-the-present tendency to consolidate the law, most of-the usages are contained in-the Sales-of-Goods-Act of | 1893. (393 words)

Exercise 226

Read, copy and transcribe

1. Inevitable
2. Value
3. Avail
4. Convulse
5. Evolution
6. Violent
7. Converse
8. Support
9. Separate
10. Situate
11. Station
12. Structure
13. Consider
14. Secret
15. Secretary
16. Secrete
17. Sacred
18. Consist
19. Short
20. Emigrate

Exercise 227
Write in Shorthand

The assuming of risks, the shouldering of responsibility for bearing losses that-may arise, is incident to all business and it-is inevitable. However far one pushes the invaluable practice | of insurance, this-will-not avail entirely, and something must needs be left to chance. Nor, on-the whole, would it-be good for-man if chance were altogether eliminated | from-life and separated from business. Uncertainty adds considerable piquancy to a drab existence though, of-course, nobody desires convulsive or violent changes for-the-sake-of variety. Though-we- | are, taking-us all-round, a very cautious race there-are-never wanting among-us those willing to-take-the chances inseparable from business. And taking one with another the | risk-takers profit because, since more are ready to devolve risk from themselves than are ready to assume it, they can put a premium upon-their services. Those services are | real. What people call "remuneration for risk" is really earned. Unless plans were made for a more-or-less distant future, no progress would-be possible ; but as-soon-as | futurity comes into-the account, chance enters too. The Time Element—"the changes and chances of-this mortal life," as-it-is expressed—implies uncertainty. A natural instinct prompts us | to-consider enjoyments now as more eligible than enjoyments that are to-come. Few future events are quite free from uncertainty ; gilt-edged securities of-the-most unblemished reputation fluctuate in- | value, as anyone with secretarial experience will-know. The man that sinks a mine, even though-he acts upon-the advice of a geological expert, runs risks ; for geology itself | is-not-yet infallible. The emigrant frequently risks a good-deal. The rubber planter in Ceylon takes risks of-political upheavals that-might conceivably sweep away his property rights, | takes some risk that-the secret researches of scientists may devise a suitable substitute, takes risks of-market, of-weather, of any number-of factors that no foresight can predict. | Even when-we-take seats in-the luncheon car, signifying by-the act that-we accept-the offer of-the railway-company to-provide a good meal for five-shillings, | we run risk of not getting the meal we anticipate. The company, too, runs some risk ; for-we-may-be short of-money, or we-may-have-no money to | pay, or having it, may evade payment.   (397 words)

Exercise 228

Read, copy and transcribe

1. Immigrate
2. Murder
3. Define
4. End
5. Need
6. Ingenious
7. Ingenuous
8. Labour
9. Elaborate
10. Learn
11. Write
12. Rot
13. Regret
14. Regard
15. Refer
16. Rough
17. Revere
18. Human
19. Heart
20. Hard

Exercise 229

Write in Shorthand

By-no-means the least of-the business-man's many duties is-that of-finding such an outlet for-his goods as will enable him to continue at work. Indeed | this-is sometimes his hardest task. The weekly payments of-wages in-the factory are dependent upon-the profitable sale of-the calico or cutlery made in-the factory; the | regular salaries of-clerks and-travellers, of warehouse workers, labourers, and-transport workers cease if-there-is a prolonged difficulty in-finding customers. Certainly the factory owner, whose overhead expenses | are-not much less when-the factory is idle than when-it-is working at full pressure, will work for stock even if sales fall off for awhile. But he- | cannot lay up stock indefinitely. An end must come to-that. There-comes a time when either work must stop or products be sold. The wholesale dealer will-not dislocate | his organization by dispensing with-his staff merely because of a brief period of slackness ; he-will hold on in hopes of better times coming when-he-will need them. | The retailer does-not discard his helpers when-the spring sales have given place to a dearth of visitors into-his shop. Any lengthy failure to dispose of-goods is, | however, inevitably accompanied by unemployment, unemployment of workers, of capital, and-of business ability. However regrettable it-may-be, we-must regard this as a fact. We-may elaborate the | argument, but labour it as-we-may, there-is-the fact, and-no ingenuity can get over-it. How then are markets to be-found ? The most effective method of increasing | sales is a cut in price, or a rise of-the quality or attractiveness of-the commodity. This method is at-times applicable ; and when-it-is, there-is a | benefit all-round. The consumer gains in-the quantity or-the quality of-the-goods ; the producer has-the advantages resulting from production on a larger scale. From-the customer | in-the retail shop ; through-the warehouseman, to-whom-the retailer offers bigger orders on condition of-more favourable terms ; to-the-manufacturer who looks to-the warehouseman for an | interpretation of-the-market, there-is exerted a constant pressure to-reduce prices. Neither-the ingenious manufacturer nor anyone else can fix these at-his whim or caprice. The material | incentives to increased purchases need only to be brought effectively to-the notice of prospective buyers. (406 words)

Exercise 230

Read, copy and transcribe

1. Hero

2. Assure

3. Found

4. Collect

5. Elect

6. Event

7. History

8. Liberal

9. Patriot

10. Precise

11. System

12. Local

13. Matter

14. Sceptic

15. Sincere

16. Signature

17. Certain

18. Ascertain

19. Insist

20. Exist

Exercise 231

Write in Shorthand

To an extraordinary extent the modern business-man is dependent upon-the banker and-the banking system. One enthusiastic writer, proud of-the dominating influence exercised by-the banks, insists | that-the cessation even for a day or-two of-the banker's activities would certainly cause a complete paralysis of-the economic life of-the nation. Such a cessation would | assuredly be-found to-produce swifter and-more far-reaching effects than-the strike of-the-most effective Labour Union. The merchant works by-means-of-the credit facilities he enjoys, | and he-would-have-no facilities either to-collect or to pay his accounts. Unable-to discount-the bills he held, unable-to cash the cheques paid to-him, he-could- | not meet-the obligations constantly falling due, and must eventually become bankrupt. His signature on a cheque would-be useless. The manufacturer making for a market distant in-time-and- | place, depends upon-the support · of-the banks ; and-that support failing he-must cease work, no matter how sincerely he-might desire to-carry-on. Whether money is scarce | or plentiful, whether over-drafts are hard or easy to obtain, is-a-matter of supreme importance to-the trader. The stock he-has bought is carried on credit ; if-the | banker, the interpreter of-the financial state-of-the country, restricts-the credit then-the trader is obliged to unload, to-sell his stock with as little sacrifice as-possible. | He-could-not exist without-the liberal help of-the banker. The picture drawn of-the banker's work is little exaggerated. True, the banker is only a middle-man ; he connects | the people who save with-the people who-are-able-to employ savings in-the creation of wealth. In-our-country, at-any-rate, people have a deep-rooted confidence in- | the security of-funds entrusted to others. They-are willing to deposit with bankers and content themselves with moderate-interest upon-their deposits, the rate-of-interest being precisely ascertainable | at-any-time. Unwilling or unable-to use their accumulated savings themselves, they provide-the means whereby-the banker meets the needs of-those-that work and-trade on borrowed- | capital. This-is absolutely-certain. There-is-no room for scepticism on-the-matter. " Our people," says Bagehot, " are bolder in-dealing-with their money than any continental nation." (389 words)

CHAPTER XLIV
SHORTHAND IN PRACTICE

In taking notes of a speech, the employment of certain significant marks will be found necessary or desirable, in order to facilitate the production of a correct verbatim transcript or a good condensed report, or to prevent misunderstanding. The use of these signs is described below—

Mishearings, etc. 223. When a word has not been heard distinctly, and the shorthand writer is uncertain whether he has written the right one or not, a circle should be drawn round the character, or a cross (×) placed under it. When the note-taker has failed to hear a word, the omission should be indicated by a caret (___) placed *under* the line. Should a portion of a sentence be so lost, the same sign should be employed, and a space left blank corresponding to the amount omitted. Or the longhand letters *n h* (*not heard*) may be written.

Errors. 224. In cases where a reporter has failed to secure a correct note of a sentence, this may be indicated by an inclined oval, thus *()* (*nought or nothing*). When it is noticed that the speaker has fallen into an error, the mark ✕ should be made on the margin of the note-book.

Reference Marks. 225. When verbatim notes of a speech are taken, but only a condensed report is required, a perpendicular stroke should be made in the left-hand margin of the note-book to indicate an important sentence or passage which it is desirable to incorporate in the summary. The end of a speech or the completion of a portion of a discourse may be indicated by two strokes, thus // When the reporter suspends note-taking, but the speaker proceeds, the words *continued speaking* may be written.

Quotations, etc. 226. Quotations from well-known sources, such as the Bible or Shakespeare, familiar to the reporter, need not be written fully if time presses. It will suffice to write the commencing and concluding words with quotation marks and a long dash between, thus "*The quality of mercy* —— *seasons justice*." A long dash may be used to denote the repetition of certain words by a speaker, instead of writing them each time, as in the familiar passage, "*Whatsoever things are true,* —— *honest,* —— *just,*" etc.

Examination of Witnesses. 227. In reporting the examination of witnesses in questions and answers, the name of each witness should be written in longhand. The name of the examiner may be written in shorthand before the first question. If the judge, or other person, intervenes with questions during the examination, his name must be written before the first question; it need not be repeated, but care must be taken to write the name of the original examiner when he resumes his questions. Various methods may be employed for dividing questions from answers, and the answer from the succeeding question, but, whatever plan is employed, it should be one which is absolutely distinctive. When a document is put in, write *document* between large parentheses, thus 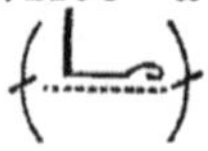 When a document is put in and read, write 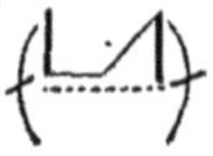

Applause, Dissent, etc. 228. The following words, descriptive of the approbation or dissent of an audience, should be enclosed between large parentheses :— ⌐ *hear,* ⌐ *hear, hear,* ⌣ *no,* ⌣ *no, no,* ℮ *sensation,* ⌐ *applause,* / *chair,* ⌐ *cheers,* ⌐ *laughter,* ∨ *uproar,* ℮ *hisses.* The adjective, or adjectives, descriptive of the kind of applause must be written after the first word. For example, what would be described as *loud and continued applause* would be written ⌐ ⌐ ⌐ in reporting.

Reference Books. 229. In most offices the shorthand writer will find some reference books. But he will soon discover that it is needful to have on his own bookshelf or in his desk certain books of reference for his own use. The most indispensable work is undoubtedly a good English Dictionary. *Pitman's Shorthand and English Dictionary* will be found to answer the purpose. Next in importance, if his work is of a literary character, will be a guide to all proper names in biography, geography, mythology, etc.

Business Knowledge. 230. It may not be out of place to observe that the more thoroughly equipped the shorthand writer is in the matter of general knowledge the more accurate and reliable will his shorthand prove to be. If, in addition to the necessary dexterity in the writing of shorthand, he possesses a good knowledge of business and other matters, it is obvious that his work will be performed with much greater ease and satisfaction to himself and to his employers. He should consult *Pitman's Commercial Catalogue* for suitable books on business.

OUTLINES FOR THE NAMES OF THE CHIEF
CITIES AND TOWNS OF THE EMPIRE.

Adelaide

Belfast

Birkenhead

Birmingham

Blackburn

Bombay

Bradford

Brisbane

Bristol

Calcutta

Cape Town

Cardiff

Cork

Derby

Dublin

Dunedin

Edinburgh

Gateshead

Gibraltar

Glasgow

Halifax

Hong-Kong

Huddersfield

Hull

Johannesburg

Leeds

Liverpool

London

Madras

Manchester

Melbourne

Middlesbrough

Montreal

Newcastle-on-Tyne

Norwich

Nottingham

Ottawa

Plymouth

Portsmouth

Preston

Pretoria

Sheffield

Singapore

Southampton

Stoke-on-Trent

Sunderland

Swansea

Sydney

Wellington

Winnipeg

Wolverhampton

GRAMMALOGUES

Arranged alphabetically

a *or* an	cold	his
accord-ing	come	hour
advantage	could	how
ah !	dear	however
all	deliver-ed-y	importance-ant
and	deliverance	impossible
any	difference-t	improve-d-ment
are	difficult	in
as	do	influence
aught	doctor, Dr.	influenced
awe	during	information
aye	eh ?	inscribe-d
balance	equal-ly	inscription
be	equalled	instruction
because	first	instructive
been	for	is
behalf	from	it
belief-ve-d	general-ly	itself
beyond	generalization	justification
build-ing	gentleman	language
but	gentlemen	large
call	give-n	largely
called	go	larger
can	gold	liberty
cannot	great	Lord
care	guard	me
cared	had	member
chair	hand	mere
chaired	has	more
cheer	have	most
cheered	he	Mr.
child	him	much
circumstance	himself	myself

near		should		told	
next		significance		too	
nor		significant		toward	
northern		signification		towards	
number-ed		signify-ied		trade	
O! oh!		southern		tried	
of		speak		truth	
on		special-ly		two	
opinion		spirit		under	
opportunity		subject-ed		usual-ly	
ought		subjection		valuation	
our		subjective		very	
ourselves		sure		was	
over		surprise		we	
owe		surprised		what	
owing		tell		when	
own		thank-ed		whether	
particular		that		which	
people		the		who	
pleasure		their		whose	
principal-ly		them		why	
principle		themselves		wish	
put		there		wished	
quite		therefore		with	
rather		thing		within	
remark-ed		think		without	
remember-ed		third		wonderful-ly	
satisfaction		this		word	
school		those		would	
schooled		though		writer	
selfish-ness		thus		yard	
sent		thyself		year	
several		till		you	
shall, shalt		to		young	
short		to be		your	

GRAMMALOGUES. *Arranged phonetically*
(Numbers refer to the position of the outline)

\ 3 put	/ 1 much, 2 which
⟍ 2 special-ly, 3 speak	⟋ 2 chair, 3 cheer
⟍ 3 principle, principal-ly	⟋ 1 chaired, 2 cheered
⟍ 3 people	⟋ 1 child
⟍ 1 surprise	
⟍ 1 surprised	/ 1 large
⟍ 1 particular, 2 opportu-	⟋ 1 larger
⟍ 2 spirit [nity	⟋ 1 largely
	⟍ 2 general-ly
\ 2 be, 3 to be	⟍ 2 generalization
⟍ 2 subject-ed	⟍ 2 justification
⟍ 2 subjective	⟍ 1 gentleman, 2 gentlemen
⟍ 2 subjection	
⟍ 1 liberty, 2 member,	
remember-ed, 3 number-ed	_ 1 can, 2 come
⟍ 3 belief, believe-d	⟍ 1 because
⟍ 1 behalf	⟋ 2 care
⟍ 2 been	⟋ 1 accord-ing, 2 cared
⟍ 1 balance	⟋ 1 call, 2 equal-ly
⟍ 2 build-ing	⟋ 1 called, 2 equalled, cold
	⟍ 2 school
| 2 it	⟍ 2 schooled
⎩ 3 itself	- 1 quite, 2 could
⎱ 2 truth	⟍ 1 cannot
⟍ 1 tried, 2 toward, trade	⟍ 1 inscribe-d
⟍ 2 towards	⟍ 1 inscription
⎾ 2 tell, 3 till	
⎾ 2 told	_ 1 go, 2 give-n
⎰ 2 circumstance	⟍ 1 signify-ied-ficant
⎰ 2 satisfaction	⟍ 1 significance
⎧ 2 instructive	⟍ 1 signification
⎩ 2 instruction	⟍ 1 guard, 2 great
	⟍ 2 gold
| 1 had, 2 do, 3 different-	
-ence	
⎾ 1 Dr., 2 dear, 3 during	⎩ 1 for
⎾ 2 deliver-ed-y	⟍ 2 from
⎰ 2 deliverance	
⎩ 1 advantage, 3 difficult	

⟍ 2 have	⌒ 1 me, 2 him
⟍ 2 several	⌒ 1 myself, 2 himself
⟍ 1 over, 3 however	⌒ 1 most
⟍ 1 valuation	⌒ 1 more, remark-ed, 2 Mr., mere
⟍ 2 very	

(1 thank-ed, 2 think	⌒ 1 important-ance, 2 improve-d-ment
) 2 third	⌒ 1 impossible

(1 though, 2 them	⌣ 1 in, any, 3 own
(1 those, thyself, 2 this, 3 thus	⌣ 1 influence
(2 themselves	⌣ 1 influenced, 2 next
) 2 there, their	⌣ 1 nor, 2 near
(3 within	⌣ 2 opinion
(2 southern	⌣ 1 northern
' 1 that, 2 without	⌣ 1 information
) 3 therefore	⌣ 1 hand, 2 under
	⌣ 1 sent

○ 1 has, as, 2 his, is	⌣ 1 language, owing, 2 thing, 3 young
○ 2 first	

) 2 was, 3 whose	(2 Lord

⟋ 2 shall, shalt, 3 wish	⟍ 2 your, 3 year
⟋ 2 wished	⟍ 1 yard, 2 word
⟋ 2 selfish-ness	⟋ 2 are, 3 our, hour
⟋ 3 sure	⟋ 3 ourselves
⟋ 1 short	⟋ 2 rather, writer

⟋ 2 usual-ly	⟋ 2 we
⟋ 2 pleasure	⌣ 2 whether
	⟋ 2 wonderful-ly

VOWELS

DOTS. ⸺ a, an, . the; ⸺ ah !
· aye, eh ?

DASHES. ⸺ of, ⟍ to; ⸺ all, ⟍ two, too; ⸺ on, ı but ; ⸺ O, oh ! owe, ı he; ⸺ and, ⟋ should; ⸺ awe, ought, aught; ⟋ who.

DIPHTHONGS

∧ how;

⸺ with, ᐸ when; ⸺ what, ᐳ would; ⸺ beyond, ∩ you, ⸺ why.

SPECIAL LIST OF CONTRACTIONS

Arranged alphabetically

A

acknowledge
administrator
administratrix
advertise-d-ment
altogether
amalgamate
amalgamation
anything
arbitrary
arbitrate
arbitration
arbitrator

B

bankruptcy

C

capable
certificate
character
characteristic
circumstantial
commercial-ly
cross-examination
cross-examine-d

D

defective
deficient-ly-cy
denomination-al
description
difficulty
discharge-d
distinguish-ed

E

efficient-ly-cy
electric
electrical
electricity
England
English
Englishman
enlarge
enlarger
enthusiastic-iasm
especial-ly
esquire
establish-ed-ment
everything
exchange-d

executive
executor
executrix
expediency
expenditure
expensive
extinguish-ed

F

falsification
familiar-ity
familiarization
familiarize
February
financial-ly

G

govern-ed
government

H

howsoever

I

identical
identification
immediate
imperturbable
incandescence
incandescent
inconsiderate

inconvenience-t-ly
incorporated
independent-ly-ce
indispensable-ly
individual-ly
influential-ly
inform-ed
informer
inspect-ed-ion
insurance
intelligence
intelligent-ly
intelligible-ly
interest
investigation
investment
irrecoverable-ly
irregular
irremovable-ly
irresponsible-ility

J

January

K

knowledge

L

legislative
legislature

M

magnetic-ism
manufacture-d
manufacturer
marconigram
mathematical-ly
mathematician
mathematics
maximum
mechanical-ly
metropolitan
minimum
misfortune
mortgage-d

N

neglect-ed
negligence
never
nevertheless
nothing
notwithstanding
November

O

organization
organize-d
organizer

P

parliamentary
peculiar-ity
perform-ed
performance
performer
perpendicular
practicable
practice
practise-d
prejudice-d-ial-ly
preliminary
probable-ly-ility
proficient-ly-cy
proportion-ed
proportionate-ly
prospectus
public
publication
publish-ed
publisher

Q

questionable-ly

R

ratepayers
recoverable
reform-ed

reformer

regular

relinquish-ed

remarkable-ly

removable

represent-ed

representation

representative

republic

republican

responsible-ility

S

satisfactory

sensible-ly-ility

something

subscribe-d

subscription

substantial-ly

sufficient-ly-cy

sympathetic

T

telegram

telegraphic

thankful-ly

together

U

unanimity

unanimous-ly

uniform-ity-ly

universal-ly

universality

universe

university

unprincipled

W

whatever

whenever

whensoever

whereinsoever

wheresoever

whithersoever

Y

yesterday

INDEX

The figures refer to the paragraphs, except where the page is mentioned.

PRINTED IN GREAT BRITAIN AT THE PITMAN PRESS, BATH
B9—(4)

AN ABRIDGED CATALOGUE OF THE SHORTHAND, TYPEWRITING

AND

STATIONERY PUBLICATIONS

OF

SIR ISAAC PITMAN & SONS, LTD.

LONDON: PARKER STREET, KINGSWAY, W.C.2.
BATH · Phonetic Institute. MELBOURNE : The Rialto, Collins St.
TORONTO: 70 Bond St. NEW YORK : 2 West 45th St.
INDIA : A. H. Wheeler and Co., Bombay, Calcutta, and Allahabad.

SOLD BY ALL BOOKSELLERS THROUGHOUT THE WORLD

The prices contained in this catalogue apply
only to the British Isles.

TERMS—

Cash MUST *be sent with the order*, AND MUST INCLUDE AN APPROXIMATE
AMOUNT FOR THE POSTAGE. *When a remittance is in excess of the sum
required, the surplus will be returned.*

*Sums under 6d. can be sent in stamps. For sums of 6d. and upwards, Postal
Orders or Money Orders are preferred to stamps, and should be crossed and
made payable to* SIR ISAAC PITMAN & SONS, LTD.

*Remittances from abroad should be by means of International Money Orders
in Foreign Countries, and by British Postal Orders within the British
Overseas Dominions. Colonial Postal Orders are not negotiable in England.
Foreign stamps* CANNOT BE ACCEPTED.

All the Books in this Catalogue are New Era Editions, and in foolscap 8vo
size, unless otherwise stated.

SHORTHAND INSTRUCTION BOOKS

PITMAN'S SHORTHAND TEACHER. An elementary work suited
for self-instruction or class teaching . . . . **9d.**
Key . . . . **9d.**
PITMAN'S SHORTHAND EXERCISES. A Series of Graduated
Sentence Exercises for use with the *Shorthand Teacher* . . . **3d.**
PITMAN'S SHORTHAND PRIMERS. For use in Day Schools and
Evening Classes. In three Books : Elementary, Intermediate,
and Advanced . . . . Each **9d.**
Keys to Books I, II, and III . . . . Each **9d.**

B9—7

PITMAN'S SHORTHAND READING LESSONS, No. 1 . . . . 8d.
Key . . . . 4d.
PITMAN'S SHORTHAND READING LESSONS, No. 2 . . . . 8d.
Key . . . . 4d.
PITMAN'S SHORTHAND READING LESSONS, No. 3 . . . . 8d.
Key . . . . 4d.
PITMAN'S SHORTHAND COPY BOOKS. Nos. 1, 2, 3, and 4.
  Foolscap 4to (8¾ in. × 6½ in.) . . . . . . Each 6d.
PROGRESSIVE STUDIES IN PITMAN'S SHORTHAND. A simple
  and extended exposition of the principles of Pitman's Shorthand 2/-
PITMAN'S SHORTHAND INSTRUCTOR. Complete Instruction in
  the system . . . . Cloth 4/6
Key 2/-
                                      Cloth 2/6
SUMMARIES FROM "PITMAN'S SHORTHAND INSTRUCTOR."
  Size, 2⅞ in. × 4 in. . . . . 4d.
GRADED SHORTHAND READINGS—
  Elementary, with Key. In crown 8vo, oblong . . . . 10d.
  Intermediate, with Key. In crown 8vo, oblong . . . . 10d.
  Advanced, with Key. In crown 8vo, oblong . . . . 10d.
PITMAN'S SHORTHAND MANUAL. Contains instruction in the
  Intermediate Style with 120 exercises. Paper 2/6
Key . . . . 9d.
SHORTHAND MANUAL READING AND DICTATION EXERCISES 9d.
PITMAN'S SHORTHAND GRADUS. Writing Exercises in ordinary
  print for Manual . . . . 3d.
PITMAN'S SHORTHAND REPORTER. Containing instruction in
  the Advanced Style, with 52 Exercises 2/-
Key . . . . 9d.
REPORTING EXERCISES. Exercises on all the rules and contracted
  words. In ordinary print, counted for dictation . . . 6d.
Key . . . . In Advanced Style 1/-
PITMAN'S SHORTHAND WRITING EXERCISES AND EXAMINA-
  TION TESTS. Contains exhaustive classified lists of words illus-
  trative of every rule in the system, and graduated sentence exercises
  in ordinary print for writing or dictation practice. In crown
  8vo 2/-
Key. In crown 8vo, cloth 3/6
PROGRESSIVE WRITING AND DICTATION EXERCISES. A collec-
  tion of 82 letters and narrative exercises taken from the larger
  work, Shorthand Writing Exercises and Examination Tests. In
  crown 8vo, 62 pp. 1/-
Key 1/6
PROGRESSIVE WORD EXERCISES. Containing exercises selected
  from the larger work, Shorthand Writing Exercises and Examination
  Tests. In crown 8vo, 64 pp.. . . . . 1/-
Key 1/6
EXERCISES ON THE POSITION RULES OF PITMAN'S SHORT-
  HAND. In crown 8vo, 62 pp. 1/-
GRADUATED TESTS IN PITMAN'S SHORTHAND. Illustrating all
  the rules in the Intermediate Style. In notebook form, post 8vo
  (6½ in. by 4½ in.), with ruled paper . . . . . . 8d.
PITMAN'S SHORTHAND DRILL EXERCISES (8¼ in. × 6 in.) . . 8d.
RAPID COURSE IN PITMAN'S SHORTHAND. A series of Twenty
  Simple Lessons covering the whole of the system. Complete with
  supplementary exercises. In crown 8vo, cloth, 200 pp . . 4/6
RAPID COURSE IN PITMAN'S SHORTHAND. . . . Paper 2/-
                                      Cloth 2/6
Key 2/-

Lightning Source UK Ltd.
Milton Keynes UK
UKHW021313231222
414389UK00015B/302